SAN DIEGO BAY

A STORY OF EXPLOITATION AND RESTORATION

San Diego Waterfront 1890, San Diego Historical Society

by the students of
THE GARY AND JERRI-ANN JACOBS
HIGH TECH HIGH

Designed and Edited by
Natalie Linton and Gwen Michael-Jones

Dedication

This book is dedicated to the memory of Janet Marie Murphy Linton (2006)—leader in education, resident of Pt. Loma and good friend to all.

Table of Contents

Waterfowl Hunting   58

Tuna   86

Salt 114

Kelp Additives 144

Kelp to Gunpowder 160

Sea Lions 184

Dolphins 204

White Seabass 230

Abalone 256

Mussels 282

Diamond Reflection — Shawn Teeter   304
Bibliography   312
Photo Credits   322
Graphs

Foreword

the Jane Goodall Institute

San Diego Bay: A Story of Exploitation and Restoration is a wonderful book. It will be hard for the reader to believe that it is based on the research results of a group of high school students. This book demonstrates clearly that young people, when motivated and inspired by outstanding teachers and mentors, have the ability to make major contributions to our understanding of the damage that we have inflicted on the environment and the steps that can be taken to put things right. Much of the thinking behind this truly unique book is grounded in traditional classroom teaching in the disciplines of biology, math and the humanities. This was interwoven with an innovative hands-on approach pioneered by Jay Vavra and his dedicated group of High Tech High (HTH) school students. Jay introduced the Jane Goodall Institute's Roots & Shoots program to HTH students and, incorporating its philosophy into their studies, they have conducted an in-depth, multi-faceted study of the San Diego Bay area. With Jay's vision, the support of dedicated teachers Tom Fehrenbacher, Rod Buenviaje, and an energetic, imaginative and extremely creative group of students, the original idea—learning about the problems of San Diego Bay through hands-on study—has expanded far beyond its original scope. *San Diego Bay: A Story of Exploitation and Restoration* is the outcome. This is not just a field guide, nor is it just a biological study. It provides meticulous descriptions of the flora and fauna that inhabit San Diego Bay. It describes the long-lasting effects that certain human activities have had upon these animals and plants. The students have used traditional scientific methodology, the careful collection and analysis of data, enriching their research, and adding to its veracity, through the use of GIS technology. In addition, they researched the history of human activities in and around the Bay and conducted their own interviews with selected individuals whose experience and knowledge could help to shed new light onto aspects of their investigations.

These students have also researched the age-old human drive to exploit the natural world for increased material wealth and the power that this can bring to the exploiters. The consequences, for the environment, have often been dire in the Bay. And these facts are presented as part of a much wider picture of the effect of human greed and short-sightedness on environments around the globe. Much of this information is depressing—human impact on the Bay and the surrounding habitats has, in many cases, been truly devastating. But the students have also collected information on a whole variety of restoration projects undertaken by the government, industry or concerned individuals trying to make amends. And each chapter provides an inspiring account of one or more of the successful activities of this sort. These stories of hope are particularly encouraging as we are given information about new approaches, based on new understanding of the problems and the technology and/or perseverance needed to overcome them. Thus there is an important nature center, a refuge for waterfowl and other salt marsh dwellers, where during World War I the area was used to turn kelp into—of all things—explosives for the Allied Forces! And now it is a place where children can learn about the wonders of the natural world and, at the same time, about the indignities that humans have inflicted on it. Then there is the story of the one-time seabass spearfisherman who now manages the seabass breeding program that is helping to restore the species. What I find particularly appealing are the personal reflections of the students—the young people who have, through no fault of their own, inherited a damaged world. In this book we are moved by their poetry, their opinions based on painstaking research and acquired knowledge. Some of these reflections are uncomfortable for us and challenging. These High Tech High students stand united with thousands of other committed young people who have learned, through their Roots & Shoots experience, the importance of using their lives to try to make the world a better place for people, animals and the environment. These are the young leaders of today who will soon be moving out into the adult world, armed with facts and not just theories, citizens who will be prepared to find solutions for difficult problems by keeping open minds, listening to the different opinions, and then making decisions based on an understanding of the whole picture. These students know when to stop talking, roll up their sleeves and take action. Immeasurable value is added to this book by the beautiful descriptive writing. It is rare these days to find young people who can compose clear prose. And this is made even more appealing by the students' photographs and sketches that accompany the writing.

It is immensely reassuring to me, as I travel the globe 300 days a year, to know that the energy, enthusiasm and passions of youth can, under the mentorship of dedicated and wise adults like Jay, Tom, and Rod, lead to the production of a book like this, a book that is both informed and beautiful—that contains science laced with humanity. It gives me reason for hope. Hope for the future of our much-abused planet. Hope that the youth of today will be better stewards than we have been. Hope that, together, we can gradually restore the health of this planet we share.

Dr. Jane Goodall, DBE
Founder – the Jane Goodall Institute &
*   UN Messenger of Peace*
www.janegoodall.org
www.rootsandshoots.org

II

Introduction

We hope the readers of this book will find in its chapters an original story, beautifully told. In the following pages, we have sought to relate stories of San Diego Bay's biological exploitation, record interviews of the people who conducted the harvest, document the industrialization of the natural habitat and in some cases interviewed individuals involved in the recovery of the resource. We have also attempted to chart evidence of their impact and reflect upon their significance. Our students have explored the biological resources of San Diego Bay by addressing the Bay's ecology from a historical perspective. By examining history, we discovered together the dramatic changes that have occurred over time in the Bay's ecology, as well as the past's continuing influence and explanatory power for the present. This approach brought to light the concept of "shifting baselines," as well as the need to recognize and attempt to establish the population decline of species, including the state of marine ecosystems well before our relative short stay on this planet.

San Diego is well known for its thriving, modern, biotechnological industry. Within our community, scientists have successfully established thriving pharmaceutical, medical diagnostic and bioprocessing and bioprospecting ventures. Few individuals, however, are aware of the early experimentation and exploitation that pioneered the biotech industry in San Diego. San Diego Bay and the surrounding near-shore habitats have served as a wonderful laboratory for the exploration of marine resources and their benefits. An important and yet unknown example of early bioprocessing was the exploitation of kelp for gunpowder and explosives that took place during WWI in the lower reaches of the Bay. Local industry also exploited the same fast-growing kelp for its alginates used in many things from food preparation to paint stabilization. In more recent times, little mention or focus has been placed on other explorations in the development of new biological and marine resources. For instance, few give adequate credit to the utilization of marine mammals for the benefit of humanity being conducted by the U.S. Navy.

Like the twelve hours of a clock, this book spins around twelve selected topics involving the exploitation of marine resources in and around San Diego Bay. We followed each story chronologically from the earliest human contact, through Spanish and Mexican California, to an eventual arrival at the dramatic changes of our last century and a half. We discovered in our work a pattern of human interaction: initial contact characterized by unfamiliarity, learning, and exuberant harvest; to a slow, at times fluctuating, depletion; to an eventual and optimistic transformation story. We found in the conclusion to these stories the possibility of a sustainable relationship with our environment. Thus, each story provided us with both a point of caution and advice as well as hope, which is revealed in the human ability to exploit, yet restore. While the clock may be ticking, by making ourselves aware of the hour, we may still have time to keep our relationship with nature alive.

This book, *Exploitation and Restoration*, is the third in an ongoing series of books on San Diego Bay produced by this teaching team and their innovative, creative and skilled 11th-grade students. Over the years, the Bay has continued to provide a rich and complex setting for an outdoor classroom. We found in this urban historical ecology project, an essential integration of the biological sciences with the humanities. In this dovetailing of biology and humanities, mathematics became the essential tool, which helped us to quantify and evaluate the many questions arising from each of the Bay's stories. The project allowed our students to explore their environment first hand and to begin to address the problematic separation from our natural surroundings found in the city dweller. By bringing our work to the field, we hoped to address the detachment and devaluation that can result when we lose contact with our natural environment. Finally, through the production of this book, we attempted to provide our students with meaningful work both in its production and appreciation. Sharing our stories, information, and findings with others, from the casual user to the informed specialist, through publication brings about its own importance and reward.

In order to discover the stories within the topics we selected and what the future may hold for each, a variety of research practices were undertaken. Generally this involved extensive literature review, interviews with experts and users of resources, collection of field data and direct observation. We attempted to create a learning environment beyond which students gather simple descriptions of their fellow inhabitants, so often found in the traditional field guide approach. Instead, we followed the lead of Jared Diamond's insightful historical look at human civilization, *Guns, Germs and Steel*. We designed a study of the Bay that examined different biological resources in relationship with the Bay's geography and demography. By doing so, we attempted to understand the dependence, survival and prosperity of human culture upon a successful relationship with nature. While "use has frequently led to abuse," we concluded that our rich biodiversity and geographic complexity is best maintained through preservation, prior to its essential restoration.

The book is full of unique contributions, including original interviews of experts and historical figures, archival photos from shoeboxes and desk drawers, as well as the students' own creations of timelines, maps and visual depictions of population dynamics over time. The vast majority of photos are High Tech High images captured by those involved in this project. Yet, we realized that a valid portrayal of historical ecology could not be represented only by fleeting glimpses of contemporary scenes captured by our cameras. These stories of our past have been accompanied by carefully selected original photos. The student voice, found in these pages, provides a fresh look that weaves itself into and sheds light upon the views of experts and seasoned veterans. As teachers, we commend our first-time published authors, poets, photographers, cartographers, and editors and thank them for their year of hard work and thoughtful effort.

We would like to thank those who have inspired and supported us and encouraged us to pursue this project. We would like to thank California Sea Grant and the Unified Port of San Diego for monetary support and constructive editorial suggestions. The final informative, rich, and beautiful product that is on these pages would not be possible without the intensive review of the final drafts of this book that was done by the chief student editor, Natalie Linton, in coordination with Kelly Makley of the Environmental Services Division of the Port of San Diego and Marsha Gear and Joann Furse of California Sea Grant Communications at Scripps Institution of Oceanography. We thank the National Education Association for the support of teachers like ourselves and for their vision to provide financial assistance so that teachers can explore. Other financial support came from High Tech High and the Regional Occupational Program, institutions that believe education is best when it is rigorous and meaningful. We continue to be inspired by Dr. Jane Goodall's life's work and her message of hope. Her Roots & Shoots Program continues to demonstrate what youth can achieve and contribute to the health and well being of our planet. Larry Rosenstock and all our colleagues at High Tech High have also made this possible and encouraged its innovation and risk taking.

Jay Vavra, biology teacher
Tom Fehrenbacher, humanities teacher
Rod Buenviaje, mathematics teacher

Gary and Jerri-Ann Jacobs High Tech High, San Diego

Acknowledgements

Such a book would not be possible without extensive community support. This is a story about the people of San Diego Bay, past and present, as much as it is about the creatures. Without the people of the community, it would not have been possible to collect the information necessary to make this book.

First and foremost, on behalf of the students, we must thank our teachers, Rod Buenviaje, Tom Feherenbacher, and Dr. Jay Vavra. Throughout the year, these three helped motivate us and ensure us we were experiencing the true meaning of High Tech High's project-based learning. Their unwavering dedication to this book made us, as students, even more compelled to create a stellar product, which we did.

The ones who literally made the book possible were the students. Each student was involved in this book, with the photography, the writing, the poems, the interviews, even the science experiments; each student contributed their personal style to the book, which truly highlights its uniqueness. The chapter editors helped bring it all together: Darci Daneshvari, Natalie Linton, Schuyler Marquez, Robert Stelmach, Gwen Michael-Jones, Fannie Ngo, Erin Rexin, Jane Jensen, Amelia Pludow, and Alan Shirey.

The lives of the earliest inhabitants of the Bay were understood with the help of Steve Bouscaren, Anthropology Professor at San Diego City College; Louis Guassac, a member of the Kumeyaay Nation and Founder of Guassac and Associates; and Patricia Masters, a paleobiologist at the Scripps Institution of Oceanography, who supplied us with an informative interview and allowed us to reproduce her maps of the ancient Bay. Special thanks to Dr. Bouscaren for his multiple interviews and for sharing literature with us. We would also like to thank Andy Yatsko, the archaeologist and Cultural Resources Program Manager who laid the foundation to study the artifacts found at Ballast Point. Special thanks to Ron May, the Director of the Fort Guijarros Museum Foundation, who not only provided us with two interviews, but also allowed us to photograph artifacts within the museum collection, along with Maisie Morris, Lab Supervisor. Dr. May contributed extensively to the editing of the Native American chapter. Thanks to these experts we gained a greater understanding and deeper respect of the Native Americans of San Diego.

Extensive knowledge and historical artifacts of the Chinese fishermen were provided by the generous curator of the San Diego Chinese Historical Museum, Murray Lee. Dr. May also assisted with this chapter and arranged artifacts of the nineteenth century Chinese fishing camps around Ballast Point for us to study and photograph.

The life of the waterfowl hunter was recreated and understood with the help Ron Vavra, a former duck hunter, who assisted us in creating the modern hunt, which involved shooting birds with cameras and binoculars in the early morning along the muddy shore of the Bay. He also provided us with a biology teacher and numerous stories about duck hunting in San Diego County and raising the black brant in his backyard. We also thank Jim Brown of the U.S. Fish and Wildlife Service and former director of the San Diego City Lakes, for giving expert information about waterfowl hunting around "Duckville" and San Diego Bay. Mr. Brown also put us in touch with waterfowl legend, painter and decoy carver David Hagerbaumer, who provided us with an interview and permission to reproduce his beautiful artwork. Thanks to Jim Heather, a duck hunter and former Canadian biologist who visited our school and shared his stories about living with and studying the black brant of western Alaska.

Good fortune shined upon us with a chance encounter involving Frank Sherwood, professor emeritus of Florida State University, son of Dr. Clarence M. Sherwood, chief chemist, and head nurse, Mildred Persons Sherwood, of the Hercules gunpowder plant. He provided us with a direct connection to the workings of the WWI era gunpowder factory on the South Bay. Thanks go again to Dr. Sherwood for supplying us with historic photos of his family members at the Hercules plant along with a transcontinental interview. Barbara Moore, former program manager of Chula Vista Nature Center, gave us extensive information on the gunpowder factory and the present day nature center. Special thanks to Peter Neushul, professor of history at UC Santa Barbara, for his review of the kelp harvesting and extraction methods of Hercules.

The 76 years of the kelp harvesting industry for alginate production came to an end as we wrote this book and the story of its rise and fall was told to us in part by Dr. Craig Barilotti, Marine Resource Management Consultant for Sea Foam Enterprises, and former biologist at Kelco. We also thank him for critical review of this chapter. Further review was kindly provided by Andrew Currie, production manager of CP Kelco.

The rich history and contemporary operation of the South Bay Salt Works crystallized thanks to three important people. Thank you Allen M. Jones, vice president of H.G. Fenton, who opened the gates of the salt works and gave us insight into the process of salt production. Thank you Tracy Strahl, vice president of South Bay Salt Works, for giving us a tour around the facility; it gave us such a different perspective on the Bay. Also, thank you Victoria Touchstone, a National Wildlife Refuge planner for the U.S. Fish and Wildlife Service; without her we would not have been able to understand the biodiversity of the salt works past and present.

We were able to reconstruct the glory days of San Diego's tuna fishing industry with the help of long-time residents of San Diego, Jean Immenschuh and Guy Bruni. Both Immenschuh and Bruni shared with us colorful personal stories of the tuna fishing industry in San Diego that was such a big part of each of their lives, and they generously provided us with many beautiful and previously unpublished photos. We thank Russ Vetter of the Southwest Fisheries Science Center for informing of us of the biology of the tuna and the current state of research on this amazing predator and important marine resource.

Our introduction to the Navy Marine Mammal Program (NMMP) was Phil Lamonica, a recently retired commanding officer of the Fleet ASW Base, and Tom Lapuzza, recently retired public affairs officer of the NMMP. We had the amazing opportunity to interview trainer DruAnn Clark, who shared the perspective of someone who has trained and escorted NMMP sea lions around the world. We would also like to thank Bob Lynch who took us out on the Bay and gave greater insight into the importance of the sea lions from the perspective of a former private employee.

Chris Harris, head biotechnician with the NMMP was a big help in getting extensive information on the daily treatment and training of the dolphins of San Diego. We would like to thank Jewyl Alderson, science teacher at High Tech High and former SeaWorld employee, for the insight related to the different positive reinforcement training methods for dolphins.

We were put in touch with literally thousands of white seabass with the help of Noelle Morris of the San Diego Oceans Foundation. We would also like to thank Gabe Buhr, recently retired Hubbs SeaWorld Research Institute (HSWRI) white seabass growout facilities manager, who showed us just how devoted the HSWRI and the Oceans Resources Enhancement Hatchery Program are towards restocking white seabass in San Diego Bay. And lastly, to Bob Hetzler, a former spearfisherman, who not only provided us with a fisherman's perspective and historical photos, but also noted the importance of restocking natural resources that have been depleted.

Several important individuals provided us with information on the natural history and local industry of the abalone. Thanks to David Lapota, from SPAWAR, who gave us a tour of the abalone-raising facilities near Ballast Point and for sharing photos of the outplanted abalone on the Pt. Loma kelp bed. Also, we acknowledge Howard Stacklin, who entertained us with colorful stories of his personal experience diving for abalone around San Diego Bay. And a special thanks to David Leighton, who reviewed this chapter and provided us wonderful photos.

The world of the bay mussel opened up for us with the assistance of Dr. Bonnie J. Becker, a former marine biologist at Cabrillo National Monument and a new faculty member of the University of Washington, Tacoma; John Davis, owner of Carlsbad Aquafarm; and Steve Le Page, the owner of M-Rep Consulting. Thanks to Laurel Rogers, U.S. Geological Survey, San Diego for providing us with the map used in the geography sections of the book. Special thanks to professor emeritus Richard "Pancho" Lantz for joining us on field outings and sharing his knowledge and passion for the creatures of the Bay.

Thanks to graphic arts teacher David Jean for his expertise in the realm of design and for sharing his artistic vision. The technical aspects and logistics of conducting and transcribing over thirty in-the-field interviews for this book and for an upcoming documentary would not have been possible without the assistance and skills of multimedia teacher Blair Hatch.

We were able to photograph and understand the geography of the Bay with the aerial assistance of Captain Steve Byers and his float plane. Thanks to Chris Travers of the San Diego Historical Society for her assistance with the photo archives.

Lastly, we would like to recognize the student photographers who contributed a great deal to these pages with their wonderful imagery of San Diego Bay and the themes this book elaborates on. Many thanks go to: Erin Rexin, Chris Slater, Connie Han, Gwen Michael-Jones, Justin Cadlaon, Kris Keller, Hilary Dufour, Amelia Pludow, Charlie Ziman, Shawn Teeter, Justin Desagun and Moray Black.

Student Introduction

Students from High Tech High have produced two marvelous field guides exhibiting the vast natural beauty of San Diego Bay. These books have received awards, praise from professors and scientists, and *Perspectives*, the book preceding this one, was published commercially. This year, however, the project has moved in another direction entirely. The two field guides gave people a new-found respect concerning everything in and around San Diego Bay, but this book tells stories of how the Bay came to be as it is now.

Over the years, a number of key resources and peoples have contributed to the development of San Diego and its Bay. If we were to write about every noteworthy topic regarding San Diego Bay, this book would be a series. But while there were and still are countless different resources, industries, movements, and peoples that have changed the Bay, *San Diego Bay: A Story of Exploitation and Restoration* focuses on twelve preeminent topics.

Native Americans once populated much of Southern California, and now populate reservations in the desert. Chinese fishermen came to San Diego Bay from Asia with their knowledge and expertise in fishing and opened up a whole new industry. Waterfowl hunting was a way of life, became a controversial pastime, and is now a stigma. Tuna is a fish that has been caught in San Diego for decades, and these mammoth fish are brought in daily by dedicated fishermen. Salt harvesting became a prime industry along the Bay. Scientific discoveries surrounding kelp brought about the establishment of two new industries involving the conversion of kelp to gunpowder and various additives. Dolphins and sea lions, two exceedingly intelligent marine mammals, have contributed to the United States' naval power through the Naval Marine Mammal Program in San Diego Bay. White seabass was an important stock for fishermen until their population began dwindling, and now efforts to restock the fishery may one day restore them to that position. Abalone was a profitable marine resource that now has its own conservation program with the government. The contributions of mussels to the fishing industry and Bay clean-up efforts are fascinating.

While researching each topic, we focused on three key ideas: utilization, exploitation, and restoration. Through these key issues, this book is meant to both inform and advise. Through this book we want the reader to realize the importance that local resources have on a city; and also, how easily their availability can diminish, which ultimately has a larger effect than most people realize. As students we wanted to blend personal narrative and perspective with expert opinion and thorough research. The product is a book that looks to the past, analyzes the present, and speculates on the future.

"We fished the Bay—even the Spaniards talked about how the Kumeyaay were found far out into the oceans spearing fish."
-Louis Guassac

Native Americans

The San Diego region has been home to Native Americans for thousands of years. Some of these early natives chose to settle near San Diego Bay and take advantage of the abundant and diverse marine life that existed there. They lived in balance with the ecology of the Bay, and often ate shellfish such as mussels and abalone, and used the creatures' shells for a variety of constructive and decorative purposes.

Around 1769, Spanish missionaries and settlers came to San Diego. A Native American tribe known as the Kumeyaay was settled near San Diego Bay and took full advantage of the Bay's bountiful resources. The arrival of the Spaniards disrupted the lifestyle of the Kumeyaay, which was forever changed. Missionaries from the Roman Catholic Church recruited Kumeyaay as laborers to produce agriculture for the presidios, and the Spanish government disenfranchised Kumeyaay families of their traditional rights.

Many families responded to these changes by appealing to their relatives at inland villages for a place away from the domineering Europeans. Others remained in San Diego, where they had no choice but to adapt with the changing times as well as they could. The Kumeyaay drifted away from their original hunter-gatherer lifestyle and were lured into the cash economy system as their traditional rights were invalidated by new U.S. property laws. As a result, they came to live in reservations and now act as the owners and operators of multi-million dollar casinos.

Geography of the Native Americans of the Bay

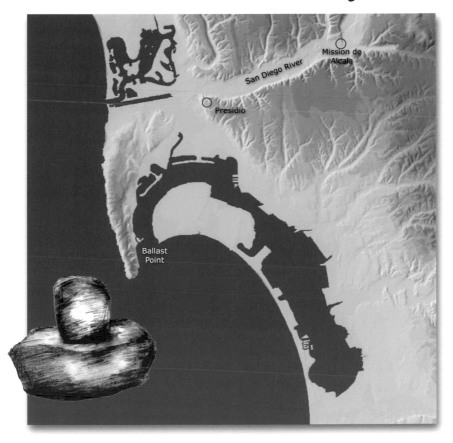

The coastal region of California centering on San Diego Bay was once a diverse habitat ideal for subsistence hunting and gathering. Within close proximity to the Bay, the natives who practiced such a lifestyle also had a year-round freshwater source in the San Diego River, among other sources. Their foraging areas included rocky shore, sandy beach, bay, lagoon, mudflat, estuarine salt marsh, coastal sage scrub and riparian woodland.

The lives of the earliest inhabitants of the region were forever changed by the arrival of European explorers and missionaries. Strategically placed fortifications were built at the Presidio, Ballast Point, and Mission de Acalá—representing the first fortifications of the Spanish government and the foundation of the Roman Catholic church in California.

History of the Natives of the Bay

Anthropologists and archaeologists have amassed substantial evidence proving that humans have resided in the region around San Diego Bay for thousands of years. According to this evidence, Native Americans arrived at the coast of San Diego around 8,000 to 12,000 years ago. However, due to their type of lifestyle, they were largely left unstudied by historians. The tribes in and around San Diego did not acquire horses or engage in elaborate war campaigns; they did not wear decorative headdresses, colored beads, or buckskin clothing, and they did not live in tipis. They lived a hunter-gatherer lifestyle that was simple and without flair. (Carrico 1987) (May 2006) (Showley 1999)

A stone tool used by the natives of San Diego Bay.

What cultural documentation there is of these natives dates back to as early as 12,000 BCE, during what is called the San Dieguito Complex. The cultural attributes of the Complex were uncovered through the excavation and discovery of tools characteristic of the era such as knives and scrapers. The San Dieguito natives were hunter-gatherers who found numerous coastal estuaries rich in bountiful food and utilitarian resources, which attracted the Native Americans to settle along the coast rather than the more barren inland. (Showley 1999) (Masters 2006)

Around 5,000 to 10,000 years ago, the sea level was 400 feet lower than it is today. With the rise in sea levels and the depletion of local resources, the San Dieguito natives moved inland, creating a form of ancient urban sprawl. At this time of geographic expansion, from our understanding of local archaeology, a second people emerged—they were known as the La Jollan people. A controversy exists among experts as to whether these were a different people that had emigrated to San Diego or whether they were the result of rapid changes undergone by the San Dieguito natives. It is believed that the La Jollan people lived along the coast in the winter time, moving to higher elevations during the summer. (Bouscaren 2005)

The La Jolla Complex presents a picture of natives in the early milling stage of development. This stage was "characterized by grinding tools reflecting the greater dependence of these people upon exploiting plant resources" (Carrico p. 7). It can be surmised that the Native Americans moved around a great deal, finding fresh food sources once the existing ones were exhausted—most likely due to seasonal weather changes. The

Kumeyaay are believed to have been good at managing the resources they used, having an excellent sense of ecology and taking advantage of seasonal harvests and marine resources. (Carrico 1987) (May 2006)

Supporting this hypothesis is the discovery of the many shell middens found at La Jolla Shores, which document the natives' dependence on gathering local shellfish. The Native Americans likely moved inland because of the loss of that food source. The natives probably visited the Bay from November to March, because during those months there were no

SHELLFISH DIET OVER TIME

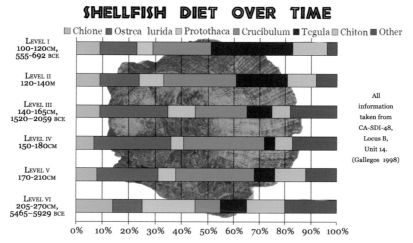

☐ Chione ■ Ostrea lurida ☐ Protothaca ■ Crucibulum ■ Tegula ☐ Chiton ■ Other

LEVEL I
100-120CM,
555-692 BCE

LEVEL II
120-140M

LEVEL III
140-165CM,
1520-2059 BCE

LEVEL IV
150-180CM

LEVEL V
170-210CM

LEVEL VI
205-270CM,
5465-5929 BCE

0% 10% 20% 30% 40% 50% 60% 70% 80% 90% 100%

All information taken from CA-SDI-48, Locus B, Unit 14. (Gallegos 1998)

Excavation of cultural material (artifacts and ecofacts) from the Ballast Point site was controlled using stratigraphic levels, wherein the highest and lowest points of each stratigraphic unit were used. In some cases, these stratigraphic levels appear to overlap, however they are mutually exclusive, and reflect subsurface soil changes and occupation levels.

red tides that made filter-feeding shellfish poisonous to eat. The La Jolla Complex lasted from around 5,000 BCE to 500 BCE, and the end of the Complex marked a shift in the types of tools used by the Native Americans. (Carrico 1987)

After the La Jolla Complex, another people moved into the region. They are often referred to as Yuman-speakers, however they are more commonly known as the Kumeyaay people. Other Native American tribes thrived in the area as well—including the Luiseño of the North County, the Cahuilla farther northeast, the Cupeño around Warner Springs, and the Ipai, often referred to as the Northern Diegueño, who lived from San Dieguito River Valley to Mission Valley. The Kumeyaay lived the closest to San Diego Bay, ranging from Mission Valley to south of Ensenada, and most lived along the coast and around the Bay. (Showley 1999)

The Kumeyaay could have derived from the San Dieguito or they may have arrived from desert around 1000 C.E. Some families were migratory, while others lived in villages year round. They hunted birds and fish in the marshes, and gathered shellfish along the coast. In addition, they were able to get seafood by building traps from shaped rocks and setting these out during the tidal exchange. The Kumeyaay used more than 60 different species of flora as food sources. The Kumeyaay hunted year round, but many gathered together and settled in permanent villages called ran-

A Native American bone tool discovered at Ballast Point.

cherias. Eight rancherias have been found along San Diego Bay, evidenced by the discovery of chipped stone tools and broken fragments of pottery. (Carrico 1987) (Hammock 1974) (May 2006) (McKeever 1985)

Trade was a part of these early Native Americans' lives. The coast was an important source for collecting or making products to trade. The Tipai and Ipai tribes traded salt, dried seafood and dried greens with the Yuman-speakers—which in Southern California include the Kumeyaay, Pai Pai, Cocopah, Kiliwa, Quechan, Yuma, and Seri—who obtained their salt by extracting it from the sea water. (Showley 1999)

Though considered to be a band level society, the Kumeyaay had a deep religious cosmology, intricate kinship systems, and a complex political network. Because their food supplies were relatively abundant, they did not have a hard time thriving in the San Diego area. Their construction efforts were focused on those objects and tools they used to catch fish or take abalone from rocks. Some of these tools, such as fish hooks made of bone, have been recovered from the midden in Ballast Point. (Carrico 1987) (Heizer 1980)

In September 1542, Juan Rodriguez Cabrillo sailed to California and landed in what is now

A reenactment of Cabrillo's landing.

known as San Diego Bay. He and his crew stayed for seven days. He noted in his journal that the Native Americans were fearful of the Spaniards and fled. He conveyed disappointment in the natives because they provided no help in finding gold. After this brief visit, over two centuries passed before a Spanish ship would again arrive in San Diego. (Showley 1999)

In 1769 an expedition from Spain arrived in California to consolidate the Crown's claim to the area, and San Diego was established as a presidio—a military outpost—and as a mission. When Junípero Serra and a group of missionaries founded Mission San Diego de Alcalá, it was for the purposes of creating an agricultural economy in the area and bringing the Kumeyaay into a cash economy that supported the Spanish Crown. Many Kumeyaay grew to resent the Spanish intrusion, despite the efforts of the missionaries and soldiers to convert and suppress them. After six years filled with tension, in November 1775 several hundred Kumeyaay surrounded Mission de Alcalá and set fire to the then wooden building in an attempt to drive the Spaniards away. They attacked a small group of Spaniards, and the Roman Catholic priest who went down to the San Diego River to negotiate with the incited na-

Mission de Alcalá.

tives in the misguided belief that religion would calm them, died of arrow wounds. The natives retreated only once they were satisfied that they made their point. Though the Spaniards did not leave, and instead simply rebuilt the mission using adobe architecture, the Kumeyaay attack did manage to weaken Spain's already tenuous hold on the area. (Carrico 1997) (Johnson 1903) (May 2006)

The natives knew how to utilize San Diego Bay and understood it, having lived off the Bay for thousands of years, but the local Spanish government had no interest in pursuing a maritime economy; they already had a well-developed system for pressing Native Americans into following their agricultural economy. After the Mexican War of Independence (1810–1821), the Mexicans continued the trend. As a result, the natives' invaluable knowledge of the Bay was ignored, and the opportunity for utilizing that knowledge was soon lost as Native American families retreated inland to live with relatives in areas removed from the new settlers. Over time, the Bay would undergo such extensive changes that it would become unrecognizable to the original inhabitants. (Gallegos 1998) (Masters 2006) (May 2006)

At the time of the Spanish arrival, the Kumeyaay population was estimated at 25,000 to 50,000 living in San Diego County. Today, an estimated 2,300 to 3,000 Kumeyaay live in the area's 12 inhabited reservations.

The drastic decline in the number of Kumeyaay since the arrival of the Europeans can be attributed to the changes in lifestyle they underwent as the colonization of North America progressed. After the U.S.-Mexican War (1846–1848), control of California was transferred from Mexico to the United States. Under the Mexican Republic, the Kumeyaay, who had been permitted to kill stray cattle for food, could dry the relatively valuable skins of the cattle on a bush and recover them for sale. However, with the transfer of control to the United States, all concepts of "property" that the natives had known under Spanish and Mexican rule were completely altered, and the "family use right" previously enjoyed by the Kumeyaay and Mexican Californians was eliminated. Unfortunately, no one bothered to inform the natives about this change. (Carrico 1987) (Guassac 2005) (May 2006)

Ratified in 1848, the Treaty of Guadalupe Hidalgo gave cities the right to "pueblo lands"—old Mexican land grants. The United States government regarded the pueblo lands as private land grants, Native Americans had the right to file papers to get these land grants until the year 1883. However, because no one ever told the Kumeyaay that this was possible, no Kumeyaay ever filed papers with the U.S. Lands Commission. Instead, U.S. citizens that moved west to California filed claims on Kumeyaay land, and from 1846 through 1900 the natives were treated as squatters. U.S. property laws completely displaced the Kumeyaay and many Mexican Californians. By 1883, the Kumeyaay were denied access to "family use rights" of resources around San Diego Bay. This was perhaps the most dreadful time for native Californians, and entire tribes were wiped out by disease and the breakdown of their economic systems, in many cases even before their oral histories could be taken and recorded. This is yet another reason why there is so little knowledge about many of the California Native American tribes. (Guassac 2005) (May 2006)

In 1887, the Dawes Act was passed, eradicating the Native American tribal system. The act declared that each head of a family would be able to claim 1/4 of a section of tribal land as a place for farming. A section contained 640 acres. Each orphan and adult over 18 would receive 1/8 of a section, and each minor would receive 1/16 of a section. The federal government held the land in trust for 25 years, allowing the natives to handle all of their own affairs. However, again, no one told the natives how to file these land claims, and speculators were able to find loopholes within the law and purchase over two-thirds of what should have been reservation lands. The allotment of what land *was* given to the natives in many cases further disrupted the kinship that formed the base of their social system as many were given land far away from their kin. (Jordan 1985) (May 2006)

Education was another large problem for Native Americans.

Children were forcibly put into "Indian Schools" where they were forbidden to speak their native languages, were forced to cut their hair, and dress in Euro-American clothes. Adding insult to injury, the teachers taught the Native American children that their own people were barbarians and savages. The children grew up to be uncomfortable with life on the reservations. In the San Diego area, some Kumeyaay children lost their identity and became absorbed in the Mexican-American community. Consequently, once they finished their schooling, they faced a multitude of problems. Having strayed from their own culture, and barred from the dominant American culture, the Native Americans were left in an in-between world of alienation. Many of them left to move to the cities to work, but found that the "whites" discriminated against them. Alcoholism and depression became a widespread problem on the reservations, and it was a very harsh time for the Native American community. (Jordan 1985) (May 2006)

A century later, in the 1980s, casinos began to be built on some reservations for, as sovereign political entities, Native American tribes could operate casinos free of state regulation. The casinos were built in the hope that they would provide a source of income for Native American communities. Tribes such as the Pauma Mission, the Luiseño, the La Posta Mission, the Diegueño, the Viejas, the Ewiiaapaayp, the Sycuan, and the Pala Mission Indians, employ 13,000 workers at their casinos, and their combined annual gross revenue is an estimated $1.5 billion. San Diego County has the largest number of Indian casinos in the country, and they have a significant economic impact upon San Diego through the amount of jobs they offer both Native Americans and people of other ethnic descents.

Viejas Band Tribal Chairman, Anthony Pico (top), Chairman of the Sycuan Tribe, Danny Tucker (left), and Louis Guassac (right).

The casinos also give millions of dollars back to the San Diego area. For example, the Barona Casino has made it a goal to build the physical, educational and cultural facilities and other infrastructure necessary to ensure the survival of many Barona generations to come. With their casino funds they have provided college scholarships, spent $1.8 million on a new sewage treatment plant, and $1 million to build 12 new homes for families with children. In fact, many other tribes have accomplished similar deeds, looking to ensure the survival of themselves and their invaluable historic traditions, an endeavor that should definitely be supported and developed.

12,000 BCE
Prehistoric people live on
the San Diego Coast

9000 BCE
The San Dieguito Indians
arrive in San Diego County

12,000 BCE
(Before Common Era)

10,000 BCE
La Jolla Complex:
Early Milling Stage

6000–1500 BCE
Native Americans inhabit
Ballast Point

1542 CE
Juan Rodriguez Cabrillo discovers San Diego

2006 CE
Five primary tribes live in San Diego, today:

Cahuilla
Cuepeño
Ipai
Kumeyaay
Luiseño

2006 CE
(Common Era)

Circa 1883
Indian reservations are established

1769
The Spanish Army, missionaries (like Junípero Serra), and colonists land in San Diego with every intention to stay

13

Louis Guassac

As we attempted to follow the history of San Diego Bay and imagine what it was like to live here thousands of years ago as a Native American, we sought out someone with the knowledge to fill in the gaps in our understanding and the consideration to support our endeavor. This person was Louis Guassac, the tribal historian of the Mesa Grande Band of Mission Indians. The Mesa Grande Band is one of 18 federally recognized tribes in San Diego County, and one of the 12 of these 18 recognized as Kumeyaay/Diegueño Indians. Mr. Guassac has also worked as a volunteer and in a career position advocating tribal self-determination. We met with Mr. Guassac in Seaport Village in December. As we battled the ambient noise of the modern Bay, we heard tales of the olden days of San Diego Bay, when Native Americans lived along its shores. Mr. Guassac was an invaluable resource concerning the Native Americans of San Diego Bay, providing a more complete perspective of just how much change the Bay has undergone.

Student Researcher (SR): What tribe does your family belong to?

Louis Guassac: The Kumeyaay/Diegueño, Kumeyaay being the original and Diegueño being the Spanish-given name … they named us after their mission … Mission de Alcalá. When Kumeyaay [were baptized], they became … Christianized, civilized Diegueño Indians, and were no longer heathen Kumeyaay. For a long time in California we were known as Mission Indians. There are 18 reservations [in San Diego County], all federally recognized, meaning that the federal government has a relationship with these Bands. Out of the 18, 12 are Kumeyaay/Diegueño.

SR: Did anyone write down your culture's history?

Guassac: No, we didn't need to write it down, because we preserved everything in our oral history... We were taught through oral history— culturally, as a people. Today, I still practice our traditional culture through participating in ceremonies as a bird singer under the direction of a lead bird singer. Everything was handed down...

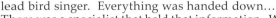
Louis Guassac.

There was a specialist that held that information. Within our structure there were specialists in every field—some that would watch the stars to see when to plant our plants or when it was time to move—that's what they did. Others were good hunters, so that's what they did. Others, who were good [resource] managers, developed the wetlands.

SR: What was the Bay like when the Kumeyaay lived there?

Guassac: When the Spaniards first came into the Bay, basically the whole area was marshlands. This was all wetlands, mud flats, lagoons—beautiful natural lagoons. But it wasn't smart to live on areas where it's flat, because periodically San Diego [Bay] would swell. So we built [our villages] on high grounds.

SR: So there were a lot of people who lived here on the Bay?

Guassac: No, resourcing from the Bay was primary—that was the purpose for being at the Bay. And the ocean was to collect things that you can have during the summer up in the mountains. Salt was important... We had salt when the marshes would move out a little bit. [It dried] naturally [just as it does] out at the salt beds today... Dehydrate the water, and you got salt.

Collection of metates (grinding stones) from the grounds of Mission de Alcalá.

SR: Because the Spaniards took over, did the Kumeyaay lose knowledge of usage on the Bay over the years?

Guassac: Yes. Our leaving the coast area removed a lot of our coastal knowledge because the people that knew that are gone. Probably the majority of what we knew has been removed and the oral history of it has been impacted negatively. The Native American population is about 3,000 in San Diego [right now].

SR: What [has been found] in San Diego Bay from the Native Americans?

Guassac: What you'll find in San Diego Bay are dump sites for shells. You'll come across shell mounds, huge shell mounds. They're underneath soils. They still periodically get [unearthed] when they do excavating or something, exploring holes for some development. In fact, [the old] Naval Training Center is mostly filled [land]. [The land really] started out on Rosecrans. When you come from Rosecrans east to the Bay that little channel [you see] there was all filled [land].

When they did their environmental review, environmental assessment and mining [at the Naval Training Center], they were running into shell mountains frequently—clams, abalone, razor clams, mussels—there was an abundance of natural resources within the Bay. There were abalone [located] where you could pick them out of the ocean. Of course, most had been fished out at the turn of the nineteenth century. The Chinese had [a fishing market] and took them out by the boatload.

SR: Can you tell us about how San Diego served as a port to more groups than just the Native Americans?

Guassac: San Diego Bay, being a natural bay, provided a natural porting opportunity. Back in those times economics was based in trade through the seas. You didn't have ... airplanes, taking things overland. It was faster going over water. So, the Bay was important—critical for trade and commerce. One of the biggest reasons why our people were removed from this area was because our economic profile [didn't fit] the Westerners' view on this Bay here.

Dedication of Kumeyaay Nation flag at the 2006 Cabrillo Festival.

SR: Were the Natives allowed to keep any lands?

Guassac: The reservations— the lands that were treated [to us]—those are ours. We have pure jurisdiction, governmental control on those lands that we currently reside on today. Under the federal statute, [our] reservations were recognized ... as domestic dependant nations—domestic meaning that we are in the continental United States. We're dependant because we still have this tie with the United States government. We can't create currency or start printing money, and we can't create an armed force. Those were the two things that they don't want to see us do; but anything in between, we can pretty much do.

SR: So what is tribal government?

Guassac: Tribal government is similar to a variety of governments in a modern, contemporary way: we have elected officials, elected chairmen, a council [government body] that is responsible for the infrastructure, health, safety, and economic vitality of the tribe, or whoever they're governing. The [council] is run by elected chairs, so the people really have the ultimate say—because they have the vote. It's a democracy, but in a tribal way of thinking. It's the community first—it's everybody first. You think of individuals second.

SR: Does the tribal community look back at the past to learn from trial and error?

Guassac: As I've mentioned, we could go back and look at history and we do often—that's what we do to remind ourselves of the shortfalls that have occurred. We can't go back and fix anything that's happened, but we can try to work together to keep it from happening again. I believe that's the model the tribal governments will work from today. Although we understand what's happened, we must help people understand that we are not here to do gaming because it's not our "pay buck." Rather, it's a function of tribal government and we can incorporate it into our government structure. And it works for us.

SR: Were there certain governments in charge of a certain part of the Bay?

Guassac: We used [San Diego Bay] as a common area for all Kumeyaay, meaning that no band had a carved out piece here. This was considered a national use area. The resources were national use, meaning that the bands came down and spent time here during the winter period. Just across the Bay in North Island, there was a fishing village over there. There were several other villages along the Bay-front here, including all the way to Point Loma.

We had many different [ways to use] the Bay. We fished the Bay—the Spaniards also talked about how the Kumeyaay were found far out into the oceans spearing fish. The kelp beds are the largest [along our] coast, [and our coast] is the wealthiest coast in the world. These kelp forests maintain a huge natural habitat in the way of species and fishes and so on. So you could imagine fishing would be great because your visibility was good to 10–15 feet perhaps. The Kumeyaay used a variety of tools for processing the food resources.

SR: Why did people want to get rid of the Native Americans?

Guassac: We didn't fit the economics. Therefore, we were an expendable people. And we weren't considered humans. It's pretty sad. I've been through the archives and researched this, and I've gotten emotional in there, 'cause you learn that these kids—these children—were gunned down just because of who they were. It's a pretty hard thing to look at. We were [considered] savages, less than human. If you do that it's easier to justify your killing.

That's why we removed ourselves from coastal areas, too; because actually, if you were caught in San Diego without any money in your pocket as a Native American, you could be arrested by the local sheriff and then put in jail. And then a local rancher could come to get you and put you to work until you paid off that fine. It was another form of slave labor, just an illegal way of doing it. You were put in jail, and the sheriff would let the ranchers know they had some laborers in their jail—and they would come and get the natives in the jail. We weren't citizens yet. We weren't citizens until 1924, so they could take us to the ranch and make us work until we could pay off that fine. But where was the judge to tell when that fine [had been paid]?

SR: Is it important that the Native Americans' history be shared with the community?

Guassac: I think it's important. In the past no one thought too much about who we were, especially here in San Diego County. Many people didn't even know that there were reservations out there. It was only when gaming came around that we became elevated where people knew about us. It's not just about gaming. Gaming is only a tool, but tribal government is about servicing the community, providing infrastructure, maintaining community services and so on. That's what tribal government is all about.

"Indian" by Arthur Putnam, Presidio Park.

Steve Bouscaren

Steve Bouscaren is a local anthropologist and an archaeologist who has been working full time as an anthropology instructor at San Diego City College since the fall of 1989. He has a B.S. degree in anthropology, M.S. degree in archaeology, and a Ph.D. in cultural anthropology, botany, and plant science. In the late 1960s, Dr. Bouscaren started to study Native American culture. He traveled to Alcatraz Island with natives in 1969, and from that moving experience he discovered a great interest in Native American culture. When he returned to San Diego, he enjoyed studying how the Natives used plants and other living organisms to survive. Ever since then, he has had an interest in finding out how indigenous peoples in places around the world use the plants native to their area for medicinal purposes. Dr. Bouscaren has worked with many different Native American tribes. He and his colleague, Miguel Wilken-Robertson, have offered workshops in Northern Baja California with the Paipai, Kumeyaay, and Kiliwa Native Americans, consisting of lessons in pottery making, agave roasting and adobe brick making.

Student Researcher (SR): Is there anything specific that you found interesting or unusual in your research of Native Americans?

Steven Bouscaren: I find all of it absolutely fascinating, and what I always think with the elders and the Native American people, is that every elder probably has the accumulation of thousands of years of knowledge and wisdom about how to live on the planet, how to take care of the resources that grow around us, and how to prevent things from being destroyed or overused... They were able to live in harmony with the environment. I think that's in direct contrast to how you see us living in the same environment and what we have done to that environment in a very short period of time compared to the thousands and thousands of years that they've lived here. I think in San Diego that's very, very obvious.

SR: How did the Native Americans impact their environment?

Bouscaren: You go back and read the early Spanish accounts of what the San Diego area looked like—for example what it looked like in 1769 when they arrived here—and then compare that to what

A Native American dwelling made of willow at Mission de Alcalá.

it looks like now. You look at the wildlife, how that's changed, how the vegetation's changed, how the waters have changed. And if you look at how the Native American people managed the environment, not only the environment that they've lived in, but the entire environment around them—how they managed water resources, and how they managed animal populations: they never over hunted. They lived in a balance … they had to. If they blew it, if they overexploited the resources that existed here, they didn't have another store they could go to down the road. So their existence depended on really wise use of those resources. And that's wisdom and knowledge that was accumulated over thousands and thousands of years.

Miss Kumeyaay Nation with bird singers.

SR: So, how did these tribes end up here in the first place?

Bouscaren: The earliest evidence that we have of someone being here in San Diego County was about 10,000 years ago. The people that lived here then we call the San Dieguito people. We don't know what they called themselves; we don't have any other reference to them, except for what we know through archaeology and the folklore and traditions passed on through present day Kumeyaay people. The San Dieguito were here for a few thousand years. They were primarily a big-game hunting population. They lived in the high areas, and there was much more fresh water around than there is now.

They lived on the edges of lakes, the ridge tops, around water sources where they could hunt the game that came to those water sources... As the environment was becoming drier and warmer and sea levels had begun to rise, we found that the estuaries, bays, and lagoons that began to form along the coast here in Southern California, and northern Baja California became very, very resource rich. Eventually, the San Dieguito people were replaced by another people called La Jollan people. We don't know if the La Jollan people were San Dieguito people that became La Jollan, or whether the San Dieguito people disappeared and were replaced by the La Jollan people. But we do know that the La Jollan people were around for several thousand years, and that they placed a heavy emphasis on exploiting marine resources for subsistence.

SR: What did they do about the red tide?

Bouscaren: Red tide generally is caused by dinoflagellates that affect certain species of shellfish, which can cause paralysis, and even death. I think that May through October is the time period during which people shouldn't consume the shellfish around here. So the La Jollan people were people that exploited the coastal areas in the winter time and probably moved into higher elevations around summer time. Around 2,500 years or so ago, the La Jollan people began to disappear.

It's possible that the San Dieguito people, the La Jollan people, were all Kumeyaay … but it's still controversial, and we're not absolutely certain. The Kumeyaay people today will tell you that they've always been here and that there weren't any other people that lived here besides them until the Europeans showed up. The Kumeyaay territory ranges from the San Diego

River in the northern county, and from the coast towards the Colorado River all the way down to the Colorado delta, and then down to Baja California, below Ensenada, towards the coast in Valle de Santo Tomas. That whole area belonged to the Kumeyaay, and at the time when the Europeans showed up there were probably at least somewhere between 25,000 to 50,000 Kumeyaay living there. Today in the 12 reservations or so in San Diego County, there are probably 2,300 to 3,000 Kumeyaay living here ... not including the Kumeyaay (Kumiai) that are living in northern Baja California, because they live on both sides of the border.

SR: Was it specifically fish and shellfish that they hunted?

Bouscaren: We know that the Kumeyaay fished. Florence Shipek recounted stories of Kumeyaay boys in reed boats that would leave around the Tijuana River and paddle all the way to the Coronado Islands to fish. We know that during the spring time, when the pelagic fish are going through this area, they hunted deep water fish. The most important time of the year for shellfish exploitation was from December to January. They also hunted small game. We know that they also used a wide variety of plants—some of which still grow here, but most of the plants are probably gone now.

SR: Are there any accessible sites on the Bay that may provide us good information?

Bouscaren: Actually there's a really interesting site right up here on Ballast Point. A local company that I've worked for off and on for several years, Dennis Gallegos and Associates, excavated a site at Ballast Point and wrote a report that was called *Five Thousand Years of Maritime [Subsistence at CA-SDI-48,] on Ballast Point, [San Diego County, California].*

Modern day Ballast Point.

SR: Do you think if the Native Americans came back today, that they'd be able to survive?

Bouscaren: I think that small numbers of people can probably survive, if [they] knew what plants to eat. I think that hunting animals would be a little problematic today in San Diego for all kinds of reasons. But if you're going to base your diet on what you caught out on the water and what you found growing out on the land, I think that probably a very small number of people could subsist that way. Could 20,000...25,000 people subsist that way? I don't think so. I think that most of those resources have been destroyed... But the San Diego Bay region was a very productive food area for the Native Americans. There weren't too many Native Americans to use those resources, and they used them wisely; they didn't overexploit them. I know that San Diego Bay looked very, very different when the Spaniards first showed up here in the late 1760s and in Delfina Cuero's time [1900–1972].

Ron May

After doing extensive research on the early inhabitants of San Diego Bay, we were referred to Ron May by Andy Yatsko, the Cultural Resource Manager for the U.S. Navy. Mr. May is the President and co-founder of Legacy 106 Inc., a company deeply involved in archaeology and historic preservation. Over the past 37 years, Mr. May has been involved in a wide range of historic and archaeological studies in California and northern Baja California, Mexico. One of his current part-time projects is located in the Navy Sub Base on Point Loma, where Mr. May and his coworkers manage the Ballast Point Repository, which archives artifacts found at Ballast Point from campsites of early natives.

One weekend, we went out to meet Mr. May. He led us past the modern war vessels and various buildings that make up the Navy base to the historical area that contained the archives. We arrived at the former handball court, which houses many of the prehistoric and historic artifacts that have been discovered on the base. There, we interviewed Mr. May.

Student Researcher (SR): So I understand that many Native American items were recovered here at Ballast Point. Can you name some items for us?

Ron May: In a prehistoric site a few blocks away from where we were doing the main excavation, we tested to see if there were Spaniards here, but we didn't find any Spanish artifacts. In the process we found cutting tools, cores, hammer stones, flake stones, and a variety of marine shells—species that indicated a different time and presence. All that led me to believe that this site had been abandoned long before the Spaniards arrived.

SR: Which tribes do you think left these items?

May: Well, the prehistoric people would be called the Milling Archaic or La Jollan Complex. We don't know what they called themselves and we

Stone tool flakes found at Ballast Point.

don't know what language they spoke. The historic people in this area were the Kumeyaay. They were Yuman-speakers. They may have been the same people but it's hard to make the connection.

SR: I understand you have found shellfish remains on Ballast Point. What kinds of shellfish and how old?

May: Well, the prehistoric people of the Milling Archaic had a lot of shellfish associated with the reef system, like the oyster and mussel… They were the kinds of things you would pick off a reef in a nonsandy environment. In historic times, the Chinese and Euro-American whalers ate a lot of Pismo clams [that are] very large—about the size of a coffee cup saucer. They also ate ...

various clam species found in sandy shell bottoms or bay bottom habitats as opposed to the rocky habitat used by the prehistoric people.

SR: I read a book about whalers and how they threw the Kumeyaay out of the Bay...

May: My understanding is that when whaling first began in San Diego in the nineteenth century—maybe as early as 1840—whaling ships came into the [Bay's] harbor

A mural at Barrio Logan—a tribute to the Bay's wildlife and cultures.

and hired Indian people to work on the ships. They would go out to sea for three to four years at a time, and ... I assume those people [were] changed [by that experience]. At various points [in time] there were Native American people working at the whaling station, but who they were and where they came from remains unknown. The other thing is both the Russian otter companies and other maritime exploiters brought in other people. We had Aleuts and Eskimos coming down into San Diego and there were even Hawaiian kanakas coming to work in the various maritime industries... All of these people were interacting with one another. It was a very cosmopolitan community.

SR: Also when the Spaniards came and took out the natives, over what period of time did that take place? How long did it take for the Kumeyaay to move inland?

May: It's mostly speculation... The Spaniards came in 1769, and they pretty much kept to their little communities and continued that [way throughout] the early nineteenth century. The Kumeyaay people that had a lot of power and authority in their communities and were important [there] probably didn't feel the need to get involved with the Spaniards—they could just retreat up to their mountain villages. [However, those] who were disenfranchised on the edge of native society and the lower class individuals, might have been more attracted to convert to Catholicism and become Spanish citizens.

SR: How has the Ballast Point site contributed to the research of Native Americans?

May: I think you really have to talk about the sites that are known here on Point Loma. Ballast Point itself is really a very small site [that is sometimes] swept over by storms during the year. There wasn't a lot of prehistoric archeological material out on Ballast Point, but here in the Fort Rosecrans historical district [there] has been [some for] around ... at least 3,500 years. Where the research contribution occurs is when the Navy needs to build something, but Section 106 of the National Historic Act requires a company to come in and do archeological work to mitigate the impact of the building. That's what happened when Gallegos and Associates were hired to do the work in advance of the construction of Jones Hall. [They tested] the idea that the shellfish and other things on the site reflect the environmental changes that had occurred. They hired Pat Masters, who reconstructed the [historic] sea levels and the whole geographic change that was occurring. That is really how we advance things—[at least] when people go in adequately funded to do the research.

SR: Can you tell us what happened when El Niños occurred?

May: That was an interesting hypothesis that Dennis Gallegos and Erin Kyle raised when they noticed a correlation between an El Niño cycle and their archeological context that was not what you would expect to see. They [thought] that there might have been some effect from El Niño cycles on the coastal environments.

[Of course], the one person that has not been mentioned that should be is Carl Hubbs. He died a number of years ago, but he was … very interested in the changing sea temperature and its effect on populations of shellfish and fish species. [In one] example, there is a *Chione californiensis* clam that has a certain ring pattern that makes it very distinctive from another *Chione* of another species. The change in sea temperature of two or three degrees caused that shellfish [to massively die off]. He had the hypothesis that when you have sudden warming or dropping of the [ocean] temperature, you'd have such a massive die-off. We are now looking at these El Niño oscillations as though they would cause a massive change in the environment to the point where people would either starve or they had to adapt to new ways of foraging food to [survive].

SR: Would the Native Americans migrate at any time of the year?

May: We were interested in the idea that they might have a long-term village where they lived all year round. They had seasonal villages. There were different times of the year when families would break up and head to different places for different things. During certain months when pine cones were ripening, thousands of people from all over the place … would all converge on these valleys to gather pine nuts and roast them, exchange news, arrange marriages, tell stories, play games, and then they would break up and move on. And they'd have local winter villages and summer villages. Not always the same people came together. As they moved from one place to another, during seasonal changes, they would gather the clothes, plants, animals, and [other] things that they needed for the next place.

Patricia Masters

We needed to find out more about the structure of the Bay from millennia past, and we found Patricia (Pat) Masters, an expert on that very subject. Dr. Masters is a paleobiologist and was involved in several paleocoastline studies around the San Diego area, including a reconstruction of San Diego Bay over the past 12,000 years. Upon arriving at Scripps Institution of Oceanography, we found her office and set up our equipment. Dr. Masters spoke to us about the Bay as it is now, and about how it looked thousands of years ago, providing us with invaluable information concerning the geographical setting the Native Americans faced when they were the primary inhabitants of it.

Student Researcher (SR): Can you tell us what the Bay was like around 15,000 years ago?

Pat Masters: 15,000 years ago, the sea level was considerably lower than the present. [It was about] 100 meters [lower] … just where the shelf break was. When the sea level rose after that time, it flooded the stream channels that were carved into the shelves and they became small estuaries. When people arrived on this coast, [perhaps] somewhere around 12,000 years ago, they encountered a lot of estuarine environments and small estuarine embayments along the coast, and I think these were probably what attracted them to the coast. These were very resourceful people who were hunter-gatherers, fishers, collectors, and foragers who would have found this a very agreeable place to live and make a living.

By 8,000 [years ago] the sea level was around 20 meters below present [levels] and that would have brought in a shoreline behind Point Loma, and that happens to be a very important mechanism along this coastline. Most of our wave energy comes from the northwest—northwest storms from the Gulf of Alaska that come down along the coast … and send high winds and high waves in front of them. … But anything that's hidden behind a promontory, like Point Loma, would be protected. And that is the key to understanding how the Bay first began.

SR: How was San Diego Bay formed?

Masters: The shoreline had to move into the shelter of Point Loma, and then a very unusual thing for our coastline occurred. If you've walked out there—visited the Silver Strand, walked on Coronado—[you know] that there's a lot of sand there now. Much of it has been supplied artificially to help build those beaches up and protect the Bay. Originally the sand was brought out of the Tijuana River by floods, and the sheltering of Point Loma provided an opportunity for a reverse eddy to occur off the Tijuana River mouth. In other words, Point Loma provided protection from North Pacific waves, allowing the sand to move to the north. Northerly transport along the California coast is a very unusual situation. So, as that sand moved, it built a spit to the north, and when that spit grew long enough, it connected to

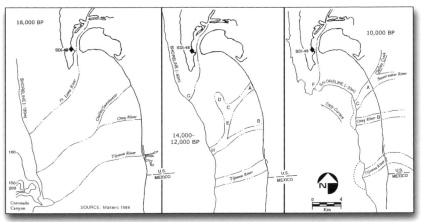

The formation of San Diego Bay (Masters in Gallegos and Kyle,
1998 p. 26). Map altered by High Tech High.

the North Island/Coronado area and created what is called a tombolo. Once
that happened, the Bay was formed.

SR: And how is that an unusual thing that happened?

Masters: Well a lot of bays such as San Francisco Bay are drowned estuaries.
They are formed behind large headlands, like Marin and the [San Francisco]
peninsula. These are high relief, high elevation, and hard structures; San
Diego Bay is not. To the north the Point Loma headland is solid rock, but the
southern part of the Bay is not—it's formed only by the sand spit. So, coastal

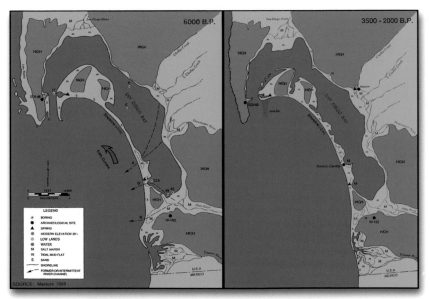

Drastic changes in the hydrography of San Diego Bay.
(Masters in Gallegos and Kyle, 1998 p. 28). Map altered by High Tech High.

processes, the movement of sediments by waves and currents ... that's crucial to the story of how San Diego Bay was formed.

SR: Were people living there when the Bay was forming?

Masters: I think that there were people living along the stream valleys, making good use of the estuaries with the fish, shellfish, birds, and sea mammals—all of the creatures that inhabit this estuarine environment. People migrated to this coastline about 12,000 years ago, but archaeological evidence around the Bay starts around 8,000 years ago.

SR: So, are you familiar with any of the marine species that have lived in the Bay at this time or even today?

Fragments of chiton found at Ballast Point.

Masters: We found [remains from the food that people harvested] at the archeological sites. There were a lot of shellfish, and the earliest levels of these sites, about 6,000 to 8,000 years ago, contain estuarine types of shellfish—scallops, clams. ... That's a little different from the archeological sites that we have up here on the northern part of the San Diego County coast without a big bay. Even around the lagoons, the earliest levels are full of ... species such as mussels and rock oysters. So, there's a bit of a difference, and it just emphasizes that estuaries were attracting people to the San Diego area, even before there was a bay. After 6,000 years—which I think is probably a reasonable estimate for when the Bay as we understand it today was formed—they would've had an amazing variety of food resources: sea turtles and all kinds of shallow water fish that prefer quiet environments. They also had access to the kelp beds around the mouth of the Bay and around the rocky side of Point Loma. There's even some archaeological evidence that they've scavenged or made use of whale resources. At a site in La Jolla ... there are circular shell fishhooks known to be one of the key traits of the Chumash, [who were] perhaps one of the earliest people on the [Channel] islands. It's a very intriguing site—[it has some] of the best evidence for [the existence of] a maritime economic base outside of San Diego Bay.

SR: Are you familiar with the diet of the Native Americans, and how it's changed over time?

Masters: The shifts in types of marine foods harvested is interesting. The site at Ballast Point indicated over 6,000 years of maritime activity and marine resource use. So, they were fishing the kelp beds, hunting the sea otters, collecting shellfish in that area of the Bay. A site on the Silver Strand is distinctive because close to 5,000 years ago, they were harvesting Pismo clams. ... The interesting thing about Pismo clams is that they are found only on a high-energy sandy coast, and that's what [the Silver Strand has]—waves crashing on a [gently sloping] sand beach formed by fine-grain sand. ... These clams can live for 20 years or more. If you have harvested them over a period of time, it means that the sand beach was very stable then. So, [5,000 years ago] the site was a wide, gently sloping fine-grain sand beach. ... [Up until] about 4,000 years ago, people [periodically] continued to come to the Strand to harvest that type of shellfish [Pismo clams].

SR: What kind of research have you conducted at Ballast Point?

Masters: I was part of the team that was analyzing the excavations there when the Navy was building some new facilities. Fortunately, it turned out to be a very significant excavation.

SR: What was found at Ballast Point? Were there tools or shellfish in that area?

Masters: There was a plethora of fire-affected rock that indicated that these people had established an area for heating rocks and roasting materials— presumably plant or animal material that they'd harvested. There were no house structures revealed, but obviously this was an area where people spent time [as evidenced by] the different densities of cultural remains in different parts of the site. There were preferred activity areas and other areas that were not as heavily utilized. So, they were there for a considerable amount of time and radiocarbon dates [indicate that some] population was making use of that site for over 6,000 years.

SR: How did the geography of the Bay affect the flora and fauna of San Diego thousands of years ago?

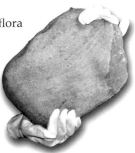

Masters: I think that's a very interesting question, and it's one I've been researching on other parts of the coast. We know that in northern San Diego County—where we have a north-south trending coastline and a relatively narrow shelf—as sea level rose, the earliest people encountered a rocky, exposed coast. They didn't find the sand beaches that we see here today and value tremendously. They found estuaries where marine waters were flooding small river valleys and creating little embayments which eventually [became the] lagoons that we're familiar with today. But the outer coast was a really rocky coast, and there was little sand. We think the transition along the San Diego coast from rocky to sediment-covered took place around 5,000 years ago, based on shellfish types found in the archeological sites.

Metate found at Ballast Point.

SR: How did the geography of the Bay influence the human prosperity in San Diego?

Masters: Well, a bay is a number of things. It's an environment that attracts sea turtles, various types of shallow water fish, and nurseries for species such as seabass—very valuable coastal fish populations. Usually a bay has a diversity of waterfowl and marine mammals. It also has the advantage of quiet water, allowing people with simple fishing methods and watercrafts to fish and hunt. It's a lot more of an energetic environment along the exposed coast outside of San Diego Bay.

SR: Any ideas on what their knowledge of kelp beds was several thousand years ago?

Masters: We know the people on Ballast Point were able to take small watercraft out through the rapid currents at the mouth of the Bay and handle the open ocean conditions on the western side of Point Loma. They were willing to take those risks and spend their time and efforts to create ways to get themselves out there because of the value of the kelp bed resources that are year-round sustainable fisheries.

On a sandy coast like the one we have today there is nothing that would attract ancient peoples. They needed rocky areas. So, that's what the west side of Point Loma was—shallow rocky reefs and kelp beds—the richest fish habitats along our coast. The kelp bed story ties in with this geography. When you have rocky coastline, you don't have sediments moving out onto the shelves and covering up the shallow, rocky reefs. This means that they don't fill up deeper areas, where the kelp grows, as well. Rocky shelves are areas … in these latitudes that allow kelp forests to grow. They were extremely vast around the Channel Islands and along the mainland coast in the early part of the Holocene. Now kelp beds are restricted by the amount of sediment that has moved out onto the nearshore shelves and the fact that the islands' shelf area decreased as sea level came up.

SR: So, the number of kelp beds has definitely decreased?

Masters: Oh yes, the peak area for kelp beds would have been during the last glacial period and at times when the sea level was creating the right depths on the shelves, say around 12,000 years ago.

Wave-eroded shore at the mouth of the Bay.

SR: What's going to happen in the future?

Masters: The reason we have a Silver Strand and the reason the Bay is still protected behind the sand dunes is artificial nourishment. We've already dredged the Bay to the extent that we can. [The dredging] occurred after WWII, and now there isn't much more to dredge out of the Bay without disrupting the South Bay area, the wildlife preserves there, or running into the contamination problems that have occurred recently. So, where is the sand going to come from? And the answer is: If not from offshore sources, [we might have to do without it]. As storms erode the coast in the winter—and we have indications that El Niños will intensify in the future—there might not be enough sand to rebuild beaches in the summer. Add rising sea level, and by 2100, we're looking at about one-half meter of sea-level rise. If the ice sheets continue to melt at their current rates, this might double. So, as the sea level comes up, the beaches are drowned and waves are sweeping into the South Bay and attacking the sea cliffs of the outer coast. Now our sand beaches are endangered. When our beaches are lost, we are going to have a very different relationship with the coastline than we have today.

A Native's Question

Why does the light skinned man
Have more cargo than the dark skinned man?
Why does the light skinned man seem closer to nature?
Though many possible answers are given
The one that will solve it is not yet chosen.

Could it be that the light skinned man was just
In the right place at the right time?
Or maybe the dark skinned man was cursed
By his harsh environment?

Could it be the resources?
Religion
Beliefs
Intelligence

Is there an answer to this question of our time?
Is it all a matter of what we think?

Or could there be a possibility that
The world
Its resources
Its treasures
Its natural materials

Have made all the difference.

Lemuel Calpito

San Diego Historical Society

Native Americans

Homo sapiens

Native American tribes have lived in San Diego Bay for thousands of years. They were quintessential hunter-gatherers, and there are many sites in San Diego, such as Ballast Point in Point Loma, where archeologists have found the discarded shells and bones of different marine animals eaten by these Native Americans. Besides consuming marine creatures, the natives used 60 different species of plants for consumption and for use in crafts. (Gallegos 1998)

Though fowl and terrestrial animals formed a part of the Native Americans' diet, the larger section of their food was drawn from San Diego

A Native American woman grinding nuts and seeds. San Diego Historical Society.

Bay and consisted of more than 30 species of fish and 64 species of shellfish. Some specific examples of what they ate include: the Giant Rock Scallop, the Butternut Clam, and the Black Turban Snail. (Gallegos 1998)

The Native Americans' material of choice for tools to catch their other, more mobile prey was bone. The bone came from the animals they captured. One example was a bone sharpened at both ends that was used as a fish hook. The Native Americans would throw the sharpened bone out into the water, and when a fish swallowed it, the bone would get lodged in its throat. Additionally, the Native Americans used stones to grind up nuts and seeds into a sort of flour that could be used in a variety of ways to complement their seafood catch. (Gallegos 1998)

Giant Rock Scallop
Hinnites giganteus

The Giant Rock Scallop was one of the more popular shellfish consumed by the early inhabitants. This scallop can be found in the waters of the Pacific from Queen Charlotte Islands in British Columbia to Punta Abreojos in Baja California. This scallop spawns during the month of April and is a plentiful source of food. (Morris 1980)

Butternut Clam
Saxidomus nuttalli

Also known as the Washington Clam, the Butternut Clam is found buried in mud and sand in the low intertidal zone of bays and lagoons, and in sandy areas near rocks on the outer coast. After eating the clam the natives would use its shell as barter for trading with other groups. (Morris 1980)

Black Turban Snail
Tegula funebralis

Another type of shellfish consumed by the Native Americans was the Black Turban Snail. It can be found along the Pacific Coast, from Vancouver to Baja California. The shell color of the snail ranges from a dark purple to a black, and it can be found by the hundreds in tide pools and on rocks. In San Diego, the Native Americans would construct tools to use for collecting the snail.

"Seven hundred tons or so of abalone would go out. Abalone were one of the largest exports in San Diego in those days." —Murray Lee

San Diego Historical Society. Ballast Point c. 1910.

Chinese Fishermen

The abundant fish and abalone present in and around San Diego Bay encouraged many Chinese to abandon the occupations they had taken up after coming to the United States in favor of work in the less competitive fishing industry. During the mid-1800s to early 1900s, the Chinese pioneered the industry in San Diego, meeting with tremendous success that enabled them to pave the way for future expansion. On the edge of San Diego Bay, the Chinese established a base for processing the abalone they gathered from the abundant waters of the Bay and all along the coast of Southern California.

The Chinese abalone harvest and fishing industry boosted San Diego's economy, but their practices, unrestricted by any monitoring or controls, were harmful to the ecology of the Bay and its surrounding waters. National anti-Chinese legislation and antipathy brought their practices under fire. Local resentment towards the Chinese grew, and rival ethnic groups that wanted the industry added to the pressure until the Chinese were driven from the very industry they had begun. Nonetheless, despite their departure from the industry, they had a significant impact on the development of both San Diego and the Bay.

Sun Yun Lee, from the Nash Collection of the Chinese Historical Society of Southern California.

Geography of the Chinese Fishermen of the Bay

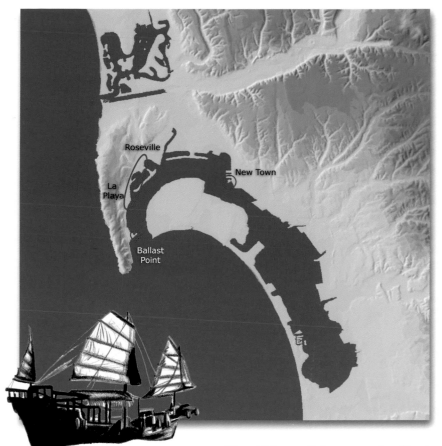

The Chinese fishermen who lived and worked on San Diego Bay operated not just in the Bay, but also all along the coast of Southern California and even down into Mexico. Nevertheless, they had several firmly established bases of operations located along the coast of San Diego Bay. The Chinese dominance of the fishing and abalone industries resulted in three bases, though they came and went with the development of San Diego. The earliest of the three was located on Ballast Point. The other two were at La Playa/Roseville and New Town, where San Diego's Chinatown became established.

History of the Chinese of the Bay

The discovery of gold in California in 1849 resulted in an unprecedented flood of Chinese immigration to the United States. At the time, domestic conditions in China were unfavorable, and it was not surprising that so many Chinese men chose to follow the lure of gold. The men departed from China hoping to strike it rich in California and return home laden with the fruits of their labor. However, mining, already a rather cutthroat venture, was made especially trying for the Chinese. Often, when some Chinese would-be miners found gold, their claims were quickly "jumped"—forcibly and illegally seized by their competitors. Alternatively, other Chinese miners "were so successful that they were soon banned from the best sites" (Lee "In Search..." p. 1). Most of the Chinese who chose to remain in the mining industry were forced to work only abandoned claims and required to pay a hefty foreign miner's tax. Consequently, before long the majority of the Chinese immigrants in California abandoned mining in favor of working in less competitive industries. (Chen 1980) (Lee "In Search..." 2000) (Lee "A History of Chinese..." 1993)

A large number of the immigrants came from the Pearl River Delta area of Guangdong Province, which is adjacent to the South China Sea and Hongshui River. Since fishing was a familiar activity for many of them, these early Chinese took up fishing in the bountiful waters along the California coast. In the San Pablo and San Francisco Bay areas, the Chinese focused on shrimp fishing. At one point, there were as many as 1,500 shrimpers. In Monterey Bay the Chinese established several fishing villages. During the 1850s and 1860s they harvested abalone, recognizing it as the same mollusk that was considered a delicacy back home. After diversifying during their boom years in the 1870s, the fishermen came to specialize in squid. (Lee 2005) (Liu 1977)

The San Diego fishing industry most likely began with some Chinese fishermen from Monterey Bay seeking new abalone sources down the coast. By the late 1850s, the fishermen had found that San Diego Bay, with its unexploited marine resources and proximity to the coastline of Baja California, would be an ideal place to set up a base for fishing and gathering abalone. The Chinese came to establish a shipbuilding industry in San Diego in order to be able to travel the distances they would need to go in order to make use of these benefits of settling in the Bay. The coastal waters of Southern California were ideal breeding grounds for abalone, and earlier Russian hunters and Aleut fishermen had stripped the coast of sea otters, the natural predators of abalone, resulting in a large boom in the local abalone population. (Lee 2005) (Lee "In Search…" 2000) (McEvoy 1986) (Richardson 1981)

In San Diego, the Chinese fishermen were among the earliest settlers along the Bay. During the 1850s, they established themselves between Roseville and Ballast Point. The Chinese fishing camp located on Ballast Point was likely the earliest camp of its kind, though the first documentation of it was not done until 1868, when San Diegan Lucy Wentworth noted that two Chinese men, Juk and Ah Sing, were fishing on Ballast Point. Gradually, the fishing camp grew, and came to lie alongside the Ballast Point Whaling Station. Three Chinese men even came to work for the whalers, and sold fish in Old Town and New San Diego. However, despite years of success, both the fishing and whaling industries were evicted from Ballast Point by the United States Army in 1873. Most of the evicted Chinese fishermen moved slightly northeast to settle in La Playa, where they began a shipbuilding yard that created numerous homemade redwood ships, called "junks," to be used by other Chinese fishermen. (Kelly 2001) (Liu 1977) (Richardson 1981)

Another fishing base for the Chinese, the Roseville colony, consisted of about ten small redwood dwellings, two or three

Map of Point Loma, 1918.
SDHS Union-Tribune Collection.

rooms deep, with sheds containing iron salting tanks and nearby wooden racks for drying fish. A second colony was located across the Bay on the waterfront at the foot of New Town, near the end of First Street, and would later become the location of San Diego's Chinatown. In due course, there came to be roughly a dozen redwood shacks in the New Town colony. Some of them were elevated on stilts out over the mudflats, as that part of the Bay had not yet been dredged. However, when the railroad was built in 1881 it interfered with access to the fishing fleet from the New Town Chinatown, and most of the fishermen relocated to the Roseville colony for easier access to their junks and sampans. (Liu 1977) (McEvoy 1977) (Richardson 1981) (Stewart 1965)

The junks used by the Chinese were homemade, built out of California redwood, and weighed between five and 15 tons. They were built according to the specifications of the owner using traditional Chinese methods. As opposed to the single-masted *cao chuan* used in San Francisco, where the shrimping grounds frequented by Chinese fishermen were within the sheltered confines of San Francisco Bay, the two- or three-masted *hong xian tuo* style predominated in the San Diegan junk fleet, as the San Diegan Chinese fishermen tended to sail in the open sea between abalone camps and met with a much harsher climate. When the Chinese fishing industry of San Diego was at its peak, there were 18 junks in the Bay, 12 of which harvested abalone. Junks in the abalone fleet tended to operate in pairs, most probably "in accordance with the China Sea system whereby one junk provided living accommodations and the other storage and transportation of the catch" (Richardson p. 9). La Playa and, more prominently, Roseville, were the centers for junk production in San Diego. Most Chinese kept their junks anchored at New Town, close to the Pacific Mail and Steamship Wharf, whose facilities they used to export their catches. (Bentz 1999) (McEvoy 1986) (Richardson 1981) (Van Tilburg 2003)

Chinese Ship Population of San Diego 1860-1895

The Chinese fishermen tended to work in groups. Usually, one member of the cooperative might own the junk and another would own the other equipment, while any other members would do the necessary manual labor. Consequently, when dividing the profits, the owners of equipment would be the first to receive a share in return for whatever equipment they provided. Then, after all expenses were deducted, the remaining profit would be divided equally amongst the crew. The Chinese fisherman operated alone, in a partnership, or in a group depending on his personal preference. Working alone, a fisherman needed to invest very little, but the return was also small, as it was limited by what he could accomplish with a single set of hands. (Richardson 1981)

Under the control of the Chinese, the San Diego fishing industry thrived. The Chinese most commonly used a technique called seine fishing, in which they used small mesh nets that they imported from China to thoroughly sweep the Bay for fish. Another technique, called outside hook-and-line fishing, was practiced exclusively by the Chinese colony living at Roseville, and the bulk of what these fishermen caught were sheephead. Another alternative, trolling in the open sea, allowed the fishermen to catch large amounts of barracuda. When trolling, the Chinese fishermen would attach a curved piece of bright abalone shell and a swivel to the back of a barbless hook, relying on the glistening of the abalone shell to attract the fish. ("The Fishes of…" 1880) (Stewart 1965) (Richardson 1981)

The fish caught by the Chinese were cleaned and salted at sea. Once the fish were brought onboard, the Chinese removed their heads, split them in half, gutted them, and layered them in wooden crates. Upon returning to port, the Chinese dried the fish, placing them flesh side up and skin side down. The dried fish were baled in bundles of about twenty-five pounds each for shipment. Typically, only

A California sheephead; one of the main fish catches of San Diego's Chinese fishermen.

the smaller fish were dried and exported, as the larger fish were brought to San Diego's Chinatown and sold fresh. By 1880, the San Diego fishery was producing 700 tons of fish annually, and had surpassed all other West Coast fisheries. By 1881, the export of dried fish was formally recognized as an important part of the San Diego economy. ("Chinese Fishers" 1887) (Stewart 1965) (Richardson 1981)

The Chinese fishermen in San Diego, like their counterparts in Monterey Bay, gathered abalone. They took the abalone from the intertidal zone and shallow water areas in and around the Bay, and all along the

coast of Southern California, down into Mexico. Using their homemade sampans and junks, the fishermen would row among the rocks at low tide, searching between exposed boulders and outcrops for the sweet delicacy. Once gathered, fishermen would dry the abalone's meat and ship it back home to China and to other Chinese around the United States. The Chinese

Sampan on the deck of a Chinese junk.
San Diego Historical Society.

abalone fishery became fully operational during the 1860s, and the abalone they harvested was San Diego's chief export to China and to Chinese colonists in other countries. (Harris 1974) (McEvoy 1977)

Once they found abalone, the Chinese would pry the mollusks off the surfaces they had attached to by using "a long-handled wedge and inserting a boat hook under the shell to draw it to the surface" (Harris p. 24). After that, they would separate the meat from its shell. The meat was pounded flat, boiled in seawater, and then spread out to dry in the sun. In the early days of the industry, the Chinese would toss the shells away. However, soon abalone shells began to be widely valued for their iridescent beauty. By 1879, $30,000-worth of cut abalone shell was being processed by the Chinese in San Diego. (Harris 1974) (McEvoy 1977) (Richardson 1981)

Cut abalone shell found at Ballast Point.

San Diego Bay had been an excellent find for the Chinese fishermen. Out of all the West Coast fisheries, it was in San Diego that Chinese fishermen were the most cordially received. Initially, at least, there was little competition from other San Diegans, so few restrictions were imposed. During the 1870s, the fishing industry grew phenomenally, and came to be more and more in the hands of the Chinese. By 1880, the Chinese were in full control, and all the fishing in San Diego was carried on by 37 Chinese fishermen. "The success [of the Chinese] was due in large part to their willingness to carry on the tedious process of sun-curing fish for shipment, their ability to make use of everything they caught, their industrious work habits, and their development of export markets" (Richardson p. 6). The fishing industry established by the Chinese brought a large income to San Diego, and the fishermen interacted positively with the local residents and businesses by purchasing lumber, food and supplies, while carrying out door-to-door sales of some of the larger fishes they had caught. (Richardson 1981)

In other parts of California, the Chinese were made the targets of violence and blatant exhibitions of racial hatred, but the Chinese fishermen in San Diego had good fortune on land as well as at sea. The fishermen's contribution to the San Diego economy, combined with locals' desire to avoid the bloodshed that characterized anti-Chinese movements in other cities, overrode most of the widespread antipathy directed towards their race. However, enough manifestations of anti-Chinese sentiment arose that the sheriff, Joseph Coyne, was obliged to "[swear] in a number of special deputies and [station] them at strategic spots" (Richardson p. 14). (Richardson 1981)

In 1880, Dr. David Starr Jordan of the California Fish and Game Commission began to direct hostility explicitly against those Chinese working as fishermen. A *San Diego Union* article recounted the report that Dr. Jordan sent to the U.S. Commission of Fisheries, which noted that the

> variety and quantity of fishes in [San Diego Bay] ... is being constantly and rapidly diminished by Chinese with their fine meshed nets; and unless proper steps are taken to prevent the wholesale destruction of young fish now going on, all the valuable food fishes will soon become extinct. ("The Fishes of..." 1880)

This statement alone scared many Chinese from the fishing industry due to fear of persecution. Two days after the publication of the *Union* article, the leaders of some of San Diego's civic organizations met with Chinese fishermen to demonstrate to them how their fine nets could soon wipe out all the fish in the Bay. For reasons that remain unclear, the fishermen suspended their fishing operations for a month. ("The Fishes of..." 1880) (Richardson 1981)

Tragically, in 1882 the Chinese junks were declared foreign vessels and banned from American waters. In the same year, Congress passed the Chinese Exclusion Act, which closed off new immigration from China. Before long, junk operators began to be implicated in smuggling immigrants and illegal commodities through Mexico. In 1887, local fisherman Captain William Kehoe continued to fuel San Diegan antipathy towards the Chinese fishermen by implicating them as the reason behind the decreasing number of large fish in San Diego Bay. A year later the

passage of the Scott Act "denied the re-entry of any Chinese laborer who had temporarily left America" (Liu p. 45), ensuring that the Chinese fishermen could not re-enter the United States if they navigated past the three-mile limit into foreign waters. The 1892 Geary Act required all Chinese to carry a residence permit or be deported, and also put fishermen into the category known as "laborers," which was an excluded class. The Chinese fishermen could no longer afford to remain as fishermen and were forced—through persecution and through adverse laws—to leave the fishing industry. (Lee "The Chinese Fishing Industry of San Diego" 1999) (Liu 1977) (McEvoy 1977) (Richardson 1981)

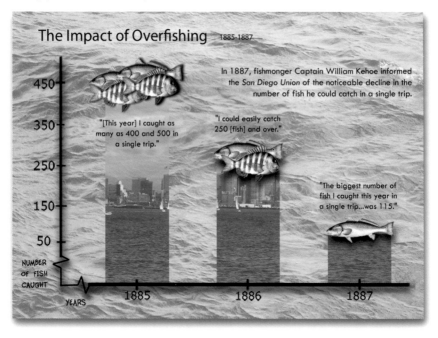

The Impact of Overfishing   1885-1887

In 1887, fishmonger Captain William Kehoe informed the *San Diego Union* of the noticeable decline in the number of fish he could catch in a single trip.

"[This year] I caught as many as 400 and 500 in a single trip."

"I could easily catch 250 [fish] and over."

"The biggest number of fish I caught this year in a single trip...was 115."

450
350
250
150
50
NUMBER OF FISH CAUGHT

YEARS   1885   1886   1887

After the departure of the Chinese, the San Diego fishing industry stagnated. The Chinese either returned to China or entered into other industries, such as market gardening. At first, only a few Italian and Portuguese fishermen remained in San Diego to supply the fresh fish market, but before long other ethnicities replaced the Chinese as fishermen. Many Japanese filled in the gap left by the removal of Chinese abalone fishers, though racial discrimination eventually drove them from the industry as well. Then, in the mid-1900s, about half a century after the Chinese were forced to stop fishing commercially, the restoration of the depleted

resources of San Diego Bay began in earnest. At the same time, the laws excluding Chinese immigration were lifted, allowing for the free immigration of Chinese back into the San Diego area. Nevertheless, though many Chinese began fishing once again, they never grasped the same level of domination of the San Diegan fishing industry that they once held. Today, most Chinese in San Diego fish for sport rather than as an occupation. (Liu 1977) (Richardson 1981)

A Chinese market gardener, circa 1922.
San Diego Historical Society.

The Catch

"Slish" goes the net as it cuts through the ocean
Ensnaring masses of fish with the force of a potent potion

But now it says "slosh" as eager hands pull it free
And revealed are treasures from the depths of the sea
Almond eyes light up with glee

"Thump" proclaims the net, as it drops into the junk
The Chinese fishermen look pleased with the result of
the day's final dunk

Returning to shore, from the net comes a
"whoosh"
As the gills of the fish give a
final push

Natalie Linton

1881
Many Chinese move back to Roseville when construction of a railroad through San Diego interferes with access to the moorings of junks

1873
The United States Army evicts Chinese fishermen operating from Ballast Point and they move to La Playa where they establish a shipbuilding industry

1879
$30,000-worth of cut abalone shell is processed by Chinese fishermen in San Diego County alone

1840

1882
The Chinese Exclusion Act passes, prohibiting Chinese immigration for ten years

1849
The California Gold Rush brings an increase in Chinese immigrants to the United States

1876
A state law regulating the size of Chinese net meshes was passed, thus reducing the size of the catches

1880
Nationwide anti-Chinese sentiment spreads to San Diego; it was noted that Chinese overfishing reduced fish population in the Bay

1915
Regulations banning the drying and export of abalone meat from California pass; Chinese participation in the industry ends

1886
12 Chinese-run fishing companies operate 18 junks

1892
The Geary Act forces many Chinese fishermen to sell their junks

1920

1887
Local fisherman Captain William Kehoe blames Chinese fishermen for the decrease in the number of large fish in the Bay

1893
San Diego Bay has only one Chinese junk still fishing

1916
The last remaining Chinese junk is sold

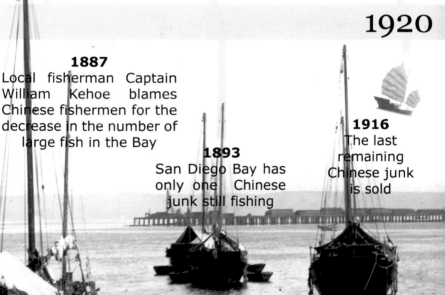

Chinese junks in San Diego Bay, 1887.
San Diego Historical Society.

45

Murray Lee

We were able to meet with Murray Lee, the curator of Chinese American History for the San Diego Chinese Historical Museum at his home. When we arrived, Mr. Lee and his wife greeted us enthusiastically and invited us inside. We entered into the house of this man who knows so much about the early Chinese community in San Diego, and Mr. Lee kindly offered to show us the resources he had that related to San Diego's Chinese fishermen.

We passed through open-aired rooms into Mr. Lee's study, where he had amassed a hoard of invaluable information through years of extensive research. The sheer amount of documentation he had was phenomenal. Piles of papers were bundled together, organized in boxes and squirreled away in various storage spaces around the room waiting to be used. Photographs were scattered here and there—a portrait of the prominent San Diegan Chinese man Ah Quin and his family; a diagram Mr. Lee created portraying the locations where the San Diego Chinese once lived—and much, much more. We set up our equipment in Mr. Lee's living room and settled down to listen.

Student Researcher (SR): What brought Chinese fishermen to San Diego?

Murray Lee: You have to go back to why the Chinese came to America, and that was primarily because of the Gold Rush, when the word got out that there was gold in California. That's one of the reasons why they called California and America "Gold Mountain." They came over like everybody else hoping to strike it rich, [but then] they found that going and doing mining was hazardous because whenever they would discover anything somebody would take away their claims, and so they started just mining a lot of the abandoned mines.

Some people say that after the mining experience the Chinese may have drifted south. But I think that when you do a little research about the first fisherman that came to San Diego you'll find that they probably came down the coast from around San Francisco and Monterey. But in Monterey, they had quite a number of fishing villages; they fished in the bay there, and one of their main catches was abalone, because nobody in this country wanted to eat abalone. They used to think it was like shoe leather, and they didn't know how to process it.

So, the Chinese went up and down the coast gathering abalone and made quite a profit out of that. And I'm sure that these abalone junks drifted on south, and they were looking to expand their range of abalone [gathering] along the coast because [abalone are] kind of coastal [and reside] on rocks, where they were gathered quite easily. They probably wandered into San Diego Harbor and they thought that this was an ideal place to set up a base for gathering abalone all the way down Baja California as the coast was ideal for abalone and nobody else was going after it.

SR: When they came to San Diego, where did they live and where did they work?

Lee: I think the fishermen may have actually started out on Ballast Point … where there was a whaling station… They also anchored off Point Loma … which is where the San Diego Yacht Club is today… I think it's still called La Playa—or Roseville—and they had a fishing village there. They had shacks, and in those days shacks were built of redwood, because it was the only wood that people could really use, because this area didn't have trees [that were] useful. All the redwood and lumber came down the coast in these big huge rafts and unloaded in San Diego at the Pacific Mail Steamship Wharf.

They established a shipbuilding industry there, too. They built the junks out there on Point Loma—made of redwood, because that was the most common wood, except that redwood wasn't strong enough for the masts and the rudders… They imported ironwood from China for the masts and rudders.

So, they built junks. [At one time] they had as many as 18 junks in San Diego… They usually had a crew of maybe two fishermen on there, and they would go out for days. They could go 400 miles or so. They'd go on the boats and gather the abalone. They took the abalone meat out of their shells and cooked it, dried it, and brought it back to San Diego and shipped it out from that pier, which is right down at the foot of where Chinatown was.

We kind of feel that the Chinese fishermen were instrumental in establishing the Chinatown where it is or where it was, because it was convenient to the Pacific Mail Steamship Wharf, [where] all the cargo went in and out. They used to ship all the abalone out [until] later on, when people decided that abalone shells were good for jewelry-making. There was a market for the shells, so they'd go back to all the places where they had put the shells, because [before] they threw the shells away [since] they were too heavy to bring back. They went and re-gathered the shells, and they used to ship tons of these shells out of San Diego through that period.

Chinatown section of San Diego, Third and Island. San Diego Historical Society.

They established a second fishing village at the foot of Third Street … and the pier was on Fifth Street. They anchored all their junks just off the coast there because at that time the harbor had not been dredged. And so they anchored the junks out there and they took their sampans, and they went up to the coast where they had these redwood shacks again… But they were up on stilts to be above the water, to be right out on the edge of the water where their sampans could go; and that's probably the land that they squatted on. It wasn't [Horton] sub-divided property yet ... and Chinatown was within a block or so.

SR: Do you have any idea how many fishermen worked there?

Lee: Well, at one time they had a total census of 52 fishermen. But then, it's kind of hard to take a census of fishermen since they're out there fishing most of the time. I mean, they do have these shacks where they stayed when they weren't offshore, but if you figure how many junks they had and how many people that maybe had to do the processing ... it's not that many: about 50.

SR: Did they catch anything besides abalone? You mentioned fish once or twice, I believe?

Lee: They caught all the fish hereabouts like barracuda that you might catch today, except albacore and tuna ... they used nets and things like that. Sometimes they got accused of having nets that were too fine and [were accused of] catching too many fish. They really weren't competing with anybody, because the last fishermen, I guess, in the area were the Kumeyaay. But anyway, they supplied all the fresh fish needs... They caught things other than abalone, but abalone was one of their main objectives, and their ships were designed just to go after abalone. That's what those two-masted ones were for—abalone.

Chinese junk in San Diego Bay, 1913.

SR: What kind of policy did the government and the other people living in San Diego have toward the Chinese?

Lee: Well, the junks were built on Point Loma, in San Diego, but they didn't consider them American-built junks. They considered them alien vessels—which is very difficult to understand. When they had to sell these junks later on in the 1890s, when they forced them out of business, and they had these junks they had to sell to the Caucasian population here. Then they had to go into what they call "add-measure," [that meant they had to] determine the size and the measurements of these boats. So, then they got this data describing the junks. Before, you didn't know; it was just an abalone junk. You didn't know how long it was, how wide it was, how deep it was, what the tonnage was.

In fact, every time the Chinese did get into anything that was profitable, there would be somebody that would want to take it away from them. In the early days, in the 1870s and the era before the Chinese Exclusion Act, [the Americans tried] to do everything they could to discourage the Chinese from living here. And if they went after their livelihood, they figured: "Oh, well. Then they will go back home."

So, [the Americans] passed this one Exclusion Law—the 1888 Scott Act—that said that anybody leaving the country—a fishing boat going beyond the three-mile limit was leaving the country—had to have papers [when they came back], and since they weren't allowed to have papers because they weren't allowed to become citizens [as per the Chinese Exclusion Act of 1882] they had to sell all their junks or go back to China... This was about the 1890s.

SR: While they were still working as fishermen in San Diego, do you think their work benefited the San Diego economy at all?

Lee: Oh yes, because they bought a lot of equipment and things like that and shipped stuff out. They had paid to ship it out on the Pacific Steamship

The Pacific Mail Steamship Wharf and San Diego Harbor c. 1890. Chinese fishing junks can be seen at the extreme upper right. San Diego Historical Society.

Wharf; tons of abalone shells and things like that. It was one of the largest exports in San Diego in those days ... 700 tons or so [of abalone] would go out. There used to be these side-wheeler steamships that would come into San Diego and go back and forth between San Francisco and San Diego. Every four days they would come in. So, that's why they moved to New Town. In the 1880s Ah Quin was asked to move to San Diego to be a broker for Chinese labor to build the railroad from National City to San Bernadino, but the railroad went right through where the village was, so they had to move back to Point Loma.

SR: When people saw how successful the Chinese were in the fishing industry, did any other groups try to come in and become fishermen and take that prosperity?

Lee: Yeah, the next group that tried to come in (that wasn't excluded yet—eventually all the Asians were excluded) was the Japanese ... and [like the Chinese] the Japanese went right into the abalone industry, and it became very profitable for them. Later on, the Italians and the Portuguese came in. They primarily went for the tuna and albacore and a lot of the deep sea fishing with poles, and it was a whole different technology.

Ron May

Not only was Ron May sought out for his expertise concerning the Native Americans of San Diego Bay, but we also looked to him for his knowledge of the early Chinese fishermen who lived and worked at Ballast Point. On a beautiful Saturday morning, we entered into the fringes of the highly guarded military base established on Ballast Point. When we arrived, a tough-looking military guard asked us the reason for our visit. We responded politely and our contact, Ron May, a volunteer historian and archaeologist at Ballast Point, was standing nearby. He signaled for the guard to let us through, and gave us a pass that would allow us temporary entry into the base. We caravanned behind Mr. May to the old, converted World War II style building where artifacts from the Ballast Point Chinese fishing camp were stored. Inside the building there were boxes upon boxes and stacks upon stacks of artifacts and written information. Amidst this organized chaos Mr. May settled himself to answer our questions on a topic he knew like the back of his hand.

Student Researcher (SR): I heard you found numerous artifacts left by the Chinese fishermen out at Ballast Point. Can you tell us a little about what you found?

Ron May: Yes, in 1991 and 1992 we had an opportunity to dig up the Chinese fishing camp where it was supposed to be according to very scant historical references. … We found a large trash pit associated with the Chinese fishing camp. In that we found brown glaze jars that stored soy sauce and alcoholic beverages. We also found their rice bowls, condiment bowls, and tea sipping bowls. They had interesting celadon porcelain spoons and we also found evidence that they used English plates, American plates and "pre-tine" forks.

SR: Where do the Chinese fishermen at Ballast Point fit in with the other Chinese fishermen during the time period?

Rim of a soy sauce dispenser found at Ballast Point.

May: We believe the Chinese on Ballast Point were the earliest. … [They were] here as early as 1860. [But they were all] evicted in 1873 when the U.S. Army came in to build a post, and the Chinese moved from Ballast to La Playa. There, they expanded their operations to build [junks]. They used redwood that they bought from somewhere—probably around Central California. They carved the boats and put them together on the San Diego Harbor. With those larger boats, they were capable of going out to San Clemente Isle … and they could harvest abalone and any other shellfish and bring it up here on a large scale, then sell it in markets like San Francisco and China.

That operation completely shut down before 1892. By then, there were all these Chinese exclusionary laws prohibiting them from engaging in shipping and requiring them to pay outrageous fees that they could never afford. So, eventually they sold all their boats and moved down to what was called the Stingaree district in downtown. They changed their employment again to the fringes of society since they were not allowed to engage in their traditional business practices. You find them in the U.S. census working as laundry men and marginal employment.

SR: Are there any artifacts that you found that have been significant as a time marker or otherwise?

Remains of a Bamboo style bowl found at Ballast Point.

May: We found pieces of vegetable processing bowls here … they are very rare and very early—from the 1850s to the 1860s—they're the most significant piece [we have]. We also found several bowls that are called Double Happiness. [They are painted] a very dark blue on a light blue porcelain background, and those Double Happiness bowls date back to 1850 to 1860, certainly no later than 1870, and we [have a number of those] pieces in this collection. They're not typical of the Chinese sites from 1880 and on … it was exciting to find … that material here.

SR: Why do you think that these Chinese came to settle at Ballast Point and establish their fishing camp there?

May: Well, the Chinese … almost always suffered from ethnic and racial discrimination. Everywhere they went in the United States in the 19th century it was horrible. It was … safer for them to live on the fringes of society than to live in the city where [Caucasian] people were dominating. … Many of the Chinese who came to the gold fields in the 1850s gave up [mining] … and went back to their traditional ways of making a living from fishing along the coasts and living on the fringes of San Diego Bay.

We found lots of fish bones and shark teeth and things indicating that they were doing heavy fishing here [at Ballast Point]. … Photographs showed that they dried fish and hung them up on these racks with all these little fish bodies wafting in the sun and light to dry out. Not all of the fish was consumed; they also packed it up and shipped it to San Francisco for sale and some of it went overseas.

SR: Do you know much about the personal activities the Chinese engaged in while they were living on Ballast Point?

May: Well that's where the architecture is very interesting, and we have been able to document

Remains of a tea or condiment cup found at Ballast Point.

that they had houses that were fairly substantial. The kind of architectural remains show that they built strong buildings; that they used a lot of nails and binding materials to make a solid wooden building. We found the kind of things associated with screens rather than windows for ventilation. We found lots of tiny little tacks indicating that they may have decorated their walls or put canvas on their walls. They might have put a canvas ceiling in their rooms to prevent anything dropping [down] from the roof. We found ornamentation. We found that almost every piece of metal was scrap glass or scrap tin that was cut down and re-used in some form even though we don't know what [that form was].

SR: What can you tell us about the cut shell industry the Chinese fishermen had going on at Ballast Point?

May: I have several references that the Chinese engaged in cutting abalone shell for jewelry, and in one case for making fishing lures. But my guess is

Cut abalone shell taken from the remains of the Chinese fishing camp at Ballast Point.

that most of it was cut down into blanks and sold to some other industry. The pieces that we have from the site are, I believe, the waste from after they cut down what they could sell. We have a few good pieces that would have been useful, and had probably been lost in the dirt during that process. [They are] a very exciting find—in that I have never seen anybody publish anything on [the cut shell industry, other] than people referencing [the fact that they] knew that the Chinese did it.

SR: Is there anything we haven't covered about the Chinese fishermen?

May: I think there's a misconception among archeologists when working with the Chinese, [and that is] that the Chinese were isolated and not interactive with the other people and their communities. ... We're testing that here at Ballast Point. I know there was some evidence of some interaction because we're finding Chinese artifacts in the whalers' camp and things ... at the Chinese camp. I believe that the discrimination and bad feelings towards the Chinese developed later in time, and the people who were here in the mid-nineteenth century got along better than they did by the time the exclusionary laws were going into effect [during the] late 1880s to early 1890s. By that time, there were other things going on in China that brought people here as well; revolutions in their country were driving people back over here, too. There were a lot of people looking for work, and by then there were a lot of people in California and work was harder to find ... so you had economic problems; you had repression and ethnic interactions that are not good for people.

From the Perspective
of a Chinese Fisherman

As I fish here on the Bay
I reflect on my past
The tenacious fights with other fishermen
The way I have eluded laws to benefit those I love
How my net captures everything in sight
The White men try to stop me
But I will keep on fishing till they throw me in jail
Or chase me from here
Because I will do anything
To see that my family can eat every night

Ted Valentine

*A piece of a "Coconut Grove" dish dating
after 1900 found at Ballast Point.*

The Chinese fishermen of San Diego harvested a variety of marine species. The focus of their collection was primarily pelagic fish and abalone. The natural history of abalone will be described in detail in a later chapter. Some of the most common fish catches for the fishermen were barracuda, mackerel, mullet, whitefish, sheephead (redfish) and smelt. (Ocean Biographic Information System 2006)

California Barracuda
Sphyraena argentea

California barracuda grow to be about 4 feet long and weigh 18 lbs. They are mostly slender, but have round midsections. Their heads are flat and they have large mouths with large, sharp, triangular teeth. They are brown-blue above and white below, with silvery sides; their caudal fin is yellow. They prefer to live in deep, offshore waters, often in reef areas. These barracuda mostly prey on other fish, including small tunas, smelt, mullet and anchovies. They range from Kodiak Island to Southern Baja. (Eschmeyer 1999)

The Chinese fishermen who fished the San Diego Bay caught local barracuda by trolling. "The fishermen had a curved piece of bright abalone shell and a swivel attached to the back of a hook; it would glisten, and the fish would see that. When the fish would bite, it would be pulled right in, with no slack, as there was no barb on the hook" (Stewart p. 17).

Pacific Mackerel
Scomber japonicus

This species of mackerel can grow to weigh 1½–2½ lbs and be around 25 inches long, but are usually no bigger than 16–18 inches. They are dark green to blue-black in color above, silver with dark blotches below, and have about 30 irregular wavy streaks along their backs, passing just below their lateral lines. These mackerel live inshore or near the surface, and the young enter bays. They eat schooling fish such as anchovies and herring, as well as squid. They travel in schools and range from Alaska to Mexico, though they are most abundant between Monterey Bay and Southern Baja. (Eschmeyer 1999) ("*Scomber japonicus*" 2006)

Pacific mackerel have been a very important commercial species for well over a century. The Chinese fishermen caught these mackerel by seining, where they encircled an area in nets and drew the nets shut, scooping up the fish in the process.

Striped Mullet
Mugil cephalus

Striped mullet grow to be about 3 feet long and can weigh more than 10 lbs. They are torpedo shaped and have a broad head that is flat between the eyes. They have thin lips, short fins, two widely spaced dorsal fins, and are olive green with silvery sides. Mullet travel in large schools and feed off the ocean bottom, eating zooplankton, benthic organisms and detritus (dead organic matter). They scrape food from rocks or strain food from the ocean surface or floor through their gill rakers and teeth. They can often be seen leaping out of the water in the Bay. Mullet prefer to live in warm seas, and range from San Francisco to Chile. (Eschmeyer 1999) ("*Mugil cephalus*" 2006)

As mullet are coastal fish that prefer to live in areas with dense vegetation and sand or mud bottoms, the Chinese fishermen probably caught them using hook-and-line fishing as opposed to seining so as to avoid getting their nets caught up in the vegetation.

Ocean Whitefish
Caulolatilus princeps

This species of whitefish grows to be around 40 inches long and weigh about 13 lbs. They are yellowish-brown or tan above and white below. Their fins are light yellow with blue stripes. Ocean whitefish prefer to live in reefy, rocky bottoms, though they also live in soft sand and mud bottom environments. They dig into the substrate for food, feeding off bottom invertebrates such as worms, small sheep crabs, ridgeback shrimp, anchovies, and octopi. They presently range from Vancouver Island to Peru. (Eschmeyer 1999)

"White-fish," as they were called when the Chinese fishermen still fished the Bay, live in shallow, subtidal areas, kelp forests and rocky reefs to depths of up to 75 fathoms. They were typically caught by Chinese fishermen using hook-and-line fishing. (*"Caulolatilus princeps"* 2006)

California Sheephead ("Redfish")
Semicossyphus pulcher

California sheephead grow to be about 3 feet and weigh around 36 lbs. Females are reddish-brown to rose colored with white chins; males have white chins, blackish heads, red eyes and reddish midsections; the young are red-orange, usually with at least one white stripe along their midsection. Sheephead are "protogynous hermaphrodites." They begin life as females, but the older, larger females develop into males. ("Abbreviated..." 2006) (Eschmeyer 1999)

The sheephead prefer to live among reefs, on rocky bottoms, on sea grass beds or among kelp beds. They feed on hard-shelled organisms such as sea urchins, mollusks, lobsters and crabs. They presently range from Monterey Bay to Guadalupe Island, though they also reside in the Gulf of California. (Eschmeyer 1999) (*"Semicossyphus pulcher"* 2006)

In the early days of San Diego, sheephead were commonly referred to as "redfish" by San Diegans. Because of their tendency to live among the kelp beds off the coast, fishing for sheephead using nets was very difficult. As a result, the Chinese fishermen typically caught them using the hook-and-line fishing method. Currently, the populations of California sheephead off Southern California have declined due to fishing pressure and the reduction of kelp beds. ("The Fishes of..." 1880)

Serenity—*A Nature Reflection*

The Bay is bustling with the day's activity: sailors sailing, motorboats churning, and cargo ships embarking. Sitting on the shore, I go unnoticed. My mind wanders back to the day when life was so much simpler here. Back to when men could make a living in sleek boats pursuing a simple pleasure—fishing. It seems so different from the life I live now. I wish that I could be like San Diego's storied fishermen and take part in the harvesting of my own food. Now I never know where or who caught the fish that sits on my plate.

As I sit here on the shore, I think of my ancestors. It must have been satisfying to be a Chinese fisherman. To live a life of ease and maintain a sense of joy; to spend my days in endless waters, dreaming about the catch of the day in hopes of becoming a legend; to fulfill the age-old tradition of providing for my family. I dream about coming home at the end of the day to see the smiles on my children's faces. They would be so happy to see their father, who has worked so hard to fill their empty stomachs.

Yet, after so much imagining, I return to the here and now, wondering how our lives could have changed so much in just the last century. I inhabit the same city, I look at the same sun, yet somehow I am so different from the generations before me and I will be so different from those who are still to come. The land we inhabit, though stationary, moves with time and changes like the direction of the wind. It's hard to make out these movements and changes when we are so caught up in our own lives. The balance between me and my past seems crooked and ill-placed. If I could go back and spend a day with a Chinese fisherman, it might all be clearer.

Connie Han

"My relationship with waterfowling was for me a way of life."

-David Hagerbaumer

Waterfowl
Hunting

The annual migration of waterfowl along the Pacific Flyway once attracted countless duck hunters to San Diego Bay and local wetlands. At one point in time, ducks were so abundant in the area now known as Mission Bay that it was widely referred to as "Duckville." The actual tradition of duck hunting began with the first human inhabitants. Recently, however, the tradition has faced a serious decline. This slump has largely been the result of changing patterns of duck migration caused by the disappearance of San Diego's wetlands, local urbanization, and ultimately, the prohibition against discharging firearms within city limits, established during the 1960s.

Yet, despite all the changes that developed to prevent duck hunting from occurring on the Bay, duck hunters have continued to promote an appreciation of the birds and their habitats. Furthermore, some hunters continue to take part in several of the less lethal hunting traditions, such as the original American art form of decoy making. These men and women have also adapted to current circumstances by taking the initiative in helping to restore and inspire appreciation for the birds' habitats. Thanks to their efforts, we are now able to reflect on the significant impact the tradition of duck hunting has had on San Diego's rich history, economy, and ecology.

Geography of Waterfowl Hunting on the Bay

The marshlands and wetlands in and around San Diego Bay provide an ideal habitat for the waterfowl that frequent the area. Though no longer as extensive as it once was, such an idyllic setting provided a firm basis for a hunting culture in the region. Parts of "Duckville" and Hog Ranch Point were often visited by hunters and hunted alike.

History of Hunting on the Bay

The idea of hunting seems foreign, even ludicrous, to the average American. Yet, the sport was not always considered so. For many people, hunting represents a long forgotten instinct or a tradition worthy of regard. However, there are many inaccurate assumptions about the activity. Social changes, human population growth and modern urbanization have served as the sources for these misunderstandings. By looking at the past, we can pinpoint the events that led to changes in our attitude towards hunting.

Pintails courting on San Diego Bay.

The land that became known as San Diego was very different during the time of the Kumeyaay. "What is now Midway and Sports Arena was black wet mud and tidal flats with a river channel, which could split or go to either bay" ("Point Loma—Environmental Management of Pre-Contact Kumeyaay" par. 4). The natives hunted a wide variety of animals with rabbit sticks, including small game such as rabbits, chipmunks, badgers and foxes. For larger animals, such as deer and antelope, they would use bows and arrows. The Kumeyaay were known to have hunted the geese and ducks that flew in for the winter, using bird calls to attract their prey. They slung *bola* at them—weapons consisting of two or three round stones tied onto a rope—to bring them down. "The invention of rope for nets, lines, and snares allowed the addition of fish and birds to our diet" (Diamond p. 39). Yet, though the Kumeyaay regularly took from the land, they also maintained a certain

Mission Bay, a.k.a. "Duckville"

balance and awareness of the effects of their presence. (Diamond 1999) ("Point Loma—Environmental Management of Pre-Contact Kumeyaay") (Winterhald 1981)

However, once the Spanish arrived and established themselves in the New World, the utilization of San Diego Bay for its marine resources increased. At the same time, duck hunting seemingly lost a place in the history books. Following establishment of Spanish settlements in the area, the tradition did not reappear in any form until the latter half of the 1800s. During this time, areas of San Diego were known to have supported an abundance of ducks and large populations of these birds could especially be found at Mission Bay— "Duckville." During this time, duck hunting

transitioned from being a subsistence activity to a recreational sport, though it is difficult to identify exactly when this transition occurred. It can only be assumed that hunting became a choice, as food easily could be obtained through mass agriculture, courtesy of modern technology.

The acceptance of California into the Union in 1850 stimulated an onslaught of new changes for San Diego.

Adalaska Pearon, "Mayor" of "Duckville," 1913. San Diego Historical Society.

The previously sparsely populated region grew to 30,000 by 1900. Such rapid growth necessitated the construction of housing and commercial developments, including the dredging San Diego Bay and filling marshes and wetlands in the region. There was a drastic reduction in the waterfowl habitats and a proportional decline in the migratory bird population in the area.

In order to address the declining duck and goose populations, in 1934, the U.S. Fish and Wildlife Service created Federal Migratory Bird Hunting and Conservation Stamps. "Duck stamps" are still required for hunting waterfowl in the United States and currently

Void after June 30, 2002

Northern Pintail **$15**

U.S. DEPARTMENT OF THE INTERIOR

MIGRATORY BIRD HUNTING AND CONSERVATION STAMP

A federal duck stamp.

help generate funding for wetland conservation. Since its enactment, $670 million has been spent to purchase or lease more than 5.2 million acres of

key waterfowl habitat in the United States. In addition, the U.S. Fish and Wildlife Service regulates the dates of waterfowl seasons, bag limits, and the prohibition of live decoys, so that the number of ducks harvested is proportional to the duck population. ("The Federal Duck Stamp Program" 2006) (Scharff 1957)

American Wigeons.

During the 20th century, the tradition of duck hunting underwent many significant transformations in San Diego. The most significant of these occurred in the 1960s with the loss of duck hunting within San Diego City limits. Not only were duck hunters unable to use the Bay for hunting, because of the ban on firearm discharge within city limits, but increased urban development gradually pushed the ducks themselves from their natural habitat. In California as a whole, the sport of duck hunting has faced a continual decline. The number of legal duck hunters in the state has dropped over time, and the number of duck stamps sold has decreased. In 1952, a peak of 214,456 duck stamps were sold in California; in 2005, the number was only around 70,000, including those purchased by collectors. ("The Federal Duck Stamp Program" 2006)

A drawing by David Hagerbaumer.

The public's view of the sport has changed as well. Since duck hunting no longer takes place on the Bay or other nearby locations, fewer people are aware of the tradition. Many view the sport as inhumane or simply just wrong. Contrary to this belief, many hunters argue that the tradition provides an instinctual connection and actually helps the environment, as hunters learn to care about those practices that may threaten the natural scene. Many hunters believe that if the public were more aware of the positive role of the sport, they would gain a greater appreciation for the ecology and history of the region.

An innovative alternative would be the implementation of photo safaris in which San Diegans and visitors alike can be educated about local duck populations. The program would facilitate a mock hunt in which participants would enjoy the waterfowl on the Bay by learning about their biology and duck hunting traditions such as decoy carving and placement, and duck calling. Participants would appreciate the waterfowl by "shooting" them with their cameras, rather than with guns. This type of "hunt" would help educate both tourists and residents about this part of the city's history. The public would become familiar with their environment and gain a better sense

Ron Vavra and students from High Tech High out on a mock hunt to "shoot" ducks. Vavra gives a duck call as the group lies in wait.

of their place in nature. Proceeds from the mock hunt could be used to benefit species conservation and awareness, while more funds would allow several different programs to have a larger impact on duck conservation.

Another example of positive changes can be seen through the precedent established by Ron Vavra. Once an avid waterfowl hunter,

Brant raised in Ron Vavra's backyard.

Vavra took the restoration of ducks into his own hands by setting up a conservatory for black brant in his backyard. Vavra's efforts to help restore the birds may seem ironic to the general public. Yet, hunters see this need to restore and maintain nature as essential to their sport and the natural world of which they are a part.

While the practice of duck hunting has changed over time, some essential elements are found to recur. The use of decoys to lure ducks originated when hunter-gatherers used tule reed and skinned ducks to create the illusion of a live duck. Later,

decoys would be made out of cork or wood. Today a majority of hunters purchase mass-produced decoys made of plastic. The creation of custom-made decoys has become regarded as a traditional American art form, with some artists even creating decoys for display only. Artist and duck hunter, David Hagerbaumer started his own decoy-making business in San Diego in 1946. Hagerbaumer carved and painted decoys using redwood and balsa for the bodies and pine for the heads. The decoys were sold for $3 each, and though the business did not make a huge profit, today the decoys can fetch hundreds to thousands of dollars. (Hagerbaumer 2006) (Hooper 2006)

Knowledge of our region's rich history provides answers to important questions regarding the practices we continue today. While duck hunting may no longer have relevance to our everyday lives, it has had a profoundly positive effect on saving and restoring coastal wetlands. The desire to hunt that we inherited from our ancestors now helps influence environmental rules and regulations. A new awareness and appreciation for our relationship with our natural environment might someday allow us to know what duck hunters have long held as the truth.

Her Fate

I see better
When I'm hiding behind the blind
She can't see at all
When I shoot her from behind

How satisfying she is, you would not guess
In this game, she's the checkmate of chess

I love that duck at the day's end
I rest my head on a pillow … inside are the feathers of a friend

On a shelf, in my room, I love the way she looks
She really fits in nicely, sitting next to my books

But I love her most
When she's sitting on my plate
Next to my potatoes
This is her fate

Jamie Spiegel

1000
Early inhabitants of the Bay used a weapon made of rope and a stick called a *bola* to hunt ducks

1000

1592
Juan Cabrillo arrives in San Diego, establishing Spanish contact

WATERFOWL FEEDING AREA
NO SHOOTING ZONE
NO SHOOTING BEYOND THIS SIGN

1960
Duck hunting is deemed illegal as the use of firearms is prohibited around the Bay

1888
The dredging of San Diego Bay begins, altering the future of the marshlands

2006

CALIFORNIA DUCK STAMP

2001-2002
$10.50

1934
The U.S. Fish and Wildlife Service begins to regulate duck hunting with the creation of duck stamps, bag limits, etc.

David Hagerbaumer

The process of locating and committing to an interview with renowned artist David Hagerbaumer seemed at first to be a daunting task. However, we were delighted to find him readily available and perfectly willing to answer questions and provide us with some of his beautiful artwork pertaining to our research on duck hunting on San Diego Bay. Mr. Hagerbaumer has hunted waterfowl for more than 70 years, shooting his first duck at the early age of nine.

Although hunting has been a large part of his life, he is best known for his outstanding waterfowl artwork, including the duck decoy. His artwork is one of a kind—most likely the result of his extensive experience waterfowl hunting and his great passion for nature. Mr. Hagerbaumer has been quoted as saying, "A man like me without a duck hunting boat is like a man without a soul."

Mr. Hagerbaumer received us warmly from his home in Washington and responded to our questions with valuable insight. He was able to share with us his hunting experiences on San Diego Bay in the 1940s, when ducks were abundant. The information we received provided a valuable extension of the story he began in his book, *Waterfowling These Past Fifty Years*, which was published in 1998.

Student Researcher (SR): What was it like when you were living in San Diego?

Hagerbaumer: In the mid-forties, when I came back to San Diego, it was a grand place. Waterfowling on the Bay and nearby fresh water lakes, fine quail and dove hunting in the river bottom and mesa above, no freeways and moderate traffic. The air was clean and folks had the time and inclination to stop and chew the fat. A large city even then, but [still with] a good many qualities of a smaller town. Today, it is a cesspool of humanity!

SR: How did you first start duck hunting?

Hagerbaumer: I started with my father and tutor at age eight.

SR: What kind of ducks did you hunt?

Hagerbaumer: On South Bay, we hunted black brant, [a sea goose], for the most part. However, several species of ducks were also common. These were pintail, lesser scaup, surf scoter and now and then a few teal.

SR: What was duck hunting like in the 1940s on San Diego Bay?

Hagerbaumer: Duck hunting in South Bay in the forties was very good. Very few hunters—a lot of "shooters," perhaps—but still fine waterfowling.

SR: Would you say ducks were abundant at that time?

Hagerbaumer: Yes.

SR: Where on San Diego Bay did you duck hunt?

Hagerbaumer: Only on the west shore of the Bay at the very south end; [South Bay]. There was a long and narrow point at this location that held a pit blind made by hunters, unknown years before. An adjacent hog "ranch" close by induced us to name it "Hog Ranch Point."

SR: What would you say was different about hunting on San Diego Bay, compared to other locations in San Diego?

Hagerbaumer: The main difference was the limited number of species and that brant were numerous, as opposed to inland waters.

SR: What happened to duck hunting on San Diego Bay?

Hagerbaumer: I cannot be certain, but I'll wager that development and anti-hunting forces shut it down.

A drawing of Hog Ranch Point by David Hagerbaumer.

SR: Can you tell us about the duck decoy business you started in San Diego?

Hagerbaumer: My cousin and I were discharged from the U.S. Marine Corps in early 1946. This took place in San Diego. In need of work, we both agreed to start Custom-built Decoys. More of this in my book, *Fifty Years.*

SR: How would you describe your relationship with duck hunting?

Hagerbaumer: My relationship with waterfowling was for me a way of life. I grew up doing it and have never stopped, slowed down perhaps, and not "so mad at the ducks" today, but the urge is still there and now at 85 years, I look forward to the coming season.

SR: How would you say it has impacted your life?

Hagerbaumer: Mainly, it has kept me out of doors and away from the hordes of *Homo sapiens*. From hunting ducks, I've learned the ways of waterfowl, which has aided me very much in my work. It taught me respect for all wildlife and their habitats.

SR: How do you think American society would be affected if we were to lose the duck hunting tradition?

Hagerbaumer: The vast majority of folks that make up the American society would clap their hands and shout in glee.

SR: What do you think the effect of duck hunting is on ducks?

Hagerbaumer: Today, limits are too large. For whatever reason waterfowlers, for the most part, are most interested in "limiting out." Unlike grouse and woodcock hunters who are content with a bird or two, waterfowlers (a majority) rate the quality of their hunt by the number killed and wounded. Sad!

A drawing by David Hagerbaumer of a duck hunter taking aim.

SR: Is there a significant effect on the duck population?

Hagerbaumer: The critical effect on any wild population is the loss of their habitat. A classic example in San Diego is the rape of Mission Bay for the great expansion of homes and businesses north and east. Be advised that this takes place in *all* states. There is no turning back.

SR: Do you think it is possible to revive the sport?

Hagerbaumer: I doubt it, as those of us who do still hunt are shrinking in numbers each year. If there is a way to halt this decline, I am not aware of it… I doubt that a single soul can come forth with an idea that would re-establish the tradition. Far too many folks are in opposition, too many acres are lost yearly in places where public hunting is possible. I am sorry to say that I see no future (in the long term) for the sport and tradition of waterfowling.

SR: For example, a simulated hunt with cameras instead of guns?

Hagerbaumer: Photography and shooting [with] a shotgun are two different things. Since 1950, I've gone every year to the marsh and Bay, set out my decoys and taken pictures of waterfowl decoying. I've found these photos invaluable in my work and, of course, just plain fun. Should I still be [alive] when we can no longer shoot [ducks with guns] I'm all set! I doubt, however, that to substitute camera for gun would set many waterfowlers on fire! Amen!

Jim Brown

It was an overcast, "ducky" morning by a hunter's standards when we ventured down to Seaport Village to meet with duck hunter Jim Brown. An avid angler, hunter and birder, Mr. Brown is a native San Diegan who has long been fascinated with the human and natural history of the region. In addition to serving a 30 year career as the manager of the San Diego City Lakes Program, he has worked as a writer, educator and consultant. As a recognized specialist in the field of outdoor recreation, he has taught at San Diego State University and worked closely with such agencies as the California Department of Fish and Game and U.S. Fish and Wildlife Service. To this day, Mr. Brown continues to hunt and fish. When we interviewed him, we were delighted by his enthusiasm and great insight into the transformations that have occurred in duck hunting over the last 50 years.

Student Researcher (SR): What is the impact of duck hunting on San Diego?

Jim Brown: I don't know you could say there is an impact, since waterfowl hunting hasn't taken place on the Bay for probably… I would say 25–30 years. If we look back at the history of San Diego, we know that waterfowl hunting—ducks, geese, and especially the Pacific black brant that are so familiar around San Diego Bay and Mission Bay—were important items prior to the turn of the 19th century and into the early 20th century, when waterfowl hunting was a particular subsistence issue for a lot of people. It would supplement their food and whatnot. Then it evolved into a sport hunting issue, which it remains today throughout North America.

Because of all the development that has occurred around the San Diego Bay, as well the intersection of the various city limits, all of … San Diego Bay is now within the city limits of the jurisdiction of the various [cities of] Chula Vista or National City, San Diego or Coronado or Imperial Beach, and the discharge of a firearm within a city limits is not permitted. So kind of, in a *de facto* way, waterfowl hunting, which was a considerable tradition here in San Diego, has been eliminated.

SR: Do you think duck hunting is important today?

Brown: I think the tradition of waterfowl hunting is important if we honestly interpret how San Diegans have utilized the resources in this region and San Diego Bay. In particular, if we were to be honest about our historical interpretation of that, we have to talk about waterfowl hunting. Now, whether or not waterfowl hunting can be reintroduced, at this point in time, after so many years … I think it'd be very unlikely.

SR: What do you think should be done on the Bay?

Brown: I'd personally like to see the Fish and Wildlife Service, [through the] new San Diego [Wildlife] Refuge, feature an interpretation of the history of waterfowl and waterfowl hunting—the impacts of man and waterfowl upon each other in that region. I think it would be very instructive for people to have the opportunity to go on a mock, nonshooting, duck hunt, in which maybe they go out with an old experienced duck hunter who used to hunt on the Bay. They [would] go out and pick up their decoys, create a blind, lay out their decoys, sit in the blind, call the ducks and shoot [them] with a camera rather than with guns. I think it's important to have an honest interpretation.

SR: What would you say about changes in duck populations in San Diego?

Brown: Well, waterfowl populations have fluctuated a great deal. If we go back historically, we can find people describing the skies [as being filled with waterfowl] in Southern California, at lakes like Cuyamaca, at San Diego Bay, and also over at Mission Bay, which at the time was known as Duckville— and a lot of people don't realize that Duckville was one of those wonderful marshes along the Pacific coast that was dredged to create a recreational area for people. So, Duckville became Mission Bay, and by dredging, it was no longer as attractive to waterfowl as it once was, and they used to say that [ducks] blocked out the sunlight. Of course, that was an exaggeration, but the idea was that there were so many ducks and brant in the sky over Mission Bay that it was a very striking issue.

SR: What has contributed to the decline in duck populations?

Brown: The populations of waterfowl, not just along the West Coast and the Pacific Flyway, but all over the country, have been greatly impacted by development and encroachment by man. … So I think if you take a look—historically, the numbers have gone down because of reduction primarily in habitat. Generally speaking, the waterfowl hunting has not had so much an impact as the deprivation of their habitat. I believe in California, [there was] around 6% of the habitat that was original. So, if you take [away] 94% of the places that something can live, you're going to have a corresponding drop in the population.

Ron Vavra

Our interview and introduction to former duck hunter Ron Vavra took place on Shelter Island along the coastline of San Diego Bay. He bears a close resemblance to our biotechnology teacher, but that is not surprising—Mr. Vavra is our teacher's father. Mr. Vavra was an avid duck hunter in San Diego for 50 years, a devoted member of the California Waterfowl Association, and the first person to ever raise Pacific black brant in captivity.

Although we expected him to go into scientific detail about the waterfowl in San Diego, the moment he started speaking we were drawn into a vivid recount of his duck hunting days and his experience hunting and rearing black brant. Mr. Vavra is an incredible storyteller; his ability to animate his memories led our imaginations to roam the world of duck hunting. As he sat on the rocks next to the decoys he had carved, with a wooden duck call around his neck, a large smile on his face, and speaking of the good old days, we realized how fortunate we were to hear him recount the art of duck hunting.

Student Researcher (SR): How long have you been duck hunting?

Ron Vavra: I've been duck hunting for about 50 years.

SR: How often do you duck hunt?

Vavra: I would duck hunt about once week [during the] three-and-a-half month period ... that the duck season actually lasts. ... It starts in October and runs through January.

SR: What type of waterfowl did you hunt?

Vavra: Mainly puddle ducks or ducks that live in shallow water. ... If you like prime rib, they tend to taste like that. So, that's why I tend to hunt those birds.

Ron Vavra out hunting with his dog.

SR: Can you describe a typical day of duck hunting?

Vavra: A typical duck hunting day is kind of a long story, but I'd arrive at the duck hunting club with my dog, and maybe a friend. This is in the

Imperial Valley, and we would go out in the evening and set the decoys out … He and I would spend a relaxing day in the cabin and the next morning get up before daybreak and go out in the duck blind, hide, wait for birds to come in to the decoys, call them, hopefully get a few for dinner that night, and then

pick them, clean them, drive back to El Cajon … and have wild duck and red wine with the most beautiful woman in the world—my wife.

SR: What role does the bird dog play in the hunt?

Vavra: Dogs have always been a big part of my life and when the dogs that I train "mark" birds, they take hand signals. I can send them out 100 yards and stop them on a whistle. I

Loyal Labrador makes a retrieve.

give them different directions, and it's really a conservation means, because sometimes … a bird would be crippled, and without a dog you probably couldn't recover it.

SR: Would you say all duck hunters go out with a dog?

Vavra: If I had to guess, I'd say about 25% do—and out of those 25%, 10% [of their dogs] are well trained.

SR: What methods do you use other than just decoys and duck calls?

Vavra: I think that's what separates a hunter from just a [shooter]. What a hunter does is go through the whole scenario and decoying [and calling] ducks are important. Well, about 90% of the people that [use a duck] call probably scare the ducks away.

SR: What led to your interest in making decoys?

Vavra: [Not] a lot of people are aware that decoy making is an American art form. It

Ron Vavra demonstrating decoy use.

didn't come from Europe; it started here in the United States. I'm kind of a traditionalist and like to follow traditional paths, and this led me into making my own decoys.

SR: Have you noticed the impact of duck hunting on the Bay?

Vavra: Well, there is no longer duck hunting on the Bay. It really didn't have to do with hunting, mainly human encroachment. About 85% of all the wetlands in California are gone, and so the duck population and hunting has really been affected by human encroachment and population.

SR: Do you think the population can ever level off again?

Vavra: Do I think the ducks will make a comeback and so forth? I'd say [it would be] very difficult, not because of hunting at all, but because of loss of wetlands. I mean that's the primary [factor]. ... I think the best we can do is try and slow [the loss of the wetlands] down.

SR: Do you think duck hunters help the environment?

Vavra: I don't think there's any question about it. [I have spoken] with John Howard, vice president of California Waterfowl Association, and Dick Bauer, who's a [former] migratory coordinator for the U.S. Fish and Wildlife Service. They both gave me the same statistic: 60–70% [of wetlands] are [owned by] private duck clubs. So, if duck hunting were to be eliminated, it would eliminate [about] 70% of wetlands.

SR: Are you in any duck conservation organizations?

Vavra: Yes, I've been a member of California Waterfowl Association, Ducks Unlimited, Delta Waterfowl Association. These are basically hunter groups, but they raise a tremendous amount of money for conservation of wetlands.

SR: And also I heard that you got the Silver Eagle Award?

Vavra: That's a long story, [about how I] received the Silver Eagle Award. [At the time] duck baiting, which had been outlawed in 1934, was still going on in Southern California in certain

Brant being raised in Ron Vavra's backyard.

duck clubs. ... So, for ten years I, along with certain other people, fought this battle and eventually ... in, I think, 1989, the Federal Court met here in San Diego, and they overturned the baiting of the ducks in this part of the state, and I was presented with the Silver Eagle Award by the U.S. Fish and Wildlife Service. It had only been given out five times in the United States, so it was quite an honor for all those involved.

SR: We also heard that you raised brant in your backyard.

Vavra: The brant [live in] the Bay here. I hunted brant for about three years and during that hunting experience, for some reason, I fell in love with them. I was concerned about them because they are a maritime goose. They live in bays and estuaries, and they live off eelgrass. Pollution really affects eelgrass, and so I got off on a ten-year odyssey through the U.S. Fish and Wildlife Service, drove the highway to Alaska, flew commercial from Anchorage to Bethel, flew bush pilot out on the tundra and with the help of the Service, picked up eggs that were just about to be hatched and brought them back on the plane to Southern California.

They hatched out, but they don't reproduce until they're three years old, and we had students from Grossmont College bring in eelgrass from the Bay. Nothing happened after three years, so I called a friend at the World Waterfowl trust in Slimbridge, England—Janet Keer. She said, "Ron, try the photoperiod." (The photoperiod is the length of a day.) So, we set up lights in my back yard and we had a timer and we duplicated the Alaskan time until we had 24 hours of daylight, and then brant hatched out like chickens. The whole [key] was the photoperiod; and it was the first time [the brant] were raised in the United States in captivity.

Ron Vavra's decoy workshop with decoys
in various stages of completion.

Jim Heather

We caught Jim Heather on his annual migration to San Diego from the cold Canadian prairie. Mr. Heather has had a long history as a duck hunter and biologist. After receiving a college degree in ecology in 1974, Mr. Heather worked as a field assistant on a behavioral study of the Pacific black brant goose in western Alaska. His experiences and extensive knowledge of the black brant made him an ideal interviewee for our project.

The interview was based on a recommendation made by Ron Vavra, who met Mr. Heather during his research of the brant on the Bering Sea. The interview took place along the shore of the boat channel on San Diego Bay—an occasional brant stop-over, far from the tundra of Alaska. As he began to recall his experiences and share his thoughts on the duck hunting tradition, we knew that his contribution would be a valuable addition to our knowledge of the primary species historically hunted on the Bay.

Student Researcher (SR): What would you say makes brant different from other waterfowl?

Jim Heather: They're strictly a marine goose, so they're very coastal. You rarely find them any further inland than 15 miles. Most geese have a long, slow wingbeat, but brant fly more like ducks. They're very quick. *Very* quick.

SR: Can you talk about how you came to live with the brant?

Heather: Well, in 1974, John Eisenhauer, who was doing a master's thesis on the nesting ecology and behavior of Pacific brant in western Alaska, needed a field assistant, and he picked me to go with him; and that's how I ended up there. We went back there in 1976 and continued our study, which we finished in that year.

SR: What was your favorite part of the experience?

Jim Heather working with John Eisenhower to tag young brant.

Heather: I think that seeing the variety of birds that are up in the Yukon Delta in western Alaska … it's just incredible. There were so many different kinds of shore birds and waterfowl that it was really an interesting experience.

79

SR: What do you think was the most important thing you learned from living on the tundra?

Heather: I think the main thing is that you realize when you're up there that anything you do affects other animals. So, when a bird is sitting on its nest and you scare the female off the nest, there are gulls flying around waiting for an opportunity to steal those eggs or to have a baby brant for lunch. So, you have to be very careful about impacting wildlife when you're studying them.

Jim Heather (second from the left) banding brant on the tundra of western Alaska.

SR: Did you have any challenges with how you were impacting the brant when you were there?

Heather: Well, one of the biggest challenges was that traditionally the Eskimo people eat brant eggs and they hunt birds for food. In 1974, we trapped and banded, put identification rings on their legs, a group of moulting flightless brant. A party of native people were waiting further downriver and began shooting the birds shortly after they were released from our traps. So, that was pretty frustrating, and on several occasions while eggs were being layed and incubated, some people removed eggs from brant nests we were observing.

SR: Do you think their nesting habitat has changed since your study?

Heather: I think it's stayed pretty much the same as it has been, but continued human activity in the area might change that. Alaska is a very big place and the wildlife refuges are pretty isolated, but though human disturbance is not widespread, it needs careful scrutiny in the future.

SR: What was the biological significance of your study?

Heather: Well, we identified some of the behavior patterns and we tried to gather natural history information about the Pacific black brant in terms of how many eggs they lay, what percentage of the young survive to maturity, and the impact of the indigenous people on the population. Occasionally, strong winds combined with a high tide would blow the water inland. It was so flat up there that it would flood the nesting habitat and when that happened a lot of the eggs and young would be lost—the embryos inside the eggs or the goslings would become chilled and die. So, that kind of environmental phenomenon is something we tried to get a handle on—what kind of impact that would have on nesting success. We also looked at avian and mammalian predation and how these activities affect the birds.

Patience —*A Nature Reflection*

I have been lying here all day. It's surprising how accustomed I have grown to the sounds that were so foreign to me only a couple hours ago. There were a couple of seagulls nearby, but they have left me here alone. The ambling pedestrians that pass me by seem to be confused by my presence. I try to convey to these passersby through silent means that I am in search of game—that I'm on a duck hunt—but the sight of a soaring beauty erases my impatience. I hold my breath in excitement as a duck slowly makes its way from left to right across my field of vision. I'm trying to imagine what it would be like to fly in search of a home. The freedom to move on my own, unrestricted by the laws of gravity or social expectations.

I have been waiting so long, peering up at the sky. I'm envisioning the lives of my forefathers, the freedoms they once retained. I imagine a swarm of ducks circling smoothly above my head. I wish I had decoys to lure my prey and a gun to shoot them, as to renew the tradition that my grandfather spoke of once. Yet there is something that holds me back; I am restricted by this city. This city I call home is sprawled so easily across the water, its tall buildings and bright lights intimidate. The sight makes me a foreigner. The contrast between cityscape and untouched water is too great for me to be a part of either.

I wish I could find a balance between myself and nature. My upbringing did not prepare me for my introduction to this special place. I can hear the water flow, and I wonder how such music could ever be forgotten. I question my purpose and my place in this world; my place in such an honest environment.

I feel out of place. My clothes are much too brightly colored for the landscape that surrounds me. I grow cold, unprepared, and unwelcomed by the remaining residents of this place.

I realize that no ducks are coming; my ambitions, lost.

Jamie Spiegel

81

Waterfowl Biology

Ducks and geese are classified as waterfowl, or birds that are dependent on wetland habitats. The species of waterfowl that temporarily live in and around San Diego Bay vary in composition, coloration, voice, flight pattern and feeding habits. However, all species of wild waterfowl follow a continuous, eight-step seasonal cycle. This cycle consists of migration south to warmer climes in the fall, rest during the winter, migration again in the spring and pre-nesting, nesting, brood rearing, post breeding and then molting. This cycle occurs every year, and the steps involved inevitably pose challenges for waterfowl populations and determine when the majority of these birds appear on and around the Bay. (Ducks Unlimited 2006)

Duck species can be placed in two categories: divers and dabblers. Divers have short legs with large feet, both of which help in obtaining food under the water. Dabblers have longer legs and smaller feet that help keep them afloat so they can find food on the surface. (Ehrlich 1998)

Pacific Black Brant
Branta bernicla

At one point, the brant were prominent in the San Diego area. However, it has been noticed that this small goose has shifted its terminal migratory destination toward Baja California, possibly due to dredging and development projects around the San Diego Bay. Nevertheless, the Bay is still considered a wintering site for brant, with about 750 to 1,500 of the birds migrating annually from October through January. The south San Diego Bay is the main attraction for the brant, as the area contains an abundance of eelgrass (*Zostera*), their primary food source. When eelgrass is not present, brant are also known to feed on sea lettuce (*Ulva*) or other aquatic plants.

The black brant is dark in color, has a small frame for a goose and has long wings. All brant have black heads, breasts, bills, tails and legs. White markings located around their necks contrast their predominant solid black color and are very appropriately called "necklaces." Typically, brant have small heads and beaks attached to short necks, but there are subpopulations of brant with some variation in physical traits. It is difficult to determine the sex of the species from afar, but a common indicator is that the males tend to have a larger "necklace" above their chest region. Brant typically fly in groups of five to 20 birds in a ragged "V" formation.

Surf Scoter
Melanitta perspicillata

When startled by a boat or other activity, the surf scoter can be seen doing its mad "dash" across the water in attempt to get in the air. This heavy diving duck does not oil its feathers like other ducks, and this makes its takeoff and flight appear very labored. The presence of the surf scoter on the San Diego Bay ranges from mid-October to early December. During the late fall and early winter, San Diego Bay hosts more surf scoters than any other location. Due to the surf scoters' reliance on mollusks and their significant susceptibility to pollution from boats, their health and abundance is an indicator of the Bay's health. They are commonly found in mid-water on the Bay, south of the Coronado Bridge, and are the dominant waterfowl species during winter. (Unitt 2004) (Vavra 2005)

The difference between female and male surf scoters is visible in their physical traits. Male members of the species are entirely black except for a white patch on their forehead and triangular white patch on their neck. Females, however, range from brown to black shades with an occasional white feather. Also, females have small white patches below their eyes. The male beak contains white, red, yellow and black, while the female beak is generally either greenish black or bluish black. The height and weight difference between male and female members is slight. (Ducks Unlimited 2006)

Pintail
Anas acuta

The pintail, or "sprig," as it is coined by duck hunters, is often the most desired for the dinner plate, along with the black brant. Though the pintail was once San Diego's most plentiful dabbler, it is now ranked average in relation to the rest of the population around the Bay. In the San Diego region, pintails spread out in large groups in North County lagoons, northeastern Mission Bay, San Diego River Flood Control Channel, south San Diego Bay and the Tijuana River Estuary. The short whistle of a pintail, sounding like a soft, distant train whistle, can be a distinctive sound of the salt marsh. (Unitt 2004)

Often known as the "greyhound of the air," pintails have a sleek look formed by long and slender features. Pintails were named after the central tail feathers—pintails—of the drakes, which account for a quarter of their body length. Pintails have brown heads, grey bodies and the drakes have white stripes along the sides of their neck and white patches on each side of their rump. (Ducks Unlimited 2006)

Our Exhausted Bay

Our bodies are exhausted
The day was long and hard
We spent time lying still
Using mimicry to lure in our reward

Our Bay has been exhausted
Its resources overdrawn
Exploited, unappreciated
The migration so far gone

Our time has been exhausted
We await a new beginning
A day we will see
A sky of returning wings

It is only through our efforts
That our passion can be restored
Our desires finally exhausted
Not wishing or wanting more

Schuyler Marquez

Tuna

"*You got all wet and broke your back.*"

-Guy Bruni

Since the early 1900s, the tuna fishing industry has been extremely important to San Diego Bay. Originally, immigrants to San Diego fished in the Bay because fishing was a skill they brought with them to the United States from their own countries. Italian, Japanese and Portuguese were among the most common immigrants to form tuna fishing communities along the Bay. They pioneered the local tuna industry, and once the leading shipyards, such as Campbell Machine Co., built larger fishing boats they eventually gathered together to form a tuna-fishing fleet, covering nearly the entire Pacific. Throughout the 1900s, the tuna industry in San Diego boomed, and the Bay became home to the largest tuna fishing fleet in the world.

Starting in the 1980s and 1990s, the tuna industry in San Diego began to move elsewhere as Japan became the vanguard in tuna capture and canning. Moreover, worldwide monitoring of tuna schools became possible, helping fishermen regulate their catches to avoid overfishing. However, such monitoring—coupled with other advances in fishing technology—also brought about more effective methods of catching tuna, which had a dramatic effect on the tuna population in San Diego.

As a result, today the tuna fishing industry in San Diego has almost completely disappeared. Nevertheless, it still carries the legacy of generations of tuna-fishing communities. A large portion of the tuna fleet has now converted to sportfishing, which has become a popular pastime and a successful industry in its own right. These ships go out on long-range trips, usually down the coast of Mexico, to fish for tuna. Recently, there has been somewhat of a revival of interest in the tuna industry, but most likely it will never return to its glory days.

Geography of Tuna Fishing on the Bay

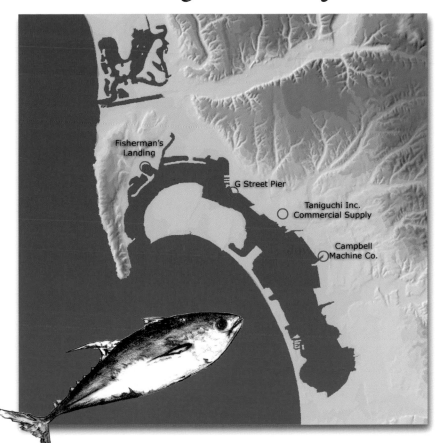

Fisherman's Landing

G Street Pier

Taniguchi Inc. Commercial Supply

Campbell Machine Co.

Campbell Machine Co., founded in 1906, was among the leading builders and repairers of tuna seiners in San Diego. Currently, the commercial tuna fishing fleet is at G Street Pier, though much sportfishing goes on from Fisherman's Landing. Taniguchi Inc. Commercial Supply, a fishing supply shop, has been in business for decades. In the glory days of San Diego's tuna fishing fleet, much of the fishing supplies were imported from Japan, and Taniguchi was a seller that many people bought from.

History of Tuna Fishing on the Bay

Before the Gold Rush of 1848, San Diego had been a small Spanish mission town. When it was discovered that the sardines off the coast of San Diego could be fished and harvested with a decent profit margin, a market resulted. The fishing fleet remained small but successful until the sardines vanished from Californian waters in 1903. Their disappearance left a gap in the market, so a new fish was found to fill the demand: albacore tuna.

Before long, San Diego became the main tuna-exporting port in the Pacific. (Bonarno 1996) (Rockland 1976)

Those who caught tuna in the early days of the fishery were immigrants from Japan, who used what would become the standard hook-and-line technique. Other cultures that came to San Diego to fish in small communities were Chinese, Italian, Spanish and Portuguese. The mix and interaction of these cultures formed a diverse, thriving community. San Diego's first tuna cannery opened in 1911, which allowed for mass production, increasing the amount of tuna available to the public. In the "boom" year of 1911, a large catch of albacore tuna drew even more fishermen to the industry, and the market skyrocketed. In 1912, four more tuna canneries were established, bringing the total number of canneries in San Diego to five. (Wolf 1980)

World War I had a significant effect on the tuna-fishing industry, as there was an increased need for fish. To fulfill the overwhelming demand, fisherman began to catch other kinds of tuna besides albacore, such as bluefin, yellowfin, and skipjack. All of these fish eventually became part of the American diet, and tuna provided soldiers overseas with a diet that included meat. At this time, a more efficient method of catching tuna—purse seining—was introduced to Southern California. Purse seining uses seine nets to encircle and catch entire schools of tuna. Fishing boats began to be built specifically for purse seining, which became a widespread technique both during and after the war. However, bait boats that used the standard fish-and-line method remained the most common fishing vessel.

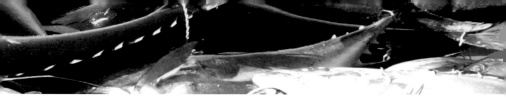

(Wolf 1980) (Rockland 1976)

In 1919, with the major boost in the tuna industry provided by the war, the number of canneries in Southern California multiplied to a total of 30. The tuna fishing fleet was made up of over 1,200 fishermen and 400 boats, with more than 100 boats in San Diego alone. However, in 1920 prices began to drop; there were simply too many boats fishing in the same area. As a result, many purse seiners began to head north, seeking less populated fishing grounds; and by 1922 the size of San Diego's fishing fleet had dropped to only 64 boats. (Wolf 1980)

In 1925, Japan and other Asian countries entered the global tuna market just as the albacore tuna was disappearing from California waters. This caused San Diego's

Large-scale production inside a San Diego tuna cannery. San Diego Historical Society Photo Collection.

tuna industry to lose some of its expected profits, creating a minor crash. Nonetheless, the United States remained the primary provider of tuna to the world markets. However, Japan used the disappearance of the albacore—the California staple fish—to jump into the American market and began selling its own brand of tuna. Californians soon accepted the "lighter" meat of the bluefin and skipjack tuna in addition to the "white" meat of the popular albacore. (Bonarno 1996)

In order to keep up with this new global competition from Japan and to make up for the Depression, local fishing technologies were updated, leading to the creation of tuna clippers—boats larger than the standard purse seiners, which could travel for more than 30 days without having to restock supplies. The creation of new clippers allowed the tuna fishermen to venture across the entire Pacific Ocean in search of a bountiful catch. Tuna clippers discovered that they could fish year-round in the San Diego area during the warmer months before moving on to warmer southern waters with the onset of cold weather. This nonstop fishing brought a continuous supply of fish to the San Diego canneries and triggered a boom in San Diego's economy, solidifying the city's place as the tuna capital of the world. (Bonarno 1996) (Bruni 2006) (Immenschuh 2006)

After WWI, the tuna industry held steady for well over a decade. However, the Great Depression affected tuna exactly as it did nearly every other industry, and there was a huge slump. Nevertheless, once the Great Depression passed, the tuna industry began to expand once again as international ports opened, and tuna became a popular and stable worldwide food commodity. With the increased fishing ranges of the tuna clippers, by 1927 over half of the annual catch of San Diego's fishermen came from areas far south of San Diego. Instead of being a prime fishing location, San Diego Bay became a very popular stopping spot for tuna clippers on long runs—even those not originating from San Diego. Consequently, the San Diego canneries were in an excellent position to increase their output. With so many tuna boats passing through the San Diego ports, the amount of tuna that was processed and canned daily soon sky-rocketed. (Bonarno 1996) (Immenschuh 2006)

Wooden fishing boats, such as those made by the Campbell Machine Co., retained their popularity though the use of metal boats became more widespread. During this time, the number of boats based in San Diego also increased. By the 1940s, there were more than 400 boats from San Diego dedicated to the tuna fishing industry. Unfortunately, with the onset of WWII, many of the larger tuna clippers were commandeered and outfitted as warships, leaving only the smaller clippers and standard fishing boats, mostly wooden, left to fish. In addition, the government limited the area of fishing during the war for the safety of the fishing boats. Thus, the local fishermen of San Diego

The Supreme, *an early tuna clipper in San Diego Bay.*

were limited to a much smaller fishing range, and the industry plummeted. Miraculously, it was at this time that the albacore tuna returned to San Diego after their long absence, allowing the fishermen to recover much of their former fishing yield, despite the short range of the remaining boats. As is usual in wartime, all fish, including tuna, were in high demand and San Diego's fishing industry quickly recovered. It is very likely that these remaining boats allowed the industry to survive during this harsh period. (Bonarno 1996) (Bruni 2006) (Immenschuh 2006)

By the end of the war, the San Diego tuna fishing industry was booming once again. The post-war era saw more international markets for the tuna trade. The San Diego industry's great success eventually faced competition from overseas competitors such as post-WWII Japan. With Japan's industrial growth, the American tuna industry, especially San Diego's, began to have serious competitors from Japan and later Latin America. The Japanese government supported its budding tuna industry through laws, such as a "Special Law," passed in 1953 to aid with the construction of fishing boats. In 1952, there were 290 Japanese fishing boats that had a carrying capacity of more then 60 tons. By 1956, the number of these boats more than doubled to a total of almost 600. This rivaled the San Diego fleet, which had a slower production rate for ships. Further need for greater catches of tuna led to the development of the "giant" tuna seiners, or super seiners—first by the San Diego industry, and then by Japan. The older, wooden tuna boats were

Content crew with a boatload of skipjack, late 1940s.

phased out even faster during this time, as metal boats were seen as much more efficient and durable for longer fishing runs. As a result of Japan's intense competition, many California canneries began to go out of business. The number of tuna canneries in San Diego dropped from five in 1952 to two in 1957. (Bonarno 1996) (Immenschuh 2006)

During this time, the scientific community began to research the impact of massive fishing, with concerns about the permanent effects of overfishing via the purse-seining fishing technique. They warned the fishing industry that unregulated and unmonitored fishing could have major repercussions, possibly eventually leading to extinction of the species. The fishing industry, however, ignored these warnings, and continued to build even larger and more complex steel boats in order to compete with foreign markets. Then, to add to these concerns, the dolphin issue arose. (Bonarno 1996) (Cary 1957) (Immenschuh 2006)

Dolphins had long been used as a means to finding tuna and other schools of fish. Since dolphins often followed tuna and were easy to spot (as they surfaced for air), they were often encircled by the large purse-seine nets. This resulted in some dolphin casualties, and became a major issue in

Single-pole tuna fishing.

the 1970s and 1980s, when laws were passed to severely limit trade with fishing companies that were not "dolphin safe." One such act, the Marine Mammal Protection Act of 1972, effectively limited the area that U.S. tuna vessels could fish to an area around Hawaii, while overseas competitors like Japan, unhampered by any dolphin-safety standards, could fish anywhere they wanted all year long. Though these dolphin protection laws were subsequently loosened by the Reagan administration, a great blow had been dealt to the U.S. tuna industry. Taiwan and several other overseas countries became major players in the industry by gaining footholds in the international market. According to the national databank of fisheries of the National Oceanic and Atmospheric Administration, the annual profits of the San Diego tuna industry fell to only $1,137,913 in 1979. (Bonarno 1996) (NOAA 2006) ("Transient ... " 1978)

The annual profits of the U.S. industry dropped from $1,236,511 in 1982 to $143,615 in 1983, but the economy quickly recovered from this slump, rising back to $1,301,492 in 1984. Between 1988 and 1989, however, the overseas tuna industries had grown enough that almost all of the San Diego tuna companies and their canneries, which were struggling to survive, were bought out by processors such as Unicord and Safcol (Thailand), and Mitsubishi (Japan). Several of the San Diego canneries continued on for a couple more years, before closing due to high labor costs and low profits. Often canneries were opened in lower labor-cost locations, and foreign tuna fleets were able to make significantly more "cost-efficient" catches, thus reducing the world price of tuna. This caused many local fishermen to relocate or leave their jobs, as they simply could not compete with the lower prices of foreign fleets. (Bonarno 1996)

The deathblow to the San Diego tuna industry came in the 1990s. Environmental groups observed that the standards for the protection of dolphins had dropped significantly. Much stronger measures of dolphin safety were instituted, and the local industry could only accept tuna that was caught using "dolphin safe" vessels and methods. This reduced the number of commercial tuna fishing boats from 40 in 1990 to 16 in 1992 and caused the industry to come to a halt. Korea and Taiwan, whose laws enabled them to fish in the restricted "dolphin-protected" waters, built boats as quickly as possible, and soon dominated the tuna industry. The surviving San Diego canneries relied almost primarily on foreign imports for tuna. Though the now much reduced U.S. fleet was still active, it had moved to the richer fishing areas of the Western Pacific, returning with its catches to nearby ports. San Diego had been cut off from the tuna industry, although some money was still made locally, presumably by sport fishermen selling to restaurants and small stores. In 1999, the annual profit of the industry had

increased to $700,000—but by the dawn of the new millennium, it had fallen to less than $100,000. (Bonarno 1996) (ABD 1991) (NOAA 2006)

Today, San Diego still harbors a few fishermen—mostly recreational. San Diego's Cannery Row is

completely empty of commercial canneries; the days when it bustled with workers are simply memories, as the last local commercial cannery shut down in 1984. But these memories have left San Diego a significant place in history, when it was known as The Tuna Capital of the World. The tuna fishing industry significantly boosted San Diego's economy in many ways. It facilitated the rise of the canneries locally, and the rise of modern corporate tuna processing companies such as Bumblebee™, Campbell™, Chicken of the Sea™, and Starkist™. (NPR 1998) (ABD 1991)

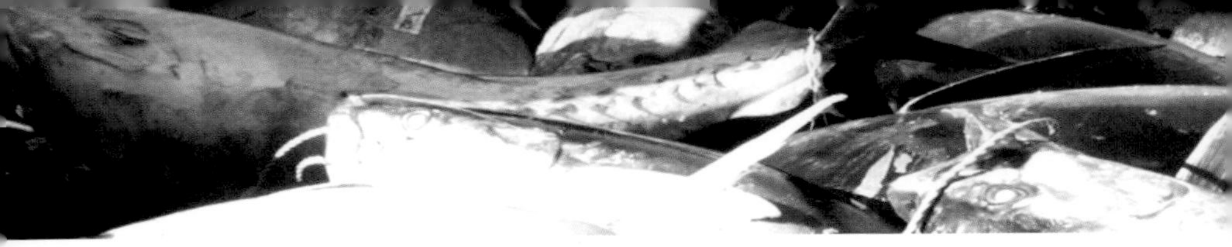

During San Diego's tuna-fishing boom, there was a great reduction in the overall population of the tuna. Tuna often migrated from year to year, and different species vanished from local waters—only to return years later. It is not known whether they were overfished or if this was simply a result of their natural migration patterns. Contemporary research conducted by scientists indicates that in the future, tuna may not return to San Diego in their previous abundance. Consequently, for any large-scale fishing of tuna, fishermen may need to sail more than 100 miles south. (Vetter 2006)

Then there are other, more positive factors that enter into the debate regarding the future of tuna. Tuna have evolved into fast, strong masters of the sea, and faster fish, like tuna, have a higher chance of survival. However, modern fishing technology enables fishermen to harvest tuna with a level of speed and efficiency that the fish are unable to match, much less overcome. The new technology that helps scientists monitor and track tuna for conservation purposes also aids fishermen in capturing tuna. The San Diego tuna industry has advanced much from the early 1900s, from standard straight-line fishing to the purse seining, from tiny hand-crafted wooden boats to massive, self-sufficient steel giants that patrol international waters. There are both good and bad aspects to these technological advances and their effects on the ecology of the ocean as a whole. (Vetter 2006)

Legacy

Tuna—gods beneath the heavenly sky
Stand great and strong in their savior's eyes
Give themselves up like wine and bread,
So a sailor's boy can, sated, rest his sleepy head

Fish in the sea do not breathe air,
Swimming about without a care
Only sharks, hooks, and whirlpools
Make these tuna lose their cool

Even if they are pulled up on deck
And tossed over a buff guy's neck
Their legacy will surely live on
Stacked by the dozens on a shelf at Vons

Peter Pham

1912
Four more canneries open in San Diego, for a total of five

1925
Albacore tuna vanish from local waters—Japan enters the international tuna market

1903
Sardines vanish from local waters, Albacore tuna begin to fill their place as a good

1941
The U.S. enters WWII using fishing boats borrowed for war efforts

1920
Prices drop as the tuna industry enters a slump

1900

1927
More than half of San Diego's catches come from areas south of San Diego

1911
First cannery in San Diego opens; the mass production of tuna increases to supply the public demand

1917
The U.S. enters WWI, fishing economy is boosted

1922
Many fishing boats leave to less crowded waters—the size of the San Diego fleet drops to 64 boats

1989
Three processing corporations (Unicord, Safcol, Mitsubishi) buy out almost all of San Diego's companies and canneries (Bumblebee, Starkist, Heinz)

1956
Japan builds a huge fishing fleet capable of outclassing America's

1988-89
Last commercial tuna cannery in San Diego is shut down due to lower operating costs in Asia and Latin America

2006

1972
Marine Mammal Protection Act is passed. American fishing boats are limited by dolphin safety measures

1992
Activity of San Diego's commercial tuna fleet grinds to a halt. The fleet moves away

Jean Immenschuh

Near the end of our project, we had covered most of the bases of the San Diego tuna industry in great detail. However, we lacked in-depth information on one major topic—the tuna-fishing boats themselves. We needed to learn more about them and gain some background of the industry, and in order to learn more about this topic, we were lucky enough to interview the daughter of the founder of Campbell Machine Co., Jean Immenschuh, at her summer home in Mission Beach, San Diego.

Jean Immenschuh, 1934, outside family home constructed by tuna-boat carpenters.

We held the interview inside, but the window scene that made up the background was bustling with activity, and we had an excellent view of the beach and its denizens—rollerskaters sliding by, bikers pedaling determinedly, and couples out for romantic walks. However, our topic of conversation bore a stark contrast to this modern day atmosphere, as we chatted with Mrs. Immenschuh about the San Diego tuna industry at its peak.

As she chose to pursue a career as a veterinarian instead of the family shipbuilding business, Mrs. Immenschuh has never been involved in the design or construction of tuna boats. The wealth of information she offered us was from her childhood memories of growing up around the tuna boats built by her family's company. Along with the photographs displayed on many pages in this chapter, Mrs. Immenschuh provided us with a deep, insightful perspective on the tuna shipbuilding industry during the years when San Diego was known as The Tuna Capital of the World.

Student Researcher (SR): We understand as you grew up, your family was involved in tuna-boat building?

Jean Immenschuh: Yes, they started in the 1920s; way before I was born. At the end of Broadway, they had a little boatbuilding place, and then they eventually moved down to the foot of Eighth Street in San Diego and had the Campbell Machine Co. there. Before, they had [the first] auto-repair shop in San Diego ... and my dad had one of the first driver's licenses ever issued around San Diego.

The Campbell Machine Co. shipyard.

Front row, far right: David Campbell (overalls) standing and George Campbell (suit) sitting.

SR: Were there any other shipyard competitors of the company?

Immenschuh: There were several [other companies] that had shipyards around San Diego, and at the same time, there were five canneries that operated around the harbor.

SR: What was it like growing up around ships?

Immenschuh: Oh, it was fun. I enjoyed it as a child. I had the whole shipyard to run around in and played on the boxes and watched the boats be launched, and we went on trial trips and on the maiden voyage of the ships—usually just out to the Coronado Islands and back—but it was fun. They were very crowded; lots of people went on that [maiden] voyage.

SR: Did the fishermen requisition their boats personally?

Immenschuh: Oh, yes. The fishermen were mostly either Italian or Portuguese. The Portuguese lived in a colony, and the Italians lived where the Italians live now, in the commercial section of San Diego. They all knew my father, and one man did all the designing of the boats—Manuel Madruga. I still have some toys that he made for me when I was little. My father did all the actual outdoor machinist type stuff, and my uncle [George] was a bookkeeper.

SR: Do you know what caused the transition from smaller to bigger boats?

Immenschuh: I think they had to expand their fishing trips. They started out just around San Diego and out in our ocean, and eventually worked down to jobs towards South America, and the Galápagos Islands.

SR: When fishermen would commission a boat, do you remember if there were differences between the Portuguese and the Italians'?

Immenschuh: I don't really remember … the Portuguese were all Catholics, and they had their little chapels on their ships. The Italians [boats] were not as fancy as the Portuguese.

The Europa *being built in the Campbell Machine Co. shipyard, four days into production.*

SR: Did you have any other interactions with the Italians or Portuguese, or any of the other cultures?

Immenschuh: Originally the Japanese were always involved too. But that ended in World War II when they were shipped out of San Diego … they never did really come back. When I was young there was a little Japanese fleet—but I don't think they lasted long [enough] to have the bigger ships that went farther away.

SR: Aside from the loss of Japanese culture in the tuna fishing industry, what effects did the World Wars bring to the tuna fishing industry?

Immenschuh: During World War II, the tuna boats were made into food-carrier boats. They were pressed into service, and a lot of the captains enlisted. They carried food in the refrigeration holds to the islands in the South Pacific.

SR: So, did very many of those boats come back?

Immenschuh: All but about two or three were sunk.

SR: Were only larger boats taken by the government to be food carriers?

Immenschuh: I don't know how they chose them—I think a lot of it was if the captains enlisted or wanted to go. The boatbuilding part changed because they built minesweepers instead of tuna boats. I remember the minesweepers, because we built some of them. They also did work on the big transport ships. They would load the ship's cargo holds, and then build bunks over them for the men to sleep in when they went overseas.

SR: How large was your family's company at its peak?

Immenschuh: During the war, I think they had 300 employees, so they built dry docks. For many years they had many ways [to build] the boats. They built one dry dock, and then ended up with three dry docks, large ones.

David Campbell standing on boat rail overseeing the placement of an engine onto the newly outfitted, 117-ft tuna clipper Invader.

SR: Eventually, the boats were built with metal?

Immenschuh: Yes, they were … by National Steel, which has been here for years. A few were built up in Long Beach, but I'm not sure we had anything to do with that.

SR: Did you ever notice any decline in the number of boats being made?

Immenschuh: Towards the end there was a vast decline because of the environmentalists. … They were seining at the time, and didn't use poles any more. Dolphins and fish and lots of other things … died in the process, so they put a stop to that. Most of the old wooden [fishing] boats were sold to Mexico or South America—[places] where they were not so far away from their fishing banks.

SR: This house was built by some of the workers from Campbell Machine?

Immenschuh: Oh yes, this house was built back during the Depression in 1933. They were not building tuna boats at that time, and my dad didn't want to lose the tuna-boat carpenters. They were skilled people … so he tried to keep them busy a day or two a week. That way they would have food for their families, and that's how this house happened to be built. We also built another house out in the country, too—a ranch.

Russ Vetter

Through our research and investigations, we had read many studies and scrolled through many historical sources, so our knowledge of the history of San Diego's tuna fishing industry was extensive. However, we needed the opinion of a fisheries expert; someone who could tell us everything about tuna from a scientific perspective. Luckily, we found a person who fit the bill perfectly: Russ Vetter, the father of a High Tech High student and a notable ecologist with the National Oceanic and Atmospheric Administration (NOAA). In his work for NOAA, Dr. Vetter and the members of the Large Pelagics Biology Program track tunas, sharks and billlfishes around the world, gathering more information about their ecological situation.

Our interview with Dr. Vetter was a scenic one, outside his laboratory high above La Jolla Shores. We had an excellent view of the beach that was the doorway to the expansive, watery home of the tuna. In our interview, Dr. Vetter kindly explained the nuances of the current tracking systems used to locate tuna, their discovered migration patterns, and their incredible biological capabilities. He then went on to explain tuna's role in San Diego's history, and the need for tighter standards to ensure their conservation and survival. When we were through, we understood the history and present condition of the species more clearly than we had before our interview.

Student Researcher (SR): Could you give some background information on tuna?

Russ Vetter: Tuna have always fascinated scientists because they are the most active, most highly evolved, most specialized fish predators in the ocean. The ocean is just icy cold water—no place to hide, no place to run, nothing to get behind. So, everything in the open ocean is built on speed—you are either quick, or you die. Tuna are the fastest swimmers; they have tiny finlets on their backs, [similar to those] actually used in jet design to break up turbulence. They are very fast growing, and as a fishery they produce a lot of fish in a short amount of time. ... Ocean sharks, [for example, produce maybe] one to ten babies a year and are easy to overfish, whereas tuna are what we call highly productive. They will grow to a large size in only a few years, and if you manage them properly you can feed a lot of people without overfishing,

Shogun *returns with a record 2006 catch.*

which is the problem with sharks and other fishes.

SR: What do tuna eat?

Vetter: Tuna like to eat flying fish. That's why they are so fast, and why flying fish fly. This is because when you are chased by a tuna in an environment with absolutely nothing to hide behind, you end up going airborne and making a sharp turn, hoping that the tuna doesn't follow.

SR: How long does it take tuna to fully mature?

Vetter: Tuna can [mature] in only a few years. It's phenomenal. They have a very high growth rate. Now in terms of fishing, they are obviously prized by sport fisherman, and highly prized by commercial fisherman. It may be that a lot of people haven't eaten this type of fish or that type of fish, but there is probably nobody in the United States that has not had a tuna sandwich. They are literally front and center for all sorts of commercial fisheries and all countries around the world.

SR: How important is your work with NOAA to the tuna fishing community?

Vetter: In the long run it's extremely important. If there are no fish to fish, nobody makes money. Which is not to say that when our agency says that they need to slow down their fishing they don't complain and say that we're wrong, and can't they take a few more [fish]? They're like kids in front of a cookie jar. They want to feed their families, they want to make money, and if we tell them that they need to slow down, they are not happy. But if they wipe out all the tuna, then nobody is happy. So, we serve as a scientific agency, but we also serve as a regulatory agency.

SR: How has tuna fishing [affected] the San Diego economy?

Vetter: Well, particularly for the students that go to school down in Point Loma, it's easy now that San Diego is a city of multiple technologies and multiple small industries to forget San Diego's roots. But San Diego was, and in many ways still is, a tuna-fishing town. Many of the families that originally settled in Point Loma were Portuguese, or Italian, and many of them still have that history and that culture of going to sea and catching tuna.

SR: What is the current state of the world's tuna fisheries? Which are the biggest? Which are the smallest?

Vetter: We rate fisheries as: not fully used, fully used, overfished, or in the extreme case, in danger. Most of the fisheries of the world are considered fully utilized, and some of them in the Atlantic Ocean are overfished. Most of the issues now are not only the overfishing of tuna, but all the things that get caught when trying to catch tuna—that's been the real heartache for the tuna fisherman in San Diego.

Hauling in yellowfin.

SR: How do they catch tuna?

Vetter: It [used to be] backbreaking work [to catch tuna]. … You would throw bait into the ocean. The fish were so big that if you watch these old videos, there were three fishermen with their poles tied together; there were so many fish that they didn't need a rod and reel. They threw [the bait] in the ocean, and there would be thousands of fish around the boat. [They would] catch the tuna, pull it out of the water, throw it onto the boat and throw the hook back into the water without any bait at all, just a silver hook, and [then] there would be another tuna. If you've never seen that video before, it's amazing.

Then they came up with the idea of purse seining, in which over a mile of net circles an entire school of tuna. But what they used to find with the tuna was dolphin. So, before they had fancy ways of finding tuna, they would see dolphins at the surface of the ocean and then surround the dolphins and the tuna. In the process [the fishermen] would kill many dolphins. The dolphins, because they are air breathers, would panic and drown in the nets. So, that's when we stepped in, and many of the nations of the world agreed that this was unacceptable; there are too many dolphins being killed in the process of catching tuna. But people got better because a lot of the [tuna boat] captains and fishermen loved the ocean, and they didn't want to kill dolphins either, so they came up with ways of letting dolphins out of the net. This is not to say that they never killed dolphins, but the numbers went way down.

Tuna sportfisherman's gear.

Also, tuna will follow a log looking for small fish, or maybe just because they're curious, so you can put one log that floated down the river to the ocean, or [a broken plank from] a ship, and you can find over 100 tons of tuna around one silly log. So, now they mimic that by putting out "FADs"—fish aggregating devices—which [are made up of] a bunch of wood or old nets. The tuna will come and circle [around] this. The beauty is that you can wrap that old piece of wood and catch tuna without catching dolphins. But you catch a lot of baby fish … you catch a lot of turtles, you catch a lot of billfish. So, we solved one problem, but now we're hurting other parts of the ecosystem.

Guy Bruni

After extensive research related to the tuna fishery and this magnificent fish, we still hadn't had much success finding any tuna fishermen for a personal account of that golden age. However, a large "fish" by the name of Guy Bruni was hooked during the 27th Annual Day at the Docks at Shelter Island. While sharing the High Tech High San Diego Bay study with visitors to this San Diego sportfishing event, we had a chance encounter with Mr. Bruni, an Italian-American whose life has been immersed in the tuna industry. When we found out Mr. Bruni had been both a carpenter for the Campbell Machine Co. and then later a veteran tuna fisherman and ship's engineer with knowledge of the ins and outs of the industry, an interview was imminent. During our time with Mr. Bruni, we covered several important areas of the tuna industry. These ranged from how the Campbell Machine Co. functioned and supported the tuna fishermen, to his own experience of the "enlistment" of fishing boats by the Navy during WWII, and even the origin of fishing technology that was utilized by the tuna crews, whether Japanese, Italian or Portuguese. He also supplied us with many precious personal photos from the glory days of tuna fishing that you see on these pages.

Student Researcher (SR): What did you do in the Campbell Machine Co. shipyard?

Guy Bruni: I was a carpenter. I started out as a carpenter's helper, but I al-

ready knew what it took to get the job done. The company had a lot of craftsmen. They brought a lot of craftsman down from Seattle to build the tuna boats, because they didn't have the personnel here that it took to build that many boats. Things were slow in Seattle, so these Norwegians and Swedes came down to Campbell's, and this is where I learned a lot. … Then, in 1937 I went fishing on the *Conte Bianco*, which Campbell had built four years earlier. It was a 115-footer, and could carry 200 tons of iced fish.

Guy Bruni (second from the left) with a crew of fellow carpenters at Campbell in 1936.

SR: Who did the Campbell Machine Co. sell their boats to?

Bruni: They never built any boats on speculation; they always had Portuguese, Italians, or a few Swedes with a contract. … There were three brothers in the shipyard: Dave, George, and John. Dave was the outside foreman, George took care of the money part—he was the accountant—and John did other work... George always got in on a contract and made sure they got their share. And Dave was a machinist and a good outside guy, but not a very good negotiator. … So, Dave would pick the machinery out, and George would go and do the bargaining. They were a pretty smooth team.

SR: How did the Campbell Machine Co. affect the tuna industry?

Bruni: I would say that Campbell helped the tuna industry by building some of the larger boats, so it was involved in all the tuna boats.

Bruni (top right) and company four-pole fishing.

SR: You did some three-pole fishing, right? Do you have any stories you could share?

Bruni: Three-pole fishing—it wasn't much to tell, really, other than you have three guys, three poles, and three lines, coming down on a ring and one hook. So, you got the guys together—the tall guy here on the left, the middle guy there in the center, and the shortest guy on the end, because he's the guy who leads the fish in. … Then, when the tuna took the squid, if you kept the tunas' heads above water, you could pull them aboard pretty easily. But if they got their heads down, and their tails slapping, you lost your poles overboard most times, and the fish came off.

SR: Did you ever get injured with the big fish; did you ever get hit yourself?

Bruni: Hit? No … some of us got hit, but not enough to cause any damage. But as to anyone ever getting hurt pulling the fish in, I don't know if anyone ever did.

SR: What did you use for bait?

Bruni: The bait was used for chumming mostly with anchovetas—they survived the warm tropical waters better than any other. On the poles we hardly ever used any bait. We used the feather lures that resembled squid. We put feathers on the hook, and we used to get—not sure where they used to get it at—but all the remnants of the banjo skins, the old banjos at that time. The white sheep skin was really good, tough stuff, and when it got wet it was even tougher. You put the feathers on the squid, tied it, and wrapped it together.

After that, you cut two or three butterflies on the end, and wrap that around the feathers so that the squid would last; otherwise the tuna would tear it up in no time. This way, you just had to renew the skin, as you still had the feathers. Though, putting the feathers on it was the hardest part.

SR: How long were your trips?

Bruni: The shortest trip on the *Conte Bianco* was 28 days. The longest trips took 128 days and were to Chile, Peru, Bolivia, Panama, and Costa Rica. [We would] refuel in Panama and get provisions there. It was a good life.

SR: How old were you when you went to sea?

Bruni: I was about 23. Then when I was 28, the war broke out. We were at the Galápagos Islands, and three of us were at the island of Culpepper, and we got the message from the government. … The operator came down to the skipper, and said: "I just got a message from the Navy. All the fishing boats in the area [must] either return to San Diego or proceed to Panama." I was with Skipper Louie, and he chose to go to Panama. In fact, all of us said we're gonna go to Panama, instead of making that longer run to San Diego. They were talking about submarines being on the coast, and the day after we left the Galápagos Islands we had an escort; a Navy ship escorted 12 of us into Panama. We spent Christmas there, and the Army, the Navy, came around and took all the crewmembers from the tuna boats over to a dinner at the barracks. We were treated well, and some chose to stay with the boats, but most of us chose to come home. So, I came home to San Diego. Down [in Panama], you could easily go get a junior lieutenant rank, especially if you had any experience as captain, navigator, or engineer.

Tuna being placed in the bait hold after a successful fishing run. Conte Bianco, 1937.

SR: Did you do that? Did you go into the Navy?

Bruni: No, I just came home. … The owner and family of the boat that I was on—the *Conte Bianco*—were the one of the few that sent enough money to the broker so that any of the crew members who wanted to fly home could do so. All of us chose to come home except two.

Collecting live bait off the coast of Mexico.
"We handled this precious bait with kid gloves" -Guy Bruni

SR: Were the crews mixed Italian and Portuguese?

Bruni: We were mostly Italian, because the *Conte Bianco* was an Italian boat. We had a couple of Portuguese guys, but most of us were Italian. The cooks were either Greek or English.

SR: Do you think the fishing techniques were developed here in America or were they taken straight from Italy?

Bruni: No, I think they came from overseas. I think they came from Japan, because everything we used came from Japan. The bamboo poles, swivels and hooks were purchased through the Taniguchi Co. The hooks were barbless and they ranged from two to four inches in length.

Crew repairs nets while en route.

SR: Is there anything that the Italian or Portuguese tuna fisherman developed independently of the Japanese technologies?

Bruni: That, I couldn't say, because when I started fishing ... the system that we all used was about the same. I'm sure there were ones who had the three-pole fishing and the two-pole fishing—they had all the equipment. But as far as any of them developing anything new? It was still the same. You got all wet and broke your back.

Connection —*A Nature Reflection*

   I try to concentrate on my writing, but am distracted by the sporadic touch of raindrops upon my paper and body as the droplets end their long journey from high above. The air is cool, but filled with the obnoxiously noisy sound of a large truck backing up. But even through that racket I can somehow hear birds calling to one another. It is unfortunate that this place, for all its underlying beauty, has become so endangered.

   I continue to sit here at the boat channel adjacent to San Diego Bay, but my thoughts are flowing with the water of the channel, far out to sea. Out on the Bay, I notice many boats docked, floating on an endless blue horizon. How many of them, I wonder, are run by sport fishermen who catch tuna? Are there any at all? I wonder where the tuna industry has gone. I know that all of San Diego's main tuna canneries have moved elsewhere, and with them nearly all the career fishermen. Only the sport fishermen remain to catch the occasional tuna in the waters of the Bay.

   I look around the docks. Nothing moves, not a single vessel stirs. Only the ripples break the water's silence. Then, a boat drifts into view. It looks like a tuna fishing boat, and although it is faded, it is still intact. The contrast between the Bay's natural beauty and the stern unattractiveness of the fishing ships is curiously alarming. Industry and nature seem always to be locked in a conflicting war of priority. This sight makes me wonder, what good will a new pair of shoes be without any ground to walk upon?

                                        Peter Pham

Members of the tuna family are champions among fish in their own right and are renowned across the globe for spectacular stamina and speed. Tuna belong to the tribe Thunnini, a subgroup of the Scombridae, or mackerel family. (Gibbs 2006)

Tuna generally reach sexual maturity three to five years after they are born. They are unique among fish for both their rapid growth and longevity. Normally, they live and migrate in small schools. However, there are some solitary tuna, and these can grow to weigh over 500 pounds. Tuna generally inhabit the upper and middle layers of the ocean to depths of 1,600 ft. (Gibbs 2006)

The most common commercially caught and sold tuna species are: albacore, yellowfin, bluefin, bigeye, and skipjack.

Albacore
Thunnus alalunga

Albacore are white-fleshed tuna, and are considered to be California's staple fish. They are very popular in the world market, but their popularity is especially prevalent in the United States. Albacore have been nicknamed "Chicken of the Sea," as their taste closely resembles chicken to some. They migrate constantly, so catches of them vary greatly from year to year. Their weight ranges from 20–45 lbs, and they are small compared to other species of tuna. ("Tuna Species Datasheet" 2004) ("Thunnus albacares" 2006)

Yellowfin
Thunnus albacares

Yellowfin tuna have been known to live up to eight years, and average about 125 lbs. They are a dark blue above with a silver-gray belly. Some have yellow side stripes, but they all have yellowish fins. They mostly feed on schooling fishes, crustaceans and squid. They are very sensitive to low concentrations of oxygen, so they're usually not found in depths of more than 800 ft. ("Tuna Species Datasheet" 2004) (*"Thunnus albacares"* 2006)

Bluefin
Thunnus thynnus

Bluefin tuna are the most expensive of all the tuna. Their wide-ranging migration pattern produces a very high fat content, giving them their flavor. Bluefin eat squid and schooling fish such as anchovies, jack mackerel, and sardines. They have a slow reproductive cycle, allowing them to live as long as 10–15 years; longer than any other tuna species. However, their sluggish reproductive cycle also puts them in danger of being overfished. ("Tuna Species Datasheet" 2004) ("Types of Tuna" 2006)

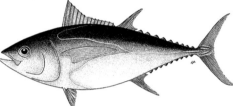

Bigeye
Thunnus obesus

Bigeye have some of the same characteristics as bluefin tuna, but they don't grow as large and they don't have the same level of fat content. They are usually a whitish color on their bellies. They spawn twice a year. Most of their diet consists of fish, cephalopods, and crustaceans. The oldest bigeye ever recorded was 11 years old. ("Tuna Species Datasheet" 2004) ("Types of Tuna" 2006)

Skipjack
Katsuwonus pelamis

Most skipjack reside in the western Pacific Ocean, though 20 percent still remain in the Indian Ocean. They are so overfished that their average life span is only about three years. Skipjack can be recognized by the presence of between four and seven stripes on their bellies. They have silvery flanks and bellies and short fins. ("Tuna Species Datasheet" 2004)

"If you think back to salary, salary is from the root word salt. 2,000 years ago, Roman soldiers were paid for their work in salt, because salt was very valuable in keeping soldiers alive."

- Tracy Strahl

Salt

Salt has been a highly prized commodity for thousands of years, and until a century ago it was considered very scarce. This scarcity, coupled with salt's natural worth, led it to be considered of greater value than even gold in many cultures throughout history. Native Americans and settlers who lived on the edge of San Diego Bay discovered, to their good fortune, that they were in a prime location, both geographically and climatically, to gather salt from the Bay. While the Native Americans harvested salt in small quantities, some of the later settlers began changing salt production into a routine industry. As a result, they profited greatly because of the purity of salt from southern San Diego Bay, or South Bay.

Over the years, the harvesting of this salt has been controlled by a number of companies, beginning with the La Punta Salt Co. in 1873. Western Salt Co., which later became a division of H.G. Fenton Co., purchased and owned the salt works facilities for 80 years, until the facilities and salt ponds were purchased by the Port of San Diego in 1999 to establish a National Wildlife Refuge in South Bay. The salt industry has been important to San Diego because the product was exported to Pacific markets and sold in the southwestern United States. A management plan adopted in late 2006 identifies the actions necessary to protect the flora and fauna of San Diego Bay—in particular the large numbers of migratory birds that are supported by the various natural and manmade habitats in South Bay, including the highly saline waters of the salt ponds. However, as the demand for salt is still strong, South Bay Salt Works will undoubtedly be a stable operation in the Bay for years to come.

Geography of the Salt in the Bay

South Bay Salt Works, though it has grown and shrunk with the times, has always been stationed at the southernmost end of San Diego Bay—South Bay—in Chula Vista. There, salt yields are abundant and the area is an ideal location for a salt works facility. The saline environment is also home to several brine organisms, as well as a wide variety of birds.

History of the Salt in the Bay

Salt is arguably one of the most essential natural materials and has some of the most unique molecular properties known to humans. It has been prized for millennia by many cultures. It is a widely used food preservative, used in religions, as a form of currency, and has been an important factor in boosting economies. Around 15,000 years ago, when mastodons roamed Earth, it is speculated that they tended to congregate around large salt seeps. Thus, early man found an easy way to obtain mastodon meat, since the creatures could be hunted at these locations. Even prehistoric peoples harvested salt and used it to season a variety of vegetables and cereals. (Strahl 2005) ("What is Salt?" 2005)

In the great eons of history, the commercialization of salt occurred with the Roman army, whose soldiers were actually paid in salt. The modern day word "salary" comes from the Latin word for salt or "sal." This

Magnesium chloride crystals at South Bay Salt Works.

example clearly shows its incredible value, as it was not only essential for human life but could be traded for other goods. (Strahl 2005)

Nowadays, salt is a bulk commodity, but it is still valuable enough to make it a viable industry here in San Diego. Since it weighs a lot, the harvesting location determines where the salt will be shipped, and ultimately where it will be used. The salt from South Bay Salt Works is sold in Northern California, where it is used as a water softener and for de-icing roads, as well as in Hawaii and the South Pacific. (Strahl 2005)

The table salt used by humans is known as NaCl, or sodium chloride, to chemists. The first commercialization of sodium chloride occurred in ancient Sudan, where various tribes warred with each other over salt supplies. This salt was often sold to European countries for seasoning food and preserving meats before the days of refrigeration. Salt was even prized for its purported ability to carry holy words into the human body. Following ancient tradition, it was mixed with ink to write prayers on slates. Then, the salty ink was washed off and drunk in the hopes of curing ills and fulfilling wishes. (Lovejoy 1986) ("What is Salt?" 2005)

One of the most important properties of sodium chloride is that it occurs naturally all over the planet. Seawater is about 2.7% sodium chloride. Given its many important uses and its availability, it was only a matter of time before people saw a profit in this resource. Just in the last century, the salt industry has experienced tremendous growth as new applications for the resource developed. Salt production has increased from 10 million to 200 million tons annually. Today, three countries produce more than 25 percent of the world's salt: the United States, 45 million tons; Canada, 12.5 million tons; and Mexico, 8.6 million tons annually. Mexico currently owns the world's single largest solar-evaporation salt-production facility, the Guerrero Negro Ponds in Baja California. ("What is Salt?" 2005) ("About the Salt Industry" 2005)

While salt can be found in large quantities throughout the bounteous Earth, its molecular structure can vary. Sodium chloride crystals are cubic in form. Different climates and traces of contaminants can determine crystal growth, resulting in larger or smaller crystals. Solar salt from seawater, for example, will always contain traces of CaS, MgS, and MgCl. Consequently, salt works produce different forms of salt depending upon their location. For example, at the Guerrero Negro facility, the crystals are very large, while in San Francisco, they are much smaller. San Diego Bay crystals are somewhere in between. (Strahl 2005)

Western Salt Co. in 1953.

The salt industry in San Diego began in 1873 with the establishment of the La Punta Salt Co. The company constructed a series of levees and ponds for solar-evaporative salt production in the southernmost end of San Diego Bay. Salt production was seen as a lucrative trade in San Diego for several reasons. First, in 1873, there were few nearby competitors geographically—the biggest being some small operations in Northern California. (Today, the biggest competitor is the Baja California Guerrero Negro facility, which produces around 5 million metric tons of salt annually—roughly 66 times that of South Bay Salt Works production [see graph].) Second, the weather—a crucial element in the solar-evaporative production of salt—was often sunny and favorable for such an enterprise in San Diego. Third, San Diego Bay is sheltered from heavy wave action and large storm surges, making it ideal for having a solar-evaporative salt operation. After several years, the industry caught the eye of George Babcock, a successful San Diego businessman, who in 1901 bought and expanded the business. (Jones 2005)

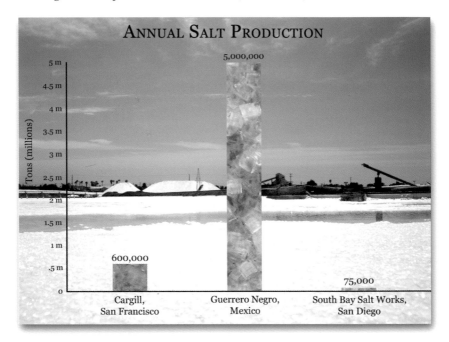

ANNUAL SALT PRODUCTION

In 1902, the enterprise was renamed "Western Salt Co." In 1916, the Otay basin experienced a major flood, causing the Otay Dam to break, resulting in colossal damage to the salt works. This disaster, coupled with some business failures related to Babcock's railroad investments, put him in a tough financial position. An associate of Babcock's, John Spreckels, who was famous for developing much of Coronado, decided to help out. Spreckels and Babcock were also able to enlist the help of Henry G. Fenton, who was a major player in the construction business in San Diego. Fenton owned several small companies and actually ended up acquiring the Western Salt Co. in 1922. Western Salt was expanded again under Fenton and has remained relatively the same size for the past 84 years. However, in 1999, H.G. Fenton sold Western Salt to the Port of San Diego. In 2002, Western Salt Co. was renamed South Bay Salt Works. The business remained profitable, but H.G. Fenton is now more involved in real estate than mining, construction and salt production. (Strahl 2005) (Jones 2005)

South Bay Salt Works, located at 1470 Bay Blvd. in Chula Vista, harvests salt using a process that has not changed much over the last 130 years: solar evaporation. The process begins when the Bay's water enters the primary salt ponds. The salt travels through a series of ponds controlled by gates, steadily evaporating and becoming more concentrated. In each of these ponds, the color of the water changes dramatically. This is due to the proliferation of halobacteria (see p. 138) and algae in addition to the precipitation (coming out of solution) of other "salts." One of the byproducts of precipitation is "gypsum," or calcium sulfate dihydrate ($CaSO_4 \cdot 2H_2O$). It is toxic if consumed by humans in large quantities. The main product, sodium chloride, travels on, eventually ending up in ponds known as the "crystallizer ponds," which are almost entirely composed of solid salt. In the South Bay every year, chiseling machines are brought in to reduce the salt mound to 4 to 6 inches of salt, leaving a thin layer of clean salt on the ground. This residue of nonharvested salt is known as the "sacrificial salt bottom." (Strahl 2005)

Once the chisel cutters have finished, the salt is loaded onto dump trucks and is washed, then dried, fired in a kiln and sorted according to size. After being sorted, it is sold to retailers and shipped out. In wet weather, the entire process from evaporation to harvest might take 15 to 16 months, but in dry conditions, around 8 to 10 months. All

Log preserved in an evaporation pond after being washed down the Otay River during the great flood of 1916.

the salt produced at South Bay Salt Works is industrial grade salt, as opposed to everyday table salt. (Strahl 2005)

Salt was previously used to de-ice areas around Lake Tahoe. However, people realized that it was washing into the lake and having detrimental effects, so de-icing was stopped in that area, although it still remains a viable market. In some parts of Arizona, the salt is mixed with chemicals and sprayed on dirt roads to keep the dust down. Salt for water softening will also increase as consumers demand more quality in their water. For example, the tap water in San Diego has large amounts of calcium carbonate, making the water "hard"—a condition that probably will not change anytime in the near future.

The production of salt has had some positive impact on the surrounding environment. Down at the Guerrero Negro facility in Mexico, water near the salt ponds has been warmed by industrial activity, and the lagoon there has created a large area of very calm water. Both of these conditions keep the area a natural haven for young gray whales. Unfortunately, ongoing coastal development threatens to endanger this sanctuary. ("Guerrero Negro" 2006)

Here in San Diego, the area in and around South Bay Salt Works hosts many birds, including: the black skimmer, elegant tern, Forster's tern, royal tern, Caspian tern, and California least tern. These birds normally nest on the soft, sandy, coastal beaches, or migrate through such areas at some point during the year. However, many of these beaches are occupied by residential and industrial developments, and the birds can no longer use those locations.

Gate system shown traversing levee that is used to move water from pond to pond.

Alternatively, the levees between the salt ponds are the perfect habitat for such birds, as they are generally undisturbed, soft and sandy. In addition, South Bay Salt Works has tried placing substrates composed of coarse sand on the levees to simulate a beach's sand to better suit the birds' needs. This substrate placement program is in accordance with the recommendations of the U.S. Fish and Wildlife Service regarding the protection of migratory birds. So far, it has been effective. Additionally, many of these birds find food in the surrounding saline ponds, which contain large concentrations of such tasty morsels as brine shrimp and flies. (Jones 2005)

However, this artificial saline environment, which is much different than a standard salt marsh, has also displaced the benthic (bottom-dwelling) organisms and various fish that would live in such a salt marsh. Thus, while South Bay Salt Works provides needed habitat to endangered and rare birds, it has also eliminated some habitat for other aquatic organisms. (Stadtlander 1994) (Touchstone 2006)

South Bay Salt Works has had more than just a biological impact on San Diego. It employs about 23 employees, all of whom work there year round. Many employees operate heavy machinery: driving or loading trucks, packing salt in bags, wrapping pallets, etc. In terms of taxes, the establishment and its employees supply about $300,000 in tax benefits to the federal, state and local economies. When the crews aren't harvesting, they do maintenance on the equipment, as the highly saline environment of the facility requires constant vigilance. (Strahl 2005)

In the past, the company has had to find new markets several times. One of the major shifts occurred with the departure of the tuna fishing industry from San Diego because of by-catch and environmental measures. Even though the tuna canneries provided about 30 to 40 percent of the salt work's business, the company simply changed marketing direction. In the words of Vice President Tracy Strahl, the departure of the tuna fishing fleet "didn't do anything [to us in the long run]." In the short run, however, it was troubling because Western Salt Co. allowed the sales department to shrink. (Strahl 2005)

The company's markets are evolving. Since it is a smaller player in the industry (compared to facilities in Mexico or in San Francisco), it can adapt and shift focus much easier. Allen Jones, the Vice President of H.G. Fenton— the previous owner of the company—and Tracy Strahl both agree that the salt industry is here to stay. "The salt industry is ever changing," Strahl says. Over time, new market niches will arise for the salt produced in San Diego, while others will be eliminated. However, there are no current plans for expansion in South Bay. (Jones 2005) (Strahl 2005)

Western Salt Co., 1915.

Though the short-term outlook for South Bay Salt Works is promising, this may change in the next couple of decades. The U.S. Fish and Wildlife Service is planning to restore salt ponds within the National Wildlife Refuge to marshes and mudflats, as well as to restore tidal flow to certain areas. Some see this as a perfect solution, as endangered and rare birds already flock to the area for nesting and protection from urban influences. For example, every year, the facility is home to the world's largest population of migratory double-crested cormorants. About 90 percent of light-footed clapper rail habitat has been eliminated by coastal developments and about 70% of all coastal wetlands in California are no longer functional habitats. Many people hope for the conservation of the few wetlands and their inhabitants that still exist. ("San Diego Bay National Wildlife Refuge Article" 2006)

Historically, the area that is currently occupied by South Bay Salt Works housed a plethora of animals that thrived off the marshlands around the Bay. Waterfowl, enormous seabass and a variety of shellfish populated

the bountiful habitat. Native Americans cultivated the salt that evaporated naturally from the Bay, but their effect on the marshlands was minimal. When others came to settle San Diego, the allure of an easy industry was overwhelming as there were many places and industries that needed salt. Over the years, the number of ponds in the Salt Works expanded, destroying some of the marshland. Some species profited from the increase of brine, while others were harmed by this change

American avocet feeding along the shores of the primary stage salt pond.

and were forced to move. Benthic organisms such as crabs and lobsters virtually disappeared from areas with elevated salt concentrations, while organisms such as brine flies and brine shrimp thrived there. Also, the construction of levees for the ponds established soft, sandy, undisturbed areas. This led to many birds, including some endangered species, building nests at the Salt Works. Nevertheless, the salt industry certainly will carry on, expanding to suit the needs of the world's population, and the industry's impact on San Diego Bay will be felt for generations to come.

Eternal Cognizance of the Saliferous Seascape —*A Nature Reflection*

I can hear the waves as they crash on the beach, flowing into the mouth of San Diego Bay. The waves travel southward along the back of the Bay where the Salt Works rests. Here is where large salt crystals form, reflecting the sunlight off a multi-faceted surface. With or without its visitors, the Salt Works slumbers in peace. Time passes by while salt keeps coming in, and evaporation continues on as wind continues to blow across this sunny, "snowy" place.

Here there are grains of salt with unique crystalline composition—so essential to us all. Humans have warred over this resource, fighting battles and spilling blood. Over the years, over the centuries, salt has been a valuable commodity. Soon, the harvesters will come to scoop up the salt.

Huge salt harvesting facilities, made of mortar, bricks and mud, have been created to collect the precious commodity, and though some believe that salt facilities have destroyed the habitat, the Salt Works in San Diego is home to many creatures. In the summer, birds like the once endangered California least tern nest serenely on the flats, picking out brine shrimp from the warm salt water. Many of the species who visit here are endangered, so the facility serves as a refuge, as a hub for the Pacific migration, a resting point for birds. I wonder where the birds will fly—perhaps they will migrate to the icy climes of the Arctic, or to the torrid, burning white sands of Mexico.

Shawn Teeter and Kris Keller

1873
La Punta Salt Co. is established in San Diego Bay

1916
The salt works is damaged by a major flood that breaks the Otay Dam

1760
French maps show evidence of Native Americans harvesting salt in the Bay

1760

1922
H.G. Fenton purchases Western Salt Co., and begins to expand the company

1901–1902
George Babcock, a Coronado developer, buys La Punta Salt Co. in 1901 and in 1902 establishes Western Salt Co.

1990-1992
The U.S. tuna fleet leaves San Diego and a large part of the salt work's income sails away, but the company continues business

1999
Western Salt Co. is now part of a National Wildlife Refuge

2006

2006
The U.S. Fish and Wildlife Service creates a management plan for the refuge

1993
The U.S. Fish and Wildlife Service conducts a study that shows there are seabirds nesting at the salt ponds at Western Salt

Allen Jones

On the drive down to South Bay, Allen M. Jones, the vice president of H.G. Fenton Co. and former vice president of Western Salt Co., began to talk about his experiences, pausing only for the occasional question from us. His company, H.G. Fenton, has a long history with salt. Mr. Jones oversaw environmental issues and land entitlement for all of H.G. Fenton's properties, including Western Salt's areas of rich bird diversity.

While working for H.G. Fenton, Mr. Jones persuaded the company that it would be more profitable to sell Western Salt for mitigation rather than develop it or continue operating. His proposal was accepted, and H.G. Fenton sold the company to the Port of San Diego and California State Lands Commission.

Through research on San Diego Bay's salt production, we knew that Mr. Jones' knowledge would give much needed insight into the local salt business. When we arrived at South Bay Salt Works, Mr. Jones pointed out the salt ponds and gave us a brief tour. His memory of the place was impeccable. After the tour, we walked over to the salt packing area and began our interview.

Student Researcher (SR): Would you tell us about the background of the [South Bay] Salt Works?

Allen Jones: There has been a salt works in roughly its present form for over 100 years. While there is anecdotal evidence of the Native Americans having made salt in a limited manner in the southern end of the Bay, the current salt operation began in [1873] and it was established as the La Punta Salt Co. It operated in the south end of the Bay for a few decades and was then purchased by Western Salt Co. in 1922 and has been operating in its current form for more than 80 years.

Western Salt Co. in 1915.

The south end of the Bay is a shallow, tidally influenced area. There are dikes that were constructed at the southern end of the Bay to create a series of ponds, and then water from the Bay is taken in through tide gates at the western end of the Salt Works in Coronado. The water is then moved through the Salt Works over a period of about 14 months and goes through a series of ponds where it evaporates. The brine then becomes excessively more and more saline, so the nonsodium salts are precipitated off. Finally, sodium chloride is precipitated in the bottom of the ponds and creates a carpet or mat of salt about 6 or 8 inches thick that is about 99.7 percent pure sodium chloride.

While this is a small salt operation, it is more efficient than most because of its size. The water can be moved very quickly and very efficiently from pond to pond. Also, there are a number of salts, four principle salts, which are created from ocean water. It is important to move the salt quickly as the brine becomes more and more saline. This small size of the operation allows for fast movement, and salt can be produced at a smaller per-unit cost. It's also much purer because of its ability to be moved more quickly than at other operations.

Aerial view of Western Salt Co. in 1920. Notice the underdeveloped surroundings.

SR: Did anyone inside the company document any effects on the environment?

Jones: When the salt works was originally established in the 1870s and 1880s, the southern end of the Bay would have been principally tidally influenced small mud flats and related habitat. Also, the creation of the pond system in the Bay established a series of shallow ponds, so there was a habitat that was eliminated. The wildlife—chiefly shorebirds and migratory birds—were affected, as they would have used the salt works as a habitat. ... This habitat is one of the most important for migratory birds and shorebirds in Southern California.

SR: What were some of the economic reasons for selling the salt works?

Jones: The salt works was, and still is, a profitable operation. It is a profitable business for us, but an issue arose with the Port of San Diego, the operator of the San Diego International Airport. The airport wanted to expand onto some property at the former Naval Training Center [NTC] in San Diego, and the property where they wanted to expand was the least tern habitat. The only way that the federal environmental laws would allow the least tern habitat on NTC to be disturbed, was to have the Port of San Diego acquire other habitats and preserve them. We had, and still have, significant least tern habitats in San Diego Bay at the salt works, so the Port [of San Diego] acquired the facility to preserve these habitats for the least tern on a permanent basis, so that the least tern habitat at NTC could be used for expansion of the airport.

SR: What is the work environment like at South Bay Salt Works?

Jones: For much of the year, it's a rather placid and quiet operation. The principal energy source is simply the sun. About twice a year, after the salt has precipitated at the bottom of the ponds, the remaining 3 or 4 inches of water is pumped off. Then there is a flurry of activity. Tractors are used to chisel through the salt. There will be a carpet anywhere from 6 to 12 inches thick of almost pure sodium chloride. The farm equipment will then chisel up the salt. The salt is loaded into trucks and then moved into stock piles that are then sifted [and sorted by size]. After the salt is washed, it is either bagged into 50-pound bags or loaded into big bulk-load trucks and sold. For a couple of months a year, there is a flurry of activity as the salt is harvested and washed. Most of the year, the activity consists of waiting for the water to evaporate and maintaining the equipment, which is always impacted by the corrosive effects of the salt. It needs to be maintained and repaired on an ongoing basis.

Packaged salt ready for transport.

SR: What are the endangered species that occupy South Bay Salt Works?

Jones: The endangered species are: the brown pelican, the savannah sparrow (a small songbird), the [light-footed] clapper rail, and the least tern. [South Bay] Salt Works is an extremely valuable site for feeding and nesting. The brine shrimp are a food source that is … found in few other locations in this part of the state. … Plus, the ponds are separated by a series of dikes that are covered either with soil or sand. A number of species [like] the least tern are ground nesters. They will build their nests on the ground, and because of the ample acreage devoted to the dikes, there are a lot of places where they can build their nests. Because the area is fenced, there are few impacts from cats or other predators, which elsewhere in the Bay might have an impact on the wildlife.

There is a dredge—a piece of industrial equipment—built back in the 1920s that is used to scoop out the dirt that had washed off the dikes into the bottom of the ponds. The dredge, which is covered with a boom, a crane and a number of wires, [scoops out the accumulated dirt]. In the nonoperating season—which is the summer—every available surface is covered with double crested cormorants, and the dredge is the most important site for cormorant nesting south of Santa Barbara. The ponds and the dikes between the ponds are the most important nesting site for black skimmers in Southern California. So, whether it's for endangered species or other shorebirds or migratory birds, this is a very valuable wildlife habitat.

SR: What is your outlook on the salt industry today?

Jones: As ancient as the salt operation here is, and as ancient as the salt operation around the world is, it's an operation that will still be here in 100 years. It's still needed in a number of businesses and as a preservative used in food. Whether we have salt taken from the ocean, as we do in this case, or from underground salt mines as is done in Texas, Louisiana and Michigan, salt will still be harvested—probably for another 100 or more years—so we will still need operations like this.

SR: Have you personally seen any major changes at South Bay Salt Works related to the habitat and wildlife?

Jones: We've had snowy plovers that are now abundant here in certain years, [but in other years] have been almost absent. So, I don't think there are any changes in the salt operations that affect the abundance of certain birds. However, I think there are changes in the quality or abundance of some of the migratory species and as those changes occur elsewhere that will change what we see here in San Diego. For the most part, there isn't anything we have done to change the habitat, and the same kinds of birds that are looking for particular niches are always able to find them.

SR: What evidence is there of the Native Americans harvesting salt?

Jones: In trying to identify the history, there was a French map from the 1760s that shows that the entire area that is now part of South Bay Salt Works … was mud flats and tidal marshes. Very small ponds were made in the south end of the Bay, where there wasn't any active movement of the salt. The water was just ponded off, and after a few years when the water would fully evaporate, there would be salt that would crystallize at the bottom of the ponds.

SR: What role does the magnesium chloride play?

Jones: After the sodium chloride has crystallized in the bottom of the ponds, there is still liquid brine that is left in

Eighteen-wheel "salt shaker" moves another load.

the ponds. The magnesium brine is then sold in tanker trucks, principally to the forestry and mining industries. They found that if they spray it on dirt roads, the magnesium chloride brine stabilizes the dirt [so that no dust is thrown up by heavy trucks driving on the roads]. The brine forms a crust on the dirt and keeps a lot of air pollution from occurring in forestry and mining operations.

Tracy Strahl

We arrived at South Bay Salt Works on a particularly bright San Diego day, as trucks hauled fresh salt from one side of the site to the other. When we entered the office of Tracy Strahl, South Bay Salt Works sales manager, we saw salt works objects from the past: publications, as well as containers, vials and jars containing the different types of salt rested on a table by the window. Mr. Strahl jovially greeted us and briefly explained his role there. We found out that he is one of the principals in the wildlife refuge plan at the site. We moved to the conference room for our interview, and as the trucks roared by the windows, Mr. Strahl shed light on the inner workings of the company.

Student Researcher (SR): Can you please tell us a bit about South Bay Salt Works?

Tracy Strahl: The [South Bay] Salt Works is in an area that has been used for salt making since about 1873. ... In a nutshell, what we are looking at is water [that has] come into the Bay and during high tides moved up [the channel to the area here].

The pickling ponds are where we begin to drop out some of the salts that are present in seawater. The primary salts in seawater are sodium chloride, calcium sulfate, magnesium sulfate and magnesium chloride. Calcium sulfate begins to precipitate here ... and it coprecipitates—meaning that it falls out of solution with some sodium chloride. ... We want to get as much of the calcium sulfate out as possible, as we are in the business of producing high-purity sodium chloride.

... When it's ripe, we move it into some of these ponds here, which have a kind of an orange color. [This is] where we are actually going to produce the sodium chloride. The sodium chloride—the brine—is introduced in these ponds.

They are fairly shallow ponds, and the salt begins to fall out of the solution. Again, you get to a [point where] you are beginning to precipitate, or run the risk of precipitating, some of the magnesium salts. We don't want those magnesium salts to fall out of the solution, so we begin moving it through the system [into other ponds] before the solution gets to the density range where the magnesium salts are precipitating. It is a dynamic, moving system, and depending on [the weather], the evaporation rate and how long you want to leave it in, one of the crystallizer ponds changes.

We move [the brine] through, and the last part of the system is where we actually produce high-quality [sodium] chloride. It still has some residual magnesium salts and magnesium sulfate, a few traces of potassium. ... It's a fairly time-consuming process.

SR: Where does the salt go?

Strahl: The salt is dropped in these crystallizer ponds. ... The process takes about 12 months—though depending on the timing of when we go to harvest, [this may vary]. When we go and harvest a pond, it may take nine months one year and 15 or 16 months another year. That dictates the thickness of a crop. On average, we get a crop of about 4 to 6 inches in our harvest. ... We actually wash the salt, removing potential debris ... in a brine solution, and then we put it into stockpiles, where it is ready for processing. ... In other cases, we actually run it through a kiln drier [and then] dry and fire it to kill any sort of impurities that might be there. [The material] is then sized in the different screen sizes and run into different bins, where we extract the material for actual packaging. We package [industrial, commercial grade salt] in 50- and 40-pound bags. We do not produce any table salt—the very fine salt that you might be familiar [coming] out of your shaker. This salt has gone through some additional processing to get the uniform, small crystal size that [is needed] for table salt. Some people do purchase [our] salt and then reprocess it and sell it as sea salt or bath salts or things like that.

SR: Can you tell me more about the quality and efficiency of the salt produced here?

Strahl: Well, ... as you move further south along the coast, due to climatic changes, you can actually produce larger crystals, and South Bay Salt Works has always prided itself on the size of the large crystals, which for certain applications [are preferred—such as] where you are putting crystals into a [container] and then running water through it and trying to create brine solutions. The actual void space between the crystals allows for good flow ... The facility in Mexico produces upwards of around 5 million metric tons annually. We produce about 70 to 75,000 [metric] tons here; we're very small as the salt business goes. Even in San Francisco, I think their latest numbers are running around 600,000 tons annually, so having much bigger facilities on either side of us allows us to perhaps be more of a "boutique" water-softening application and pick out the things that we would like to do from some of our competitors. We are not in the mass market [that others are in].

SR: What is your current outlook on today's salt industry, and how has that changed from the past?

Strahl: The large worldwide picture for salt is ever changing. There is an increasing demand for raw materials in China, but the economics of moving products from China into the United States means that a raw material like that would not be coming here. But as long as the bigger players are focused on [the large markets], as a niche player [South Bay Salt Works] is able to move into places that we would like to. We have a very positive outlook on how we can respond to the markets. … We [have been] able to pick our markets and shift to where we wanted to be. So, instead of saying, "Well, [there goes] our market. We'll just [have to] close up shop and walk away," we redirected—and we have had to do that several times over the years, finding other markets that we want to move to, [as the] times change. I have no doubt that some of the businesses we are dealing with today [are going] through either technological or regulatory change and will change some of their practices. We have to change who we're marketing our product to. But because we produce only about 75,000 tons a year, whereas our competitors are producing 4 to 5 million tons a year, … we are able to respond to those things.

Voices

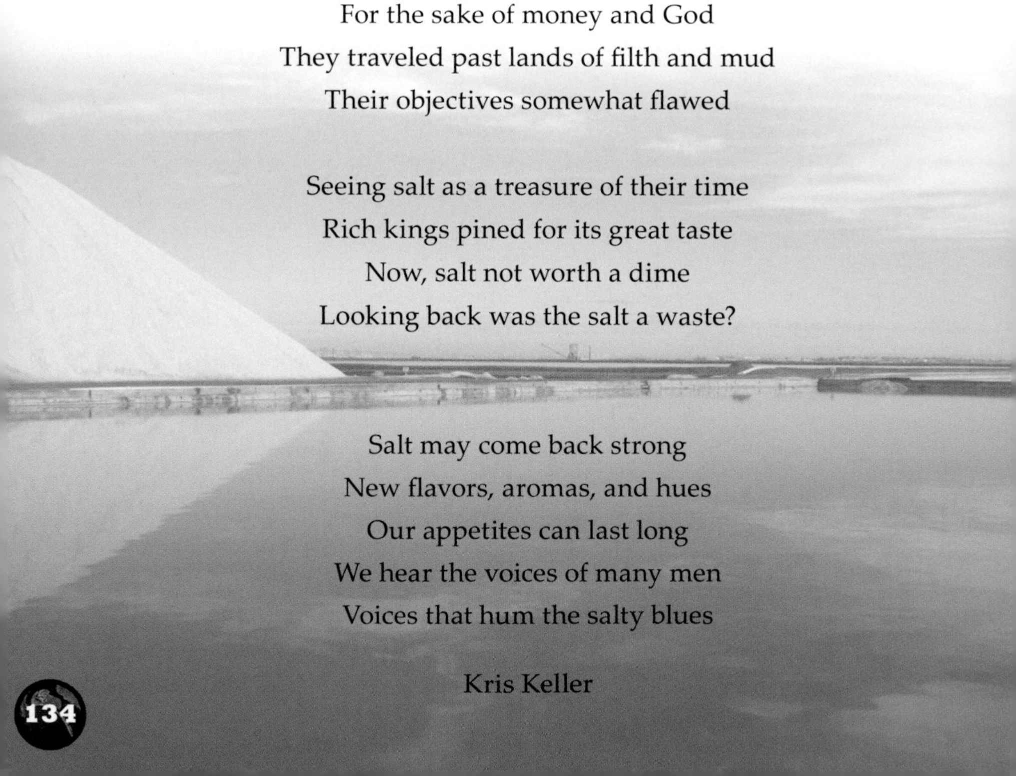

Voices hum the salty blues
Voices of many men
Many fought with their own blood
For the sake of money and God
They traveled past lands of filth and mud
Their objectives somewhat flawed

Seeing salt as a treasure of their time
Rich kings pined for its great taste
Now, salt not worth a dime
Looking back was the salt a waste?

Salt may come back strong
New flavors, aromas, and hues
Our appetites can last long
We hear the voices of many men
Voices that hum the salty blues

Kris Keller

Victoria Touchstone

The journey to the Chula Vista Nature Center was a true naturalist's experience, as we observed the flora and fauna of the South Bay, such as snowy egrets and avocets. We were excited about our interview with Victoria (Vicki) Touchstone, the lead planner for the National Wildlife Refuge at South Bay Salt Works. Ms. Touchstone is currently working on a comprehensive conservation plan with other staff for the refuge. This refuge covers an area of about 2,300 acres and includes parts of South Bay Salt Works. The planning effort focuses on assessing the condition of the wildlife and examining various management actions that would benefit south San Diego Bay's native and migrating wildlife. We sought out Ms. Touchstone to give us insight and important information concerning the biological aspects and transformation of the facility and its surrounding environment.

Student Researcher (SR): What does your work encompass and how does it relate to the facility?

Vicki Touchstone: The [South Bay] Salt Works is part of the San Diego Bay National Wildlife Refuge. … There are over 530 national wildlife refuges in the United States, [and their] land has been set aside specifically for the management of fish, wildlife, plants and their habitats. … We can serve, manage and (where appropriate) restore habitats within those areas. Because [the facility] is in a National Wildlife Refuge, we are preparing a comprehensive conservation plan that covers about 2,300 acres and includes South Bay Salt Works. We are looking at what is the most appropriate use [of the land] for wildlife there.

SR: What types of flora and fauna are found in and around the salt works?

Touchstone: There is a broad range of species. … The refuge actually includes part of the Bay and also South Bay Salt Works at the southern end of the Bay. … Primarily within the salt works … are avian species. We've got shorebirds, waterfowl such as migrating ducks … and a number of seabirds—colonial

California least terns flying through the Salt Works.

nesting seabirds that nest on the salt pond levees. There are approximately seven [colonial nesting seabirds]: black skimmer, elegant tern, Forster's tern, royal tern, Caspian tern and the endangered California least tern. We also have ... endangered snowy plovers. ... Tens of thousands of birds come through the area every year to the mudflats that are located to the north of the salt ponds, and also the salt ponds themselves.

SR: Do you know if the animal population has decreased in the Salt Works area, or [if there has been] any change in the animal population?

Touchstone: Prior to the [South Bay] Salt Works being established, the area was natural coastal wetland habitat. It was a combination of salt marsh, cordgrass, mudflats and shallow sub-tidal habitat ... [and there was] an array of species that utilized that habitat before the salt works was created. Shorebirds, ducks and marsh birds like the light-footed clapper rail—which is endangered—would have used the cordgrass and other native habitats that existed prior to the creation of the salt ponds. But you also have other species that you might not have had previously. ... Because of the loss of habitat along our coastal beaches, there are few places for terns and plovers to nest. ... Various species of terns now utilize manmade facilities like the levees on the salt ponds for nesting.

The colonial nesting seabirds are attracted to the area for a couple of reasons. We think one of the most [compelling reasons] is that it's very isolated and

so doesn't have a lot of human disturbance, although [there *are* many] predators. We have coyotes and avian predators like the peregrine falcon that will pick off the babies. But it is very isolated, which is a good thing for the birds.

SR: Has the Salt Works affected the environment around the area at all?

Touchstone: Well, it did displace natural habitat, and as you know from the settling of San Diego

Avian diversity at the San Diego Bay National Wildlife Refuge.

Bay, the Bay has lost a significant portion of its natural coastal wetlands. [However, the Salt Works] does provide benefits [for birds today], and ... we are trying to ... retain within the Salt Works what is good for the birds and [restore] what is lacking. ... For example, the light-footed clapper rail has lost most of its habitat in San Diego Bay. It requires the cordgrass habitat, so one of the proposals that we are evaluating in our comprehensive conservation plan is restoring the cordgrass habitat for the clapper rail.

SR: Do you have any statistics on this—statistics for the past and the present, and predictions for the future?

Touchstone: We have a year's worth of data that were collected from 1993–1994, and we also know that the ponds provide no benefits for fish or benthic invertebrates. We are also going to be starting some additional surveys this year to replicate what we did in 1993–1994 in order to see if anything has changed, and [we will be looking] at bird use of the ponds. … We know that a lot of the shorebirds that we observe in the ponds are actually just escaping from the high tide. When the tides go back out … that large mudflat that occurs to the north of the salt ponds is exposed. [Many of the birds] return to feed on the mudflats because there is a much higher variety of food on the natural mudflats. Other birds, such as phalaropes and eared grebes, continue to feed in ponds on the abundance of brine invertebrates which support these species.

SR: What kinds of socio-economic impacts has the Salt Works had?

Touchstone: I know they employ about 22 people, and supply about $300,000 in tax benefits to the state and local economy.

SR: Do you have any other information for us?

Touchstone: The Salt Works

Long-billed curlew hidden in the salt marsh.

actually has three separate areas... The water initially goes into the ponds in [the western] side, so those ponds are closer to the salinities of the Bay. … Some birds concentrate on those areas because they are very similar to the Bay environment. However, as you move further into the system, … the ponds are getting saltier, and that is where you are going to find your brine flies and brine shrimp. There are a lot of brine flies that accumulate on the side of this pond because of the way the wind [blows] in the Bay.

Then, there are the crystallizer ponds. These crystallizer ponds basically provide no benefit other than roosting habitat for wildlife, so that is something that we have to look at. Is it appropriate for this much of the system [to not be] providing habitat for wildlife? Or, is there enough benefit [to the wildlife] … that we should continue [the salt operation]?

We have to step back and look at the situation. Would we want to turn the area into a salt operation, or keep it as natural habitat? [Another] 1,000 acres of natural habitat in the Bay [would be] pretty significant. So, you have to look at it from all directions [and make decisions on] what is best for wildlife. Today, as a result of the railroad and the Salt Works, the river is confined … and is not in a very natural state.

Biology

The South Bay Salt Works (SBSW) is home to a great diversity of flora and fauna. Each year, a plethora of endangered, threatened, and rare birds such as the California least tern, snowy plover, and the light-footed clapper rail nest or stop at SBSW and adjacent habitats to take a rest from their migration flyways. Moreover, the highly saline waters of the evaporation ponds are home to many unique organisms such as brine flies, brine shrimp and *halobacteria*. (Touchstone 2006)

Halobacteria
Halobacterium, Haloferax, Natronobacterium

Halobacteria are members of the Archebacteria and thrive in the salt ponds of SBSW. *Halobacteria* live in highly saline conditions (4 to 5M NaCl typically) and die in more dilute water (e.g., seawater). As opposed to some creatures that simply have a tolerance for salt, these bacteria require high-sodium concentrations for membrane stability. Large blooms of these bacteria, caused by the pigment bacteriorhodopsin, appear reddish and are very apparent from the air. The pigment itself is adapted to absorb light, which provides energy to create adenosine triphosphate (ATP), a process different from other forms of photosynthesis involving electron transport. Unlike other photosynthetic creatures, the *halobacteria* are incapable of fixing carbon from carbon dioxide. ("*Halobacterium*")

Brine Fly
Ephydra riparia

Brine flies are highly concentrated around muddy areas that receive a small amount of wave action. These ideal conditions have been artificially created for them by the many earthen levees of the SBSW, which dampen any wave action. The larvae of the flies feed on *halobacteria* and algae that grows on the shores, and the adults feed on detritus and other flies. The flies themselves are an important food source for many resident birds. ("Brine Fly" 2006) (Jones 2005)

Brine Shrimp
Artemia salina

Brine shrimp are microscopic organisms that are a prime source of food for fish larvae and birds of the South Bay. They exist primarily in salty areas, such as the ocean, and can thrive in the hyper-saline conditions that occur in the evaporation ponds at SBSW, and other locales such as Mono Lake and the Great Salt Lake. *Halobacteria* are most likely the primary food source for the brine shrimp at the Salt Works. Interestingly, brine shrimp are one of the most common aquarium live-feed products. Each year, several million dollars goes into the brine shrimp industry. Also, developing embryos can survive in dormant cysts for several years in dry, harsh conditions and have been reported to survive 100 years of dormancy in sediments excavated from Utah's Great Salt Lake. Once the cysts are immersed in hyper-saline water, they resume their development. Brine shrimp are clearly important to both the economy and Bay ecosystem. ("Brine Shrimp")

Double-crested Cormorants
Phalacrocorax auritus

Double-crested cormorants have large dark bodies and sleek, skinny heads. The males have two whitish tufts during summer months that look like bushy eyebrows. During the summer months the birds crowd onto a dredge at SBSW until every last spot is occupied. In fact, there are so many birds that after they migrate, employees spend several days scraping the thick layer of guano off the machinery. Avian experts are still stumped as to why this bird prefers the artificial environment of the dredge to the soft, substrate-laden levees. Cormorants primarily feed on small fish in the open waters of the Bay as opposed to the hyper-saline waters of SBSW where there is an absence of fish. (Jones 2005) (Strahl 2005)

Marbled Godwit
Limosa fedoa

Marbled godwits are a dominant shorebird along the San Diego County coastline—especially during the winter months. Godwits are light brown in color, with dark brown barring. They can be differentiated from other shorebirds by their long, slightly upturned bill. Tidal marshes and salt flats are their main habitat, though they can also be seen on the shores of beaches and brackish lagoons. Marbled godwits occupy areas of the Tijuana River Estuary, South Bay Salt Works, North Island and Mission Bay. At South Bay Salt Works, the godwits' population reaches as high as 900 birds in November, but can be as low as 300 birds in June. Godwits migrate during the summer to the Great Plains, making only one stop along the way—at the Great Salt Lake in Utah. (Unitt 2004)

Snowy Plover
Charadrius alexandrinus nivosus

These birds are the most endangered in San Diego County. Not only have humans greatly disturbed their habitat, but they face a high level of predation from animals such as cats. Nevertheless, a protected nesting habitat and an incredible abundance of brine shrimp and brine flies allow Plovers to thrive at the Salt Works. Currently, an intensive management program is in the works for this species. (Unitt 2004)

California Least Tern
Sterna antillarum browni

California least terns are diminutive, whitish birds with slender, pointed bills, long, narrow wings and forked tails. At one time, San Diego beaches were home to the least tern, but in recent years beachgoers and development along the coastline have resulted in their habitat being heavily disturbed. The least tern was one of the first species in the 1970s to be listed as endangered by the California Department of Fish and Game and the U.S. Fish and Wildlife Service. An extensive recovery project was developed to increase their population and has proved to be quite successful, as their population has risen from approximately 500 in the 1970s to nearly 4,000 breeding pairs in 2003. The recovery of the species has been accomplished through the efforts of the San Diego Audubon Society, the Port of San Diego and the San Diego Zoological Society. (Unitt 2004)

Great Egret
Casmerodius albus

These birds are easily identifiable by their all-white plumage and are much larger than snowy egrets. They are unique wading birds that usually hold their necks in an "S" curve while in flight. Though the egrets that rest at South Bay Salt Works forage for food elsewhere in the Bay, they spend a fair amount of the winter at the facility. Egrets breed at a young age during spring, and usually nest in shrubs and trees near estuaries. Adults create nests out of plant stems and twigs for their offspring. The great egrets' diet consists of small fish, crustaceans and insects, as well as small reptiles and amphibians. A major threat to these elegant birds is human disturbance. (Unitt 2004)

Black Skimmer
Rynchops niger

Black skimmers rival brown pelicans for having the most recognizable profile and flight pattern out of all the birds of San Diego Bay. The physical characteristics of black skimmers include black plumage on their dorsal (top) sides and white plumage on their ventral (bottom) sides. Their most prominent trait is a red, laterally flattened beak. The South Bay Salt Works happens to be the most important nesting area for black skimmers in Southern California. Skimmers obtain their food by literally skimming the water with their beaks—hence their name. Their favorite foods are silversides and killi fish. ("Black Skimmer" 2006)

Brown Pelican
Pelecanus occidentalis

    Brown pelicans are almost an iconic symbol of coastal North America. They are large brown birds with a wingspan of nearly six feet, and a long bill and pouch. Their population became endangered in the 1960s and 1970s when the use of DDT became increasingly frequent in many farms and gardens. In the 1980s the use of pesticides diminished, and soon afterwards the Brown Pelican population made a quick recovery. One of the highlights of birdwatching on San Diego Bay is seeing the pelican's soaring flight and high dive that ends in a graceful plunge into the water for fish. South Bay Salt Works is an important roosting area in Southern California for these majestic fishermen. ("Brown Pelican" 2006)

Brine Shrimp Experiment

On May 22 2006, a group of students from High Tech High traveled to South Bay Salt Works to measure the salinity levels and brine shrimp activity of the ponds. Six ponds and an aquarium at the Salt Works lab were measured. Below, the data that were collected is listed in parts per thousand (ppt).

Bridge North: 300 ppt

Bridge South: 244 ppt

Pond South of Road: 416 ppt

Magnesium Chloride Pond: 336 ppt

Primary Pond: 160 ppt

Unidentified: 336 ppt

Aquarium: 32.5 ppt

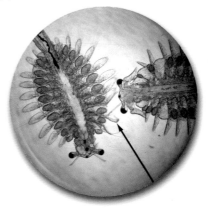

Brine shrimp were thriving in each of the ponds where water could be found, and it is interesting to note that these were surviving in salinities as high as 416 ppt, in the final stages of salt production. Much of the pond in this stage is solid salt, but there were isolated puddles of water where brine shrimp were still active. What is surprising is the maximum salinity tolerance of most *Artemia salina* is considered to be 200 ppt.

Kelp
Additives

"By harvesting it, you are really not doing much that isn't already done by nature."

-Craig Barilotti

Kelp is one of the most widely utilized resources from coastal waters adjacent to San Diego Bay. It is a practical substance that can be used in everyday items such as food, paint, toothpaste, and much, much more. The initial methods of harvesting kelp were for cattle feed and gunpowder were very crude and environmentally destructive. Harvesters would pull kelp up by their holdfasts—a method later discovered to prevent the kelp from regrowing.

As a result of efforts by the state, university scientists, and responsible kelp harvesting interests, harvesting regulations were changed in the early 1920s; only kelp from the top of the forest canopy was allowed to be harvested legally. Thus, companies have been sustainably harvesting kelp since that time.

Here in San Diego, a company called Kelco harvested kelp from 1929 to 2005, and one of their main plants was located on San Diego Bay. During its nearly century-long stay in San Diego, Kelco (now known as ISP Alginates, UK, Ltd.) played an important role in the city's economy. Unfortunately, in 2005 the company moved to Scotland for economic reasons, and as a result San Diego lost an important historical presence.

Geography of Kelp Additives Processing on the Bay

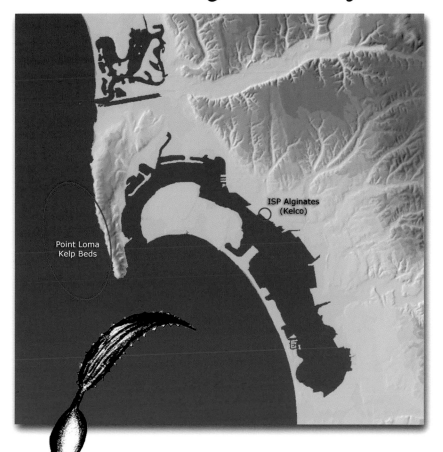

Point Loma Kelp Beds

ISP Alginates (Kelco)

On the western side of the Point Loma peninsula, just opposite San Diego Bay in the Pacific Ocean, lies
the area's largest kelp bed—the Point Loma kelp bed. ISP
Alginates, formerly known as the Kelco Co. or Kelco, annually
harvested tens of thousands of tons of giant kelp from this bed. Its facilities, located on the Bay near the eastern end of the Coronado bridge in the
Barrio Logan section of San Diego, were a testament to the business of
converting kelp to food additives—a lucrative industry that over the years
contributed greatly to San Diego's economy.

History of Kelp as Additives

Giant kelp (*Macrocystis pyrifera*) is the sea's largest marine plant, growing to lengths of more than 100 feet. Shallow waters are optimum for

its growth. Kelp attaches to rocky surfaces with root-like structures called holdfasts. Its gas-filled bladders cause its "leaves" to float to the sun-lit surface. This exposure to sunshine permits the kelp to grow as much as two feet daily. This swift growth makes harvesting the seaweed in a sustainable manner a relatively simple task. California's kelp beds are one of the state's most valuable resources, and many of the products we use daily and take for granted use a key ingredient obtained from kelp. (Carmignani 2005) (McMahon 2005) (McPeak 1988)

In 1883, British pharmacist E.C.C. Stanford discovered algin, a unique compound in kelp. This polysaccharide gives kelp its flexibility and adds to its strength. The discovery of algin was the major economic basis for commercial seaweed harvesting, as algin was a very good thickener and stabilizer. Today, algin can be found in many common commercial products, such as: salad dressing, ice cream, pharmaceutical products and paint. (Glantz 1984) (North 1971)

In San Diego, the Kelco Company, later known as Kelco Alginates, was established in 1929 to harvest kelp from the beds in and around San Diego Bay. Initially, the company produced kelp meal from *Macrocystis* to enrich livestock feed. However, Kelco soon turned to extracting algin from fresh kelp. The first use of Kelco's algin was as a sealant in tin cans. Over many years, Kelco continued to research algin, and discovered further applications for the product, many of which are unknown to the average user. In the 1930s, Kelco gathered kelp by collecting what was washed ashore, or was cut by hand offshore and then allowed to either dry onshore or pulled onboard a boat using a pole. (Glantz 1984)

As time went on and the demand for algin as a food stabilizer increased, Kelco grew in size until it was the largest producer of algin in the world. Kelco and ISP Alginates used a machine to mow kelp—a method that was first introduced around 1916. The machine has blades mounted on a conveyor system that are lowered one meter below the water's surface. A conveyor system is used to bring the cut kelp onboard. This kelp is then brought to the plant on San Diego Bay. (Glantz 1984)

Kelco developed approximately 70 algin products with many different uses. These were products to maintain foam to extend the shelf life of beer, enhance the flavor and creaminess of ice cream, increase the smoothness of desserts, gels and milkshakes, and suspend spices in salad dressings. Algin improves texture and retains moisture in bakery products, thickens liquids, holds tablets together, and lubricates and stabilizes emulsions in pharmaceuticals and cosmetics. It is an ideal product because it is nontoxic and nonallergenic, allowing for virtually universal use. Algin is also found in products such as paint, caulk, and cement to guard against separation, reduce moisture penetration, and thicken adhesives, allowing for longer shelf lives for these products. The many uses of algin keep it in constant demand. (Carmignani 2005) (Glantz 1984) (McMahon 2005) ("Search in the Aquasphere..." 1968)

In 1999, International Specialty Products (ISP) acquired Kelco Alginates to form ISP Alginates, who ran the kelp processing plant in San Diego until its closure. The company harvested 90% of the 30,000–40,000 tons of kelp harvested in San Diego County. Despite the huge quantities of kelp cut by the company, ISP Alginates was lauded for its environmental awareness. Kelp harvesting is considered to be sustainable, and scientists have pointed out that ISP is one of the few businesses that has not destroyed the marine resource it exploits. Its sustainable practices helped keep it in business. (McMahon 2005)

The kelp beds of California are owned by the state and leased to companies such as ISP. Due to a raise in rates for sewage and water, as well as higher fuel and materials

Aerial view of ISP Alginates' kelp cutters.

prices, ISP announced in June 2005 its decision to close its San Diego plant and move all of its kelp processing operations to their Scottish facilities. The company's kelp cutters stopped harvesting in mid-December 2005, and

CP Kelco, a company that ISP Alginates shared its site with, purchased the ISP kelp cutter *Kelstar* for potential harvesting in the future. The other kelp harvesters may be sold for scrap. ("CP Kelco | San Diego" 2006) (Currie 2006) (McMahon 2005)

ISP Alginates was very important to San Diego's economy and gave jobs to many citizens. The company's move to Scotland may negatively affect the San Diego economy. Its 135 employees had to find work elsewhere—perhaps at considerably lower pay. Moreover, ISP contributed approximately $20,000,000 annually to the San Diego economy; income that will be lost. (Barilotti 2006) (McMahon 2005)

The effect of kelp harvesting was not as devastating as some may believe. The most common myth was that kelp harvesting destroys the homes of marine life. In reality, very few fish or other marine life were brought onboard during the harvesting. Most free-swimming crustaceans and other fish-food organisms fell through the kelp screen and back into the water, though it was impossible to prevent epiphytes living on the kelp from being brought in with the seaweed. Kelp harvesting can help increase the density of kelp beds by allowing light to reach the bottom of the beds and promote new plant growth and, in some cases, harvesting can also thin the dense kelp canopy, lessening the problem of uprooting of the whole plant during storms. (Limbaugh 1955)

As Kelco Alginates and later ISP Alginates, the company was an important player in San Diego's development and served as a reminder of the city's roots along San Diego Bay. ISP Alginates's departure makes evident the delicate balance between protecting the environment, sustainably utilizing renewable marine resources, and providing for the economy.

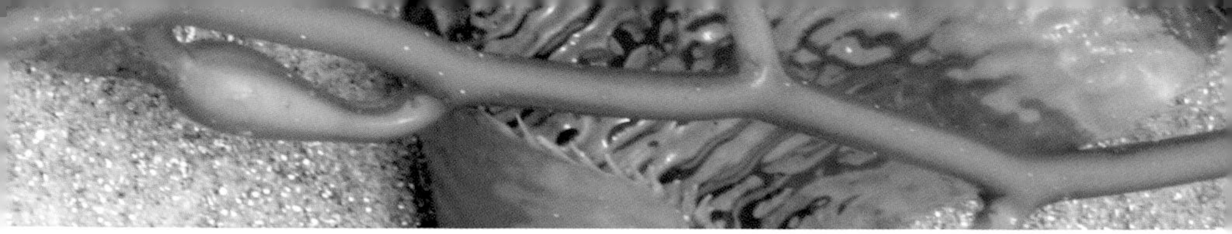

Revelations

After walking all day, I decided to sit down on a sand dune overlooking the horizon. Waves crashed down before me and seagulls flew above me, crying out loudly in search of food. Below me, rebar jutted in and out amongst the scattered concrete. There were bits of seaweed dangling from it. The gentle breeze passing through swayed the seaweed to and fro. The seaweed seemed to keep time with the waves lapping against the shore. It looked dead and lifeless.

Curious, I approached the seaweed lying there on the beach. I touched the blades of the kelp, to see if anything would happen. Nothing; as I had expected, it was just a piece of seaweed washed upon the shore. Again I touched its gooey, slimy, and disgusting skin; a skin with an opaque goop leaking out of its body. The smell of it made me gag—it made me feel like I was about to faint and vomit. I wanted to run and jump into a tub of clean water, washing out the goop left from this jellyfish-like plant.

Sand fleas buzzed around me, trying to land on my legs, tickling and annoying me. I shooed them away, but they came back. Did I remind them of the kelp? Had my closeness, my touch, now made me a part of this seaweed washed ashore? As I stood in the midst of this giant flea-fest, I wondered how anything could ever eat this smelly plant. Yet, I knew that extracts from kelp were in my favorite ice cream! And I shuddered at the thought.

Fannie Ngo

CPKelco

1929
The world's first producer of algin products, Kelco, is founded and begins operation in San Diego

1918
The increase in kelp harvesting slows down as World War I comes to an end

1880

1883
E.E.C. Stanford, a British pharmacist, discovers algin in kelp and creates methods for extracting it

1928
Philip R. Park Inc. of San Pedro began harvesting on a commercial scale. They blended the kelp meal and other ingredients for use as stock and poultry food

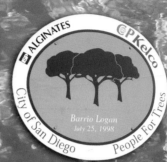

1958
Propylene glycol alginate becomes legally considered a food additive

ISP ALGINATES
CP Kelco
Barrio Logan
July 25, 1998
City of San Diego
People For Trees

2005
ISP announces they will move the company to Scotland

2006

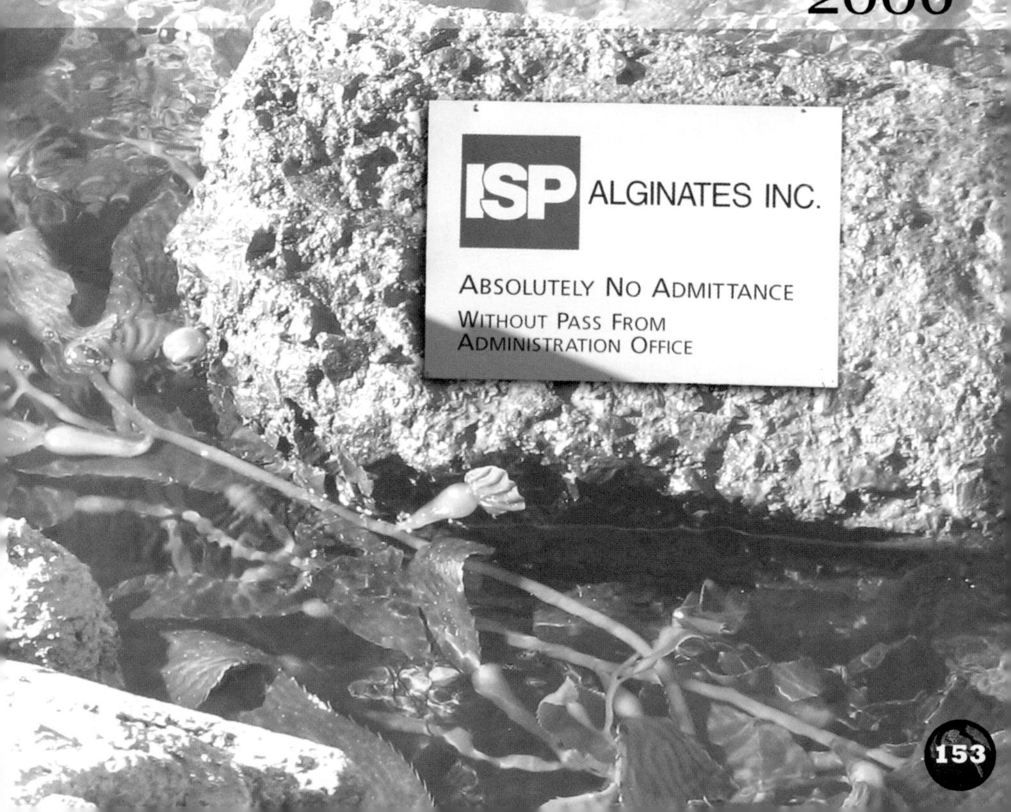

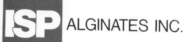

ISP ALGINATES INC.
ABSOLUTELY NO ADMITTANCE
WITHOUT PASS FROM
ADMINISTRATION OFFICE

Craig Barilotti

D r. Craig Barilotti is a marine biologist who retired from Kelco in 1996. He was inspired to study marine biology by the massive pollution issues in Southern California in the 1950s and 1960s. Dr. Barilotti worked as a professor of marine biology at San Diego State University (SDSU) and focused his research on seaweed.

Shortly after he started teaching at SDSU, Dr. Barilotti realized that to help the environment and complete his goals of reducing pollution he needed a company to support his work, and so he convinced Kelco to hire him as a marine scientist. He wanted them to know that they should start looking at the effects of pollution, especially the discharge waste from the Point Loma sewage treatment plant, on the kelp beds they harvest.

Dr. Barilotti has made managing coastal marine resources his life's work. His passion and energy for proper marine resource management is matched only by the prolific nature of the giant kelp that he has spent his career studying. His experience includes serving as a scientific consultant on resource issues to corporate and governmental entities with environmental interests. Recent field studies and management projects undertaken in Santa Barbara County include directing studies for managing kelp and sea urchin fisheries and restoring kelp for ConocoPhillips to meet the California Coastal Commission mitigation requirements.

Student Researcher (SR): What type of kelp is in San Diego?

Craig Barilotti: There are basically three surface canopy-forming kelps in San Diego… As you swim off the beach, if you're a diver or a surfer, the first kelp you see is *Egregia*. This species of kelp is called the "feather boa kelp," and it grows at depths of about 15–20 feet. Then, at depths of 25–30 feet out, to 60–65 feet, you have what's called "giant kelp" or *Macrocystis pyrifera*. … Outside of giant kelp is bull kelp, which is also called elk kelp. Harvesting is targeted on *Macrocystis pyrifera*, the giant kelp.

A tattered and beach-bound Egregia.

SR: How did you start working for Kelco?

Barilotti: Well, after teaching at SDSU and working on a contract from the Coastal Commission, it became clear to me that in order to really be successful at turning the pollution around, especially in San Diego, you needed to have a company behind you. So, I was able to convince Kelco that it was in their best interest to hire me… Kelco also happened to be interested in learning more about the kelp beds and impacts of El Niño on the kelp. I worked at Kelco as a marine scientist.

SR: Where was Kelco located?

Barilotti: Kelco, which [became] ISP Alginates, is located right by the Coronado Bay Bridge, on the San Diego side of the Bay. … Kelco was there for a good number of years, probably since the thirties. I don't believe it started there though—I think it started down in South Bay at the Hercules Powder site.

Large-scale bioprocessing tanks owned by ISP Alginates.

SR: What type of kelp did Kelco harvest the most?

Barilotti: They harvested primarily *Macrocystis pyrifera*… It lends itself very well to mechanical harvesting and you can make very high-quality products from it that you can't make from other seaweeds. … The other seaweeds have to be dried, and that makes it difficult to get the high-quality algin products that you can get from *Macrocystis pyrifera*.

SR: What was Kelco's main objective?

Barilotti: Working for Kelco was interesting because they were in business for the long haul. I started working for them in the late seventies, and even at that time they had a vested interest in protecting the kelp beds and harvesting them sustainably. Unfortunately, market factors and wages are such that the Chinese can produce algin, which is the main product that's extracted from kelp, much cheaper—at about a fourth of the price that we can produce it. So, in time the foreign market … displaced the domestic production of algin from, kelp.

SR: Could you explain the main additive from kelp that is used in food or the most popular one that we would recognize?

Barilotti: Well, you might not recognize it at all, but it's in everything. It's called algin. It's a long chain polysaccharide and it has a variety of interesting properties. It was used initially as a gel and was put on the inside of tin cans. And then, in time, realizing it could be used in food, it began to be used in ice cream. So, that was the first industrial use of algin on a large scale. … It went from there to the discovery of other properties of algin, one of which was sodium alginate, which is soluble in water, but if you put calcium in with it, a gel is formed. An interesting thing is that you can encapsulate microorganisms in the gel and they live. For instance, the Japanese used alginate to rapidly brew beer.

SR: Did anyone ever object to Kelco's harvesting of kelp, or their process of harvesting kelp?

Barilotti: Not really. I mean, there were always people who were uneasy with taking 600 tons of kelp out of the Point Loma bed or 120,000 tons of kelp out of Southern California, but no real objective, scientific objections, although there were always emotional objections. That's not to say there may not be some problems. I've spent a good part of my time trying to find problems, but haven't found any with harvesting, if it is done in the manner Kelco practiced it.

A mural in tribute to San Diego's kelp beds.

SR: How does harvesting kelp affect the surrounding area and the animals that live in kelp forests?

Barilotti: Well, harvesting kelp in itself has not been shown to have an impact that can be measured if the question is, "how does harvesting affect animals?" The way the kelp grows, it grows up to the surface and forms a surface canopy, and then the surface canopy turns with the tidal currents and there's stress on it and eventually it breaks off just below the surface, which is about where Kelco harvested it. ... The kelp washes up on the beach, or goes out to sea as kelp patties. By harvesting it, you're not really doing much that isn't already done by nature. The animals that would likely be impacted would still be. With harvesting, you will have less kelp on the beach—which most people who go to the beach would like—and so the animals that depend on the beached kelp could be impacted. But there's always so much kelp on the beach that, unless it is removed by beach-cleaning crews, I can't imagine this could be a limiting factor for animals such as kelp flies who are dependent on beached kelp. We've actually looked at other possible impacts closely, and there's nothing you could measure; let's put it that way. There could always be something we don't know about, but ... the research so far shows no particular impact of kelp harvesting.

SR: How did kelp harvesting affect the economics of San Diego?

Barilotti: That's a hard one to answer as a marine biologist—but let's say you harvest 120,000 tons of kelp and process it. You basically get about 40 pounds of algin per ton of kelp, so you're up to, say ... 5 million pounds ... and that's worth about $4 a pound. So, there's $20 million, and that stays in the community—that's jobs, that's fuel, maintenance work, and you're paying for the water and sewer and all that. All of this brings money into the San Diego economy. These are old numbers, but you can probably ... estimate it brings $30 million to the San Diego economy, and I think that's conservative. Of course, now the whole thing has moved over to Scotland, and we don't have any of that, so it's zero now.

SR: Where are some of the biggest kelp forests along the California coast?

Barilotti: Well, if the question is, "What is the largest, most important kelp bed?" It's the Point Loma kelp bed. That's the most important to Kelco, or at least it was. The product from there is the best; in part because it's the closest to the processing plant. The Point Loma kelp bed was harvested maximally. If there's kelp there, they're going to harvest it. … That's one reason we know kelp harvesting is a benign activity; because

The Point Loma lighthouse with kelp beds beyond.

this maximally harvested kelp is still doing very well, the lobsters are doing well, the sea urchins are doing well and other industries—like sport fishing—are doing well. So, based on the Point Loma kelp bed and the maximal harvesting of that resource, we can tell that kelp harvesting is sustainable. Of course, the Point Loma kelp bed is also the largest bed.

Monster Story

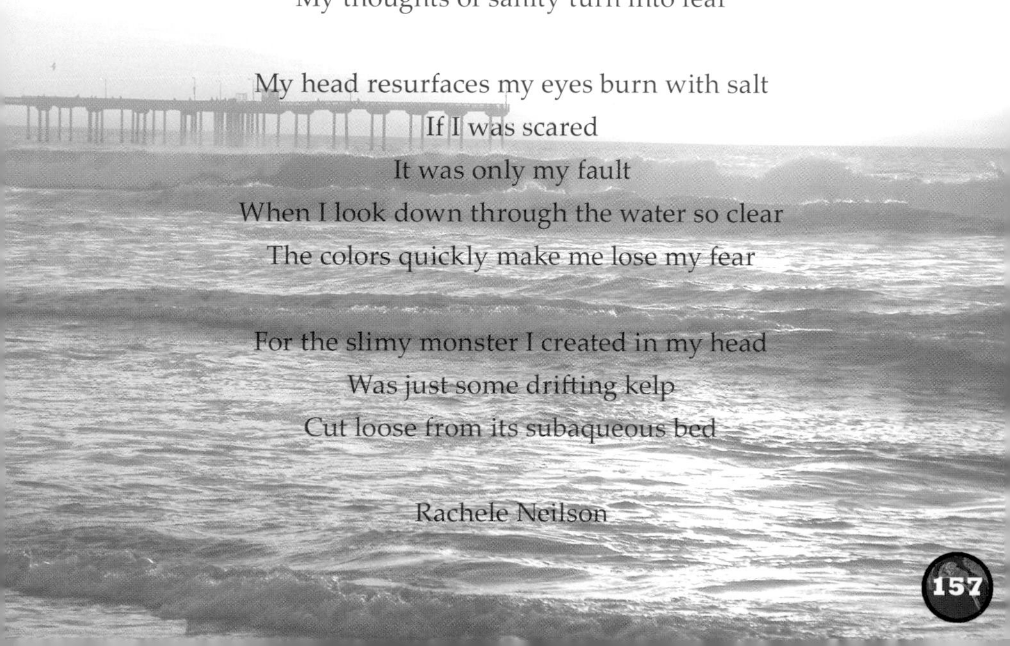

A slimy beast has grasped my feet

I drown for a moment

I cannot breathe

The water surrounds me

I cannot hear

My thoughts of sanity turn into fear

My head resurfaces my eyes burn with salt

If I was scared

It was only my fault

When I look down through the water so clear

The colors quickly make me lose my fear

For the slimy monster I created in my head

Was just some drifting kelp

Cut loose from its subaqueous bed

Rachele Neilson

Biology of San Diego Kelp

Giant kelp (*Macrocystis pyrifera*) that grows and thrives in the ocean depths along the coast of California and Baja California, Mexico is a key ingredient for many commercial products. There are three main types of seaweed: red (*rhodophyta*), brown (*phaeophyta*) and green (*cholorphyta*). Giant kelp, a brown seaweed, lives in and around San Diego Bay, grows from depths of 20–150 feet up to the surface. It also has gas-filled bladders that help pull up its blades toward the surface. There, the blades are exposed to sunlight needed for photosynthesis.

Gas-filled bladders and attached blades branching off the stipe of a frond of Macrocystis pyrifera.

Kelp beds are one of California's most valuable resources. Their growing season peaks in spring when the water is 50°–60° F. Kelp beds thrive in cold water especially during upwelling events that bring nutrients into the beds. These mostly occur in spring.

Severe storms, water with higher than normal temperatures, water with lower than normal concentrations of nutrients, and a profusion of animals that prey on kelp can all result in the destruction of kelp beds. Storms are lethal to kelp because they can uproot the plant, while warm water does not provide enough nutrients for the kelp to flourish. Also, animals such as sea urchins feed on the holdfasts of kelp, leaving the kelp unable to survive because its holdfast cannot grow back again.

The holdfasts of kelp have been found to be home to more than

Red sea urchins—predators of the giant kelp.

150 different species of marine invertebrates. They provide shelter, food, living and hiding spaces, allowing populations to flourish and keeping the

biodiversity high in the kelp forest ecosystem. Many marine mammals, such as otters and various species of fish, also live near or within kelp beds. Otters and many fish hunt and feed off the crustaceans and other marine organisms that thrive around kelp forests.

One of the key attributes of *Macrocystis pyrifera* is its amazing growth rate—a phenomenal two feet a day under ideal conditions. This growth rivals that of the fastest growing bamboo. (Bushing 2006)

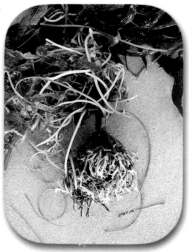

Detached holdfast of a giant kelp plant.

Sea of Wonder

Beneath mysterious blue depths
Lie the forests of the sea
Full of life
And questions

On the shore
The trees are just smelly seaweed
But in the ocean
That plain old seaweed fashions a mystical world.

Fannie Ngo

"It could be said that the Hercules plant being in San Diego from 1916–1918 was really a one-time event." -Frank Sherwood

Hercules Powder Company, 1917.
San Diego Historical Society.

Kelp to Gunpowder

Along the open coast of Southern California stretch miles and miles of kelp beds—vital resources used to produce gunpowder as well as food additives. This natural resource has not been overlooked, as San Diegan entrepreneurs have utilized this kelp forest extensively both in the past and today. One of the more unique and historically important examples of marine resource utilization on San Diego Bay was the conversion of kelp to gunpowder that occurred in the early twentieth century. The Hercules Powder Co. used giant kelp (*Macrocystis pyrifera*) to produce acetone and potash for gunpowder. In support of allied efforts during World War I, the kelp beds in San Diego were so extensively drawn upon to produce ingredients for gunpowder that they were nearly harvested into extinction.

The Hercules Powder Co., from 1916 to 1918, operated a kelp processing plant on the edge of San Diego Bay in Chula Vista, and the establishment of the factory was an exciting event in San Diego history. A large number of people worked for the company, and though the plant was short-lived, it had a great impact on its employees and the Bay. The Chula Vista Nature Center, a successful mitigation project that features a wildlife sanctuary and an interactive natural history museum, now stands on the site where the Hercules plant once existed. There, the ruins of the plant remain among brush and wildlife, a memorial to the site's noteworthy past.

Geography of Kelp to Gunpowder Processing on the Bay

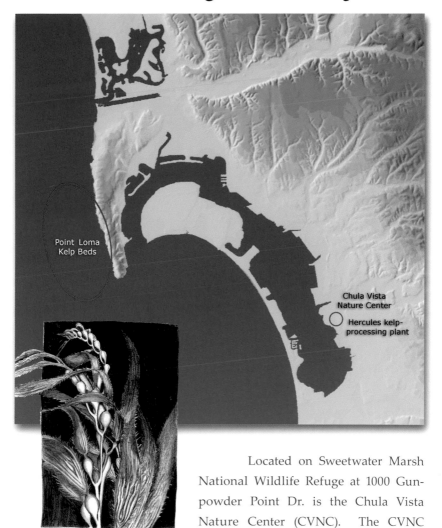

Point Loma
Kelp Beds

Chula Vista
Nature Center

Hercules kelp-
processing plant

Located on Sweetwater Marsh National Wildlife Refuge at 1000 Gunpowder Point Dr. is the Chula Vista Nature Center (CVNC). The CVNC exists where the Hercules Powder Co. once operated a plant for converting kelp to gunpowder. The company took a large volume of the kelp it used from the Point Loma kelp bed.

Kelp to Gunpowder History

San Diego Bay and its surroundings are filled with an abundance of natural resources. One of the greatest is the bountiful kelp that grows in thick underwater forests. The products that can be derived from this kelp are historically significant to San Diego and play a vital role in our everyday lives, as they are key components in products such as gunpowder, fertilizers, and food additives. Moreover, kelp is not only an invaluable asset for man-made products, it also provides a diverse and valuable habitat for hundreds of species of plants and animals. (Mondragon 2003)

The kelp ecosystem is one of the most productive and diverse in temperate waters.

The kelp forests were utilized by the earliest traders in California, who often came to the kelp beds to hunt sea otters—one of the many animals that live exclusively in the beds. However, in the early 1900s, the kelp beds were discovered to contain great commercial potential. The Hercules Powder Co., recognizing and acting on this potential, harvested kelp to extract acetone and potash—key ingredients in gunpowder.

The true origin of gunpowder remains a mystery. However, most historians think that the Chinese were the first to invent the potent black powder. It is believed that Chinese alchemists stumbled upon gunpowder while searching for the legendary elixir of everlasting life. The key ingredient of gunpowder, saltpeter, was originally used by Chinese alchemists because of its reaction with fire, the element that the Chinese believed was the source of life. Chinese experiments with saltpeter and the other two main ingredients of gunpowder, sulfur and charcoal, led China to become the first civilization to develop explosives. It was not long before the Chinese realized the true potential of their creation. However, their first use of the substance was not for war, but for pleasure—recreational fireworks. (Diamond 1999) (Kelly 2004)

Much trade prevailed between China and the West, so it is uncertain which civilization was actually the first to develop the black powder. Nevertheless, its refinement into gunpowder for use in firearms forever changed our world. The invention of gunpowder was what made offensive weapons and explosives possible. (Kelly 2004)

A gun's ability to fire was dependent on its use of gunpowder, one of whose components is saltpeter (nitrate of potash). In the nineteenth century, potash was generally taken from the water-soluble fraction of wood ash. However, at the turn of the twentieth century, people began to search for a different source. In the winter of 1902, David M. Balch noticed that the masses of giant kelp drying on the beach appeared to have salts on them. Through further study of *Macrocystis pyrifera* in his lab, he found that the salt (potassium chloride) extracted from the kelp was almost chemically pure. His groundbreaking work on the production of potash from kelp led Balch to be known as the "father of kelp." (Neushul 1989) (Sherwood 2006)

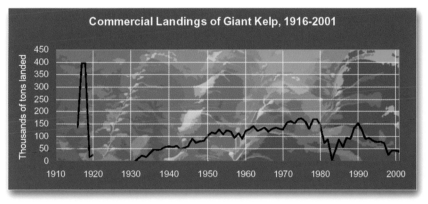

Commercial Landings of Giant Kelp, 1916-2001

In 1903, Balch received his first patent for the process he developed to extract potash from kelp. Realizing the potential of his discovery, he immediately went to work trying to sell potash. However, German potash was significantly less expensive, so his business never got off the ground. Nevertheless, though his venture failed, Balch put kelp on the map as a potentially lucrative industry. His efforts were so successful that the government sent out surveyors, including W.C. Crandall, to produce an official report on the latent possibilities in this abundant natural resource. ("A Wonderful Industry ... " 1914) (Neushul 1989)

Other entrepreneurs soon became interested in harvesting kelp, specifically for potash. The first marginally successful company to derive potash from kelp was the Coronado Chemical Co. organized by Henry S.

Firman in collaboration with Harry Wilson. Together they founded American Potash Co.. The company was located in Long Beach harbor, and focused on producing potash for use in fertilizer. ("A Wonderful Industry … " 1914) (Sherwood 2005)

During World War I, the company grew exponentially. Before the war, all of the world's potash was supplied by Germany. With Germany now an enemy, the United States and its allies had to find new ways of creating gunpowder. The Hercules Powder Co., the first kelp processing company in San Diego, sprang into action to fill the gap. (Dyer 1990)

The Hercules Powder Co. was born out of an anti-trust action against the E. I. du Pont de Nemours Powder Co. in 1913 and had an auspicious start as it single-handedly revolutionized the kelp harvesting process. When Hercules established its main plant in 1916 in Chula Vista, it discovered that kelp harvesters manufactured by other companies could not cut and gather the amount of kelp that the factory needed. Consequently, the company developed a more efficient self-propelled cutter with two center blades, in addition to the customary vertical-end cutting bars,

which could carry far more kelp than its predecessors. The cut kelp was conveyed upward on a sort of inclined conveyor belt. Once it reached the top, the kelp would be cut into small pieces  and stored in an elevated tank above the cutter. (Dyer 1990) (Neushul 1989)

There werc three such harvesters, and they remained in constant operation unless the weather was particularly bad. The harvesters "pumped their cargo through a pipe into barges that returned to the pier. At the pier, the kelp slurry was pumped out of the barges, through a pipe, and up to the processing plant on shore." (Neushul p. 578) Hercules owned nine of these transport barges, as well as four towboats. A floating machine shop serviced their harvesters right out on the water, due to the immobility of the cutters and the shallow nature of the South Bay. (Neushul 1989)

In addition to potash, a lucrative but elusive chemical needed for the allied war effort was acetone, a key ingredient in cordite—the smokeless gunpowder needed by British artillery forces during the war, for their guns were designed to fire only using cordite. Yet, due to strict British quality standards, most munitions manufacturers were not producing cordite, and North American acetone production at that time was merely a by-product of the wood pulp industry. Hercules was the only U.S. munitions manufacturer that met the challenging task of fulfilling Britain's large orders for cordite, and by the end of WWI, Hercules had tripled the amount of acetone produced in the United States. (Brown 1977) (Neushul 1989)

Because of the great demand for acetone and potash, Hercules worked to create it from kelp. In February 1916, the company invested $7 million on a new plant in Chula Vista. This was an extremely bold move considering the company had only been in existence for three years and its combined assets were a mere $10 million. The plant, which opened in July of that year, was the largest of its kind in the world, residing on approximately 30 acres, with a 2,000-foot wharf. (Neushul 1989)

Frank Sherwood with his grandfather, J.K. Persons, at the closed down Hercules plant.

During its operation, Hercules brought about $70,000 a month into the local economy through payroll and other expenses. The plant employed around 1,100 people and paid some of the highest wages in the city. In 1916, Hercules reportedly harvested 185,000 pounds of kelp off California and the next year produced about 60,000 pounds of potash. However, once WWI ended, the need for acetone and potash declined and the plant was no longer cost effective and was closed down in 1920. (Sherwood 2005)

In order to extract acetone and potash, Hercules put the harvested kelp through a "wet" process rather than the "dry" process other companies were using. In this "wet" process, the chopped kelp was loaded from the barges and placed in one of nine large redwood tanks. There, it was heated and aerated for 30 days, after which the liquid from the fermentation tanks was extracted and placed in larger tanks where lime was added to kill bacteria and stop the fermentation process. The liquid was then either heated or cooled to create various salts or a variety of other products. (Neushul 2005)

The land that once hosted Hercules gunpowder plant in San Diego is steeped in rich history. Historians think that prehistoric residents used Sweetwater Marsh to collect shell-fish and other creatures for food, and to create an intense, black dye from the sea grass beds. Cabrillo claimed the land for Spain in 1542. However, it was subsequently claimed by Mexico, who turned it over to the United States follow-ing the resolution of the Mexican-American War. Later, the land was given to the Santa Fe Railroad Company, and in 1916 it was leased to Hercules. ("The History of Gunpowder Point" 1997)

Although the plant was a great success, it operated for only four years. When it closed down in 1920, San Diego Oil Products acquired the property. The site soon became the largest cottonseed warehouse in the United States, but both the plant and warehouse burned to the ground in 1924. After the fire, tomatoes were grown there and most of the movie *Attack of the Killer Tomatoes!* was filmed on this farm. However, the land was later abandoned and became an illegal dumping site. ("The History of Gun Powder Point" 1997)

The illegal dumping only caused more havoc to an already wound-ed environment. The Hercules Powder Plant had a devastating biological impact on San Diego in addition to its huge economic impact. The plant was built on Sweetwater Marsh—an important wetland, and home to many different types of birds and mammals. Draining the wetland for the con-struction of the plant imperiled endangered species such as the light-footed clapper rail and the burrowing owl, who both made the marsh their home. (Moore 2005)

Furthermore, Hercules severely damaged another very important habitat off the San Diego coast—the kelp beds, one of our greatest natural resources. Because the need for gunpowder was so high, the kelp beds were brought to near extinction. With this came the near depletion of the thousands of different animals that call the beds their home. Today, human impact on the kelp beds is far less. However, the habitat has still gone through many obstacles such as overfishing and El Niño events, with devastating effects. Fortunately, the area appears to be on the rebound.

Today, the land is home to the Chula Vista Nature Center, a wild-life refuge resulting from the 1986 Bayfront Conservancy Trust. The main

focus of the center, which is located at 1000 Gunpowder Point Dr., is to help preserve the area and raise public awareness for environmental issues throughout San Diego County. It regularly attracts students from around the county, and is critically acclaimed for its informative and unique exhibits. The ruins of the gunpowder plant are now overgrown by

Land at the Chula Vista Nature Center.

coastal sage, and after years of hard work and diligent conservation efforts the site is now one of the most beautiful and natural locations along the shore of San Diego Bay. (Moore 2005)

Sunset —*A Nature Reflection*

Overlooking the cool blue ocean, I am struck by its vastness. A few hundred yards offshore, I can see the floating brown canopy of an amber forest below the surface of the water. I watch as the sunlight seeps through the floating foundation. It is hard to believe that without kelp, without this unique and special plant, the world as we know it would be a very different place. Kelp has been used for so many different purposes. It has been used as fertilizer to make plants grow; people consume it when they eat popular summer treats; it has even been used to military advantage as an additive in gunpowder.

Still, fish swim freely between the leaves and bulbs of the kelp, happily sandwiching themselves among the fronds. In their natural state, kelp forests are home to thousands of unique and special sea organisms. The kelp beds are an oasis of life, abundant forests of plenty. The kelp from these forests has won wars, fed plants and people, and directed the course of history.

Danika Della

1917
Hercules' plant in Chula Vista sends off its first shipment

1914
World War I begins

SENSITIVE
HABITAT
BIRDS ONLY

1909
Balch publishes an article in the *Journal of Industrial and Engineering Chemistry*, calling attention to the potential of kelp as a source of potash

1920
The Hercules plant in Chula Vista closes down and is taken over by San Diego Oil Products

1900

← Germany has a monopoly on the world's potash market

1902
In San Diego, David M. Balch discovers potassium chloride in kelp

1918
World War I comes to a close, and with it a great deal of the market for the acetone and potash that help make gunpowder

1913
Hercules Powder Co. is formed out of an anti-trust suit against DuPont

1916
Hercules leases land in Chula Vista and constructs a kelp-processing plant there

HERCULES
POWDER.

1987
The Chula Vista Nature Center opens

1970-1985
The land at Gunpowder Point is used for illegal dumping

2000

1986
The Bayfront Conservancy Trust is formed. The land at Gunpowder Point is cleaned up and the restoration of the marsh begins

1989
The Sweetwater Marsh National Wildlife Refuge is established

Barbara Moore

As we rode on the colorfully decorated shuttle from the parking lot to the Chula Vista Nature Center (CVNC), we felt that the excellent weather was perfect for an interview. We arrived at the nature refuge and met Barbara Moore, and were all calmed by her relaxed and extremely personable tone, which mirrored the ambiance of the nature center. Ms. Moore led us along a nature trail to some of the remains of the Hercules Powder Co.'s Chula Vista plant.

Ms. Moore, a naturalist, writer, and adult education instructor, is the programs manager* at the Chula Vista Nature Center. The nature center sits on Gunpowder Point, the former site of the Hercules Powder Co.'s Chula Vista plant. Ms. Moore has worked at the nature center for 15 years coordinating volunteers, public and educational programs, special events, and other activities. We sought out Ms. Moore because of her vast knowledge of the area and its inhabitants. Her background, which includes teaching, coauthoring a book and a number of other publications, is as diverse as the flora and fauna of the refuge.

Student Researcher (SR): What do you know about the Hercules Powder Company?

Barbara Moore: I know that there were [about 1,100] people working out here. They worked full time—24 hours a day. There was a trolley that brought people out to work. [The place] smelled like rotten eggs, and the people who lived in National City got the effects of the smell all the time because the wind blows towards National City. We sold a lot of the materials to make gunpowder to England and to France. The reason they started processing the kelp is because Germany had the only potash mines in the world, and during WWI Germany didn't want to sell their potash to France or to the United States for munitions … you know, gunpowder. And, so that's why they started to figure out how they could get it from the kelp. They also nearly destroyed the kelp beds, which is one of our major sportfishing and wildlife habitats off the Pacific Coast.

SR: Why do you think they chose this location on San Diego Bay for the Hercules Powder Company?

Moore: Probably because it was empty.

SR: So, do you know anything about how they actually processed the kelp to make acetone?

Moore: They fermented it. They pulled it up or cut it from the kelp bed and chopped it up. … There was a pier here and they put it on little railroad

---

*Ms. Moore has retired from CVNC since this interview was conducted.

cars and you can see the tracks that are still left here. ... They took it and dumped it into [tanks] and they fermented it to make acetone. I don't know whether they added chemicals to that or not but it rotted, and then what was left after they drained out the acetone was stored in barrels. ... They burned the leftover kelp to make potash.

SR: Have you ever noticed any negative effects that the kelp processing plant had on this land?

Moore: We're standing on it! This is the negative effect ... these old foundations. This whole area, before the kelp processing plant was here, was a native coastal sage scrub habitat with probably deer and antelope and a lot of other animals that we don't have anymore; and we don't have the plants either.

SR: Do you know of any positive effects from the Hercules Powder Company and the old plant being here?

Moore: Well, I think the positive effect is that [the area] didn't get developed. There had been plans to develop it, [but the plans were] formed after the kelp processing plant was here. And then, as it sat fallow for a long time, a lot of people dumped trash here. We managed to keep it, while not pristine, at least with open space so that children, in particular, could come out and enjoy some nature and see what it's like being close to the Bay.

SR: So, what is your view on the gunpowder production's effect on the environment?

Moore: Well, they certainly destroyed the habitat here. They dumped an awful lot of chemicals and residue into the Bay that couldn't have been very healthy for the birds, fish, or invertebrates that lived in the Bay. The fish and the birds depend on the invertebrates, so it probably caused quite a bit of damage at the time.

SR: What was the process used to turn this into a wildlife refuge?

Moore: Well, there were the lawsuits that were settled and then the owners were essentially forced to give it

Salt marsh plants found flourishing at the CVNC.

to the government ... this was the last open space on San Diego Bay and it was really important to turn it into a wildlife refuge.

SR: So, the land didn't need to undergo any special process to turn it into a refuge?

Moore: They actually did special tests out here—soil tests, because the kelp-processing plant that was here during World War I used a lot of chemicals and so they were afraid that there were spilled chemicals and residue from that, but nothing was found.

Sharks, skates and rays are appreciated by all ages at the Chula Vista Nature Center.

SR: And what about the Chula Vista Nature Center? How was it brought about and created?

Moore: The Nature Center was created as mitigation—which means lessening of damage for the mid-Bayfront development that has not yet occurred and was supposed to occur 18 or 19 years ago. It still hasn't, but eventually it will.

SR: Can you explain the development in the mid-Bay?

Moore: That's all of the open space that you can see between Sweetwater Marsh and clear down to the [South Bay] Power Plant. ... There are plans to turn it into a convention center, high-rise apartments and condos, research and development sites—that kind of thing.

SR: Since the creation of the Sweetwater Marsh National Wildlife Refuge and the Nature Center, have you noticed any improvements or positive impacts that they have made?

Moore: Yeah, I think that we have had pretty close to 50,000 school children visit, maybe even more than that, and they've got a feeling for protecting wildlife resources.

SR: What about the wildlife? Has it had any impact from this?

Moore: I think there's probably more now than there was for awhile because we've cleaned it up and we made it more habitable for them.

Garbage left at the site of the Hercules Powder Plant.

SR: Besides the building foundations, have you found any other interesting remains of the gunpowder factory on the nature reserve?

Moore: We have found a lot of pieces of broken glass from the big chemical bottles; [the kind with thick] green and purple glass. We also found remains of Navy dumping here. ... There used to be a pig farm here, and the Navy brought their garbage and fed it to the pigs. I found some little pieces of [a dish] that had a Navy anchor on it, and a few things like that.

Frank P. Sherwood

As we worked to uncover the history of Gunpowder Point, we came across many interesting people. In December, we struck gold. Barbara Moore, the programs manager at the Chula Vista Nature Center who was interviewed by us, found a manuscript left by Dr. Frank P. Sherwood at the Nature Center. She thought that it would be very useful for our research and passed it on to us. Unfortunately, she was unaware of his whereabouts, but we took the manuscript and learned a lot from its contents.

However, we decided to take things one step further. We began a search for Dr. Sherwood online by sending an email requesting personal recollections of the Hercules Powder Plant. The email was forwarded on for weeks from one colleague to another until it eventually reached Dr. Sherwood in Florida. Now an emeritus professor of Florida State University, Dr. Sherwood is the author of a series of books on his family. His father worked as a chemist, and his mother as a nurse at Hercules' plant in Chula Vista, and this connection led Dr. Sherwood to find out everything he could about the old potash plant that held so many close ties to his family. When Dr. Sherwood responded to our email, we began a correspondence that became invaluable to our retelling of the story of the Hercules Powder Company and the role it had in the history of San Diego Bay.

Student Researcher (SR): What is the connection between potash and the Hercules Gunpowder Co. your parents worked for?

Frank P. Sherwood: Potash became very important when World War I started, though today we are back to the old situation where potash is mined. About 12 countries are engaged in this process, with about two-thirds of the mined potash coming from Saskatchewan, Canada. But had there not been a need for potash for gunpowder … there probably would not have been a potash plant in San Diego. However, the need for potash for gunpowder was vitally important in the United States, and therefore in 1916 the Hercules Co. began the operation of its plant in San Diego, whereby kelp was harvested off Point Loma and then processed in south San Diego.

It could be said that the Hercules plant in San Diego, from 1916–1918, was really a one-time event. Turns out that the cost of production from potash from kelp was very high—far beyond that of mining—and so once the war ended on November 11, 1918, there was really no need to continue the production of potash from kelp and the plant closed immediately. I was born in 1920, and my father died in 1923—before I was three years old—so I never got a chance to talk to him about the Hercules plant, and kelp, and all those kinds of things. However, our family album contains a couple pictures of me at the abandoned plant with my grandfather in 1922, when I guess I had just turned two years old, and the buildings in the background looked quite old, though in fact they were then roughly only six years old.

I remember looking at the pictures and I had a feeling that this was a very ancient place. In our family, the plant was always referred to as the "old" potash plant. Yet, in fact, in 1926–1927 when I was about six or seven years old, that plant was only about ten years old. It was deserted, but as things go, it was really quite a new set of buildings, yet I had this image that it was very, very old.

SR: Can you tell us what you have discovered about the Hercules Powder Co.'s plant in the South Bay area?

Sherwood: Of course. It was the place where my mother and father met, and it played a very important role for having created an opportunity for them to get to know each other, leading to their marriage. I think my interest in this whole area—in the Hercules plant—was sparked when I went to my fiftieth class reunion for San Diego High School in 1988. It caused me to think a lot about my life in San Diego and the things that were important to me. I found that the old potash plant was a very special place, so my wife and I went to the San Diego Historical Society and went through a lot of old papers and found that there was a reasonable report on the plant and newspaper clippings. It was from these that I wrote a little monograph … on the Hercules plant as being an unusual place for a romance.

As I got into the papers and learned more about this unique process of deriving potash from kelp, I found my interest peaked a great deal. I went around to see what I could find out about what really went on at the Hercules Plant. Partly as a result. … I did learn that the site of the Hercules plant had been taken over by the Chula Vista Nature Center. So, I went down there, and found that a wonderful thing had happened to this relatively deserted piece of land—it had been taken over, and a rather beautiful facility where you can learn a lot about kelp and about harvesting and processing of it into potash had been erected.

SR: What inspired your father to move West?

Sherwood: I think the simple answer is that he wanted a job at Hercules, which was a very significant company at that time. Its origins were derived from du Pont. It was created as a spin off from du Pont about ten years earlier, when Teddy Roosevelt was very involved in trust busting. One of the first recipients of those trust-busting efforts was the du Pont de Nemours Powder Company that had long been a predominant munitions manufacturer for the United States government. So, Hercules was spun off and given munitions responsibilities among other things. Within ten years, it had become a very important company in the industrial landscape.

SR: What did your father know about extracting potash from kelp?

Sherwood: My guess is that he would've said to you or me that "I didn't know a thing about it." That's the honest answer, and I don't suppose he did, because nobody had been much involved with the process. But those were different days, and there weren't many Ph.D.s in chemistry. Those chemists were chemists in the sense that their particular awareness of chemical processes was relatively unique, and so they were called upon to look at all kinds of circumstances where chemistry was involved. My father's career can provide you with some insight as to how that went. These chemists moved from one problem to another without particularly spending a lot of time working on any one. So, I don't think it was a surprising thing that my father would've said: "Sure, I'll go out and see what I can learn about how you extract potash from kelp." It was a challenge, a new chemical issue to deal with.

I also think he may have wanted to distance himself from his preacher father. I'm fairly certain that my father, having decided that science was what he wanted to pursue, had very likely adopted a philosophy of Darwinism. These were days when Darwin was very much on everybody's mind, and that would have been unacceptable to his father, who was a devout minister and believer in completely traditional religion. On the other hand, my grandfather was a very un-assuming man; not very harsh or difficult or anything. I don't suppose he would disown his son for these kinds of behaviors, but they would be very difficult for him to accept.

SR: What kind of lab work did your father conduct?

Sherwood: I cannot describe exactly what my father did at Hercules. Our family belief is that he was the chief scientist there, and we do have a picture of him in a relatively

Dr. Sherwood's father, Dr. Clarence M. Sherwood, working in his lab at the Hercules plant sometime between 1916–1919.

small room with a lot of scientific paraphernalia around, which one would have to assume was the place where he worked. My sense is that science was not an absolutely big thing at the Hercules plant. They were already harvesting kelp and producing it into potash, so I think that the scientific contributions that my father would've made to that process would've been relatively minor and marginal. Probably just improving efficiency and so on, not making any major difference in what was being done.

SR: What did your mother do at Hercules?

Sherwood: She was the head of the infirmary there. We also have a picture of her. The infirmary was a relatively small room, and I suspect that in the scheme of things it was not a very big piece of the Hercules plant. But there were hundreds of employees and I suspect they had the usual number of colds and other ailments that required someone to be on deck all the time and make sure that they were properly cared for. Shortly after she got her R.N., she was appointed head of the infirmary at the Hercules plant, and I suspect that was either in 1916 or 1917.

SR: What happened to the company after gunpowder use declined?

Sherwood: First, I'd like to say that there was no decline in the use of gunpowder. The world would certainly be much better off if there were a real decline in its use, but we seem to be as prone to use guns to kill people as we ever were. The real decline was that potash was no longer used in the manufacturing of gunpowder. We apparently found many other ways that are more lethal and therefore preferable to us than the manufacture of gunpowder.

SR: Why didn't the economic realities of the post-war world leave kelp as a source of potash?

Dr. Sherwood's mother, Mildred Persons Sherwood, head of the infirmary at the Hercules plant.

Sherwood: I think the answer is absolutely economic. It's apparent that the cost of production of potash from kelp was far greater than from mining. So, when the war ended, and the potash mines opened in various parts of the world, the market took over and there was no place for a product that was extremely expensive to produce.

SR: Did the kelp processing plants pollute (strip) the natural environment?

Sherwood: I don't know. I do think that probably nobody was conscious of Bay pollution of the time and probably the plant did put some things into San Diego Bay that were not desirable. Many years later, in 1935, when I was active around San Diego Bay, the pollution was tremendous—largely because they were dumping raw sewage into the Bay. Since then, I understand that the Bay has been greatly cleaned up and is far better than it was in 1935.

I do think the story of this Hercules plant, operating for a relatively short period (1916–1920) is an interesting one, because it really is the first effort to develop industry in San Diego—a unique effort that goes back to the research of early scientists of San Diego. I think that's an impressive thing. They discovered that kelp had uses in industrial development and those people who were involved really deserve more recognition and more study than we've given them.

The Destruction of Kelp

This underfoot forest
That I once knew
Torn into pieces

All that was here
Now, is not
All that left
Remains only to rot
A prisoner of this aquatic war

The kelp's alginate
Is taken to a far-away land
To be used in the fight
For what is believed to be right

Dustin Blackwell

Biology at Gunpowder Point

The Chula Vista Nature Center, celebrated for its well-established endangered species reserve, strives to provide its flora and fauna with a comfortable home that emulates their natural habitats. The efforts made by the center to preserve the natural bayside habitat and its creatures have allowed many generations to enjoy the simple beauty of the area. Because of efforts like these, there is hope for the conservation and restoration of the Bay and its wildlife. Three of the threatened or endangered species that the center studies and cares for are the light-footed clapper rail, the burrowing owl, and the green sea turtle.

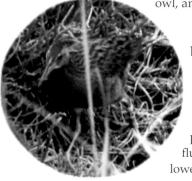

Light-footed Clapper Rail
Rallus longirostris

The light-footed clapper rail has been recognized as an endangered species since 1970. The size of the population of the clapper rail has fluctuated considerably over the years. The lowest recorded number of the species was approximately 280 living pairs. It is because of such low numbers that conservation institutions like the Chula Vista Nature Center are constantly trying to save clapper rails from extinction, providing them not only with habitat, but also a safe place to reproduce.

The Chula Vista Nature Center has released over 150 light-footed clapper rails into San Diego marshes. With efforts towards the preservation of the species such as those exemplified by the center, the number of living clapper rails is starting to increase, and in 2002, there were approximately 110 recorded pairs in the wild around San Diego Bay. (Moore 2005) (Unitt 2004)

Burrowing Owl
Athene cunicularia

Though once a plentiful species in San Diego, the burrowing owl is now on the brink of extinction in San Diego County. Due to the rapid growth of San Diego's population, the development of natural habitats for the burrowing owl needs to be drastically increased. The negative impact of urban development on the owls is exacerbated by the fact that they mainly live on the ground, which is steadily being taken over as San Diego's growth continues. Moreover, the supply of their main food source—insects—has been depleted due to the common use of pesticides by homeowners. Because of situations such as these, the Chula Vista Nature Center provides a place for burrowing owls and many other creatures to live and breed. (Unitt 2004)

Green Sea Turtle
Chelonia mydas

The latest addition to the Chula Vista Nature Center's family is the Green Sea Turtle. These sea turtles can be seen around the world in tropical waters. However, they are rarely sighted, for their population has been decreasing due to hunting of adults and eggs, and because of man-made development along the shore.

How these creatures came to the Bay is not really clear. Some believe their love of warm water drives them to migrate to the warm shores near the South Bay Power Plant. Water is taken into the power plant to cool it, and subsequently the heated water is discharged into the Bay. The elevated water temperature forms an excellent habitat for the turtles, and consequently they are sometimes found at the northern end of the South Bay Salt Works pond system, or on their dikes. However, others think the turtles' presence in the Bay may be the result of their escaping from holding pens when people imported them from Mexico for their meat. (Jones 2005) (McMahon 2006)

In Mexico, these sea turtles are still killed for their meat; their fat, which is used in soup; their fine shells, which can be used to make jewelry and ornaments; and their tough skin, which makes good leather. The Chula Vista Nature Center, noticing that coastal development has left limited living space for these turtles, is now endeavoring to keep some shore land in its natural state to supply the turtles with a safe place to live and forage. (McMahon 2006) (Moore 2005)

"It's pretty incredible because humans can't easily dive to depths of much more than 100 feet, but sea lions can recover objects from well over 500 feet."

-DruAnn Clark

Sea Lions

Sea lions have many unique features that make them amenable for human use. They are able to traverse both land and sea, reaching depths their human partners cannot. For decades, man and sea lion have worked together as entertainers and, more recently, partners in the military's protection of our coasts. In the San Diego area, these hardworking and fiercely loyal animals are not only seen at the zoo and SeaWorld, entertaining the crowds, but also in San Diego Bay, where they are an integral part of the U.S. Navy Marine Mammal Program (NMMP).

Sea lions are used in the NMMP because they are friendly, easy to work with, can dive to great depths, and have superior low-light vision. Currently, there are about 30 sea lions working in the NMMP, trained to locate inanimate objects and carry out "force protection" measures used to reduce the risk of potential harm to the Navy's security forces. The sea lions that work with the Navy continually amaze their handlers with their intelligence and diligence, and these animals will undoubtedly continue to play an important part in the workings of the NMMP for a long time to come.

Geography of the Sea Lions of the Bay

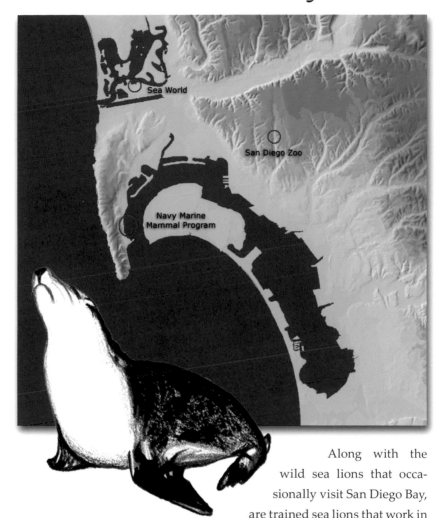

Along with the wild sea lions that occasionally visit San Diego Bay, are trained sea lions that work in partnership with humans in the U.S. Navy. This human-sea lion interaction is put to work through the NMMP, located just north of Ballast Point along the coast of the Bay. There, the NMMP sea lions make their home and are often visited by their roaming brethren. SeaWorld and the San Diego Zoo are two other locations in the San Diego Bay area where interaction between sea lions and humans regularly occurs.

History of the Sea Lions of the Bay

Sea lions are one of the few animals that can capture our attention when we are young and keep it through our adulthood. Most often seen at zoos and marine parks, these creatures have amazing abilities that enable  them to perfectly balance balls on their noses, balance on their front flippers, and jump over poles placed several feet above the water. We know sea lions for their intelligence and adaptability to living on land and in water.

Yet, despite the peaceable bond that exists between most humans and sea lions today, the first human interaction with sea lions occurred when they were hunted by mankind for food. Native American tribes along the West Coast of North America hunted sea lions, and used every part of them, wasting nothing. These early hunters harvested sea lions for their value as a food source, as well as their fur for clothing and shelter, their blubber and oil for fuel, and their bones fashioned into deadly weapons. Sea lion skin was often used to cover boats—their flippers as boot soles, their intestines as waterproof clothing, and their stomach lining as food storage containers. The Native Americans hunted the sea lions using primitive means such as clubbing them to death on land, or spearing them from their canoes. (Smith 1999) (Gordon 1994)

Over the years, many stories and myths about sea lions have been passed down. In northern Europe, sea lions were believed to be women and children condemned to a life of transience in which neither land nor sea could provide a permanent home. Sailors also had superstitions about killing sea lions, because sea lions were thought to embody the souls of dead sailors. (Gordon 1994)

When the first Europeans arrived on the West Coast of North America in the 18th century, these explorers used the Native American and Aleutian knowledge of animals and trapping to hunt and capture various sea mammals including sea lions. Soon, sea lions became an important resource for the fur trade. When Russians emigrated to America, the fur trade intensified and sea lions began to also be hunted for their oil. In those days, this oil was considered superior to whale oil. Moreover, certain parts of the sea lions were removed and sent to China to be used as aphrodisiacs. In the mid-1800s, marine mammal numbers dropped drastically along the West Coast of North America. As a result, the Europeans and Russians who had been deeply involved in industries that relied on sea lions moved on to other trades. (Coy 2002) (Folkens 2001) (Gordon 1994)

However, despite the brief respite, problems for sea lions arose again in the late 1890s when California fishermen began to complain about a decrease in the local fish supply, most notably with salmon. This decline was caused by overfishing in addition to the natural predator-prey relationship between sea lions and salmon. Often the sea lions would frustrate the fishermen further by stealing already hooked fish. To mollify the fishermen, in 1899 the U.S. Fish and Game Commission passed a law that allowed the fishermen  to shoot and kill any sea lion attempting to steal fish. In 1909, the act was repealed and a new law was put in place, this time outlawing the killing and capturing of California sea lions. Unfortunately, they continued to be hunted illegally until the 1960s. But in 1972 the Marine Mammal Protection Act was passed, providing them with protection from indiscriminate hunters. (Marine Mammal Protection Act 1994)

After many years of sea lion hunting, a new development occurred. California sea lions began to be captured, domesticated and used as a source of entertainment in circuses and zoos around the world. The first sea lion show was in 1933 at the Saint Louis Zoo in Missouri. The sea lion's name was Surfer and he was onstage for a full 27 minutes performing with rubber balls and clapping his flippers. Since then, sea lions have been trained to complete numerous other tasks, including balancing on their front flippers, retrieving items, jumping over poles and balancing objects on their nose. In San Diego, the place to see these animals performing is at SeaWorld and the San Diego Zoo, where they perform in daily shows that display their natural abilities.

One of the more scientifically oriented advantages to keeping sea lions in captivity is the ability to study their anatomy and common ailments. Not all sea lions have a fruitful and healthy life, but those that live in places such as SeaWorld tend to live longer and be in better health than their wild or circus counterparts. Sea lions are still housed in many zoos and animal parks around the world. They continue to perform for human audiences and make children squeal with joy and exclaim in amazement. ("Sea Lion Arena" 2006)

As time passed, humans changed their attitudes concerning sea lions in captivity. Rather than focusing on showing off sea lions to the public, conservationists now concentrate on rescuing and rehabilitating marine creatures such as sea lions. Facilities like SeaWorld are now rescuing stranded, malnourished, sick, and injured animals, rehabilitating them, and releasing them back into the wild. Sea lions are also being used in the effort to educate the public on the impact of humans on marine life, as well as to study sea lion biology and diseases. ("California Sea Lions" 2006)

California sea lions are commonly seen around the bait barges of Mission Bay and San Diego Bay off Point Loma. There are even tours that will take people out to their rookeries for a closer look. In La Jolla, the sea lions, along with harbor seals, currently occupy the Children's Pool. In the past couple of years there has been much debate over whether they should continue to be allowed to stay there, sharing the beach with humans, or be kicked out completely. Debate has arisen over the decrease in water sanitation due to seal and sea lion fecal matter. However, even if it were to

San Diego tourists admire the local sea lions lounging contentedly on the San Diego Bay bait barge.

be decided that the sea lions should move, the Marine Mammal Protection Act forbids any human disturbance. On the plus side, the Children's Pool provides a great area for tourists to come and observe them in their "natural habitat." (Marine Mammal Protection Act 1994)

Another concern over the sea lion residence in the area is the number of increased sightings of great white sharks, which are the primary predator of sea lions, along the coast of California. Within the past three years there have been several sightings of great white sharks off La Jolla. (Rogers 2003) (Moore 2006) (Daugherty 1979)

The Navy began to take an interest in using sea lions for military purposes in the seventies. After realizing the capabilities of these amazing creatures, they set up a program to study them—more specifically, their streamlined bodies—and apply the knowledge they gained from the study to amplifying the Navy's marine warfare technology. Currently, a number of talented sea lions are being used in the NMMP to conduct various activities, including hunting and locating training mines and enemy divers, and protecting docks where U.S. ships come into port. Under the program, they are grouped into one of two special task forces, designated MK5 and MK6. MK5 consists solely of sea lions whose task is to find and recover objects from the bottom of the ocean, while MK6 uses both sea lions and dolphins for force protection. The sea lions were most recently used in Bahrain during Operation Iraqi Freedom. They protect Navy vessels by acting as lookouts for enemy swimmers or divers. (Bonner 1994) (Clark 2006) (Lynch 2006)

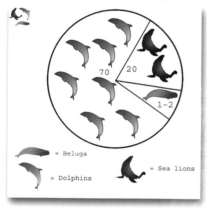

Distribution of marine mammals in the Navy's MK task forces.

As humans learn more about the California sea lion, they have come to recognize several distinctive features about them and their survival rates. New information is being released on the death of these animals due to pollution, fishing nets, fishing hooks, domoic acid poisoning, disease, and the effects of El Niño. Scientists have discovered that one subspecies of the California sea lion, the Japanese sea lion, is now extinct; another subspecies, the Galápagos sea lion, is listed as vulnerable. In the 1960s, scientists witnessed abnormal trends in the sea lion breeding rookeries. Hundreds of fetuses were aborted prematurely. The culprit was DDT and its harmful cousin DDE, an insecticide that had been dumped by Montrose Chemical Corporation, the leading DDT manufacturer, into the sea lion feeding grounds. Another discovery was made within the last decade, when dead sea lions washed ashore, poisoned by domoic acid. This poisoning is caused by blooming algae, which when ingested via the food chain, causes sea lions to have seizures. ("California Sea Lion" 2002) (California 1999) (Lefebvre 1999) (Martin 1996) (Thomas-Anderson 2003)

If humans don't step up to the plate soon and protect sea lions from irresponsible human destruction, we may not have these beautiful creatures around much longer. Fortunately, the Marine Mammal Protection Act has helped and will continue to protect sea lions. In addition, there are many programs around the world where these animals can live and breed in captivity with the hopeful goal of later release back into the wild. Right now, the future of sea lions may not be as grim as it once was, but without our help, these magnificent creatures may not continue to share the planet. (Gordon 1994)

Rewards —A Nature Reflection

As I sit here on a boat, I find myself with plenty of time to reflect on how my day has gone. I look out across the ocean, and see a few small sail boats moving swiftly in every direction. A couple of sea lions are playing in the water of the Bay and I can hear them barking to one another. Off in the distance, to my right, I see a huge green buoy with brown and black spots slowly bobbing up and down. Nearby, I notice some more sea lions sunbathing in the afternoon heat gathered on a "raft." Inadvertently, I find myself distracted by the loud grunts, barks, and squeals of the group. That's when I saw a small pup shuffling its way along, all alone.

I tell myself that he is probably exploring. Suddenly, he squeals; probably for his mother and the food she provides. I assume she's off hunting fish for him at this very moment. I imagine she's swimming somewhere in waters that unfold before me. In my mind's eye, I can clearly picture his mother diving down into a school of fish and chomping down on one of the tiny silver flashes that reflect off the fish. But she has yet to return, apparently, and I feel pity for the young pup though I know that his mother will soon come back with some food for him.

He's a cute little fellow with bulging eyes and flared whiskers. Or at least, that's what I kept thinking until I notice the claws on his front flippers. Suddenly, I realize that this is a wild animal, dangerous and unruly.

Emily Dykheng and Erin Rexin

1972
Congress passes the Marine
Mammal Protection Act

1955

1959
The Navy Marine Mammal
Program begins

1975
MK5 was added
as a sea lion only
training group

2006

2003
Sea lions are
deployed
to Bahrain

DruAnn Clark

W e set up our equipment for our interview with DruAnn Clark on a patch of grass overlooking San Diego Bay, adjacent to the sea lion cages. The sun was shining brilliantly, and its reflection on the water of the Bay created a great ambiance for the interview. In front of us, about 300 yards away, were the dolphin pens of the Navy Marine Mammal Program (NMMP).

We sought out Ms. Clark because of her experience as a trainer of sea lions in San Diego Bay and abroad in places such as Iraq, during Operation Iraqi Freedom. She is a Navy civilian and works for the NMMP. As a child, she dreamed of becoming an animal trainer. She obtained her bachelor's degree in animal behavior and began working with marine mammals at the Walt Disney World—Living Seas facility in Florida. Once Ms. Clark heard about the NMMP in San Diego she decided to move west to California. She initially worked with dolphins but soon switched to sea lions, which she found she enjoys immensely.

Student Researcher (SR): Why are the sea lions preferred over human divers?

DruAnn Clark: Well, we have the sea lions doing tasks that humans aren't that good at—tasks like object recovery. Humans can't dive down to 500 feet and recover objects that are on the bottom of the ocean in some of the low-level light situations. Humans can't see in the dark very well, whereas sea lions are very good at it. … In fact, [the sea lions'] force protection job is best utilized at night. … During the day humans can see well, but at night we are able to utilize the sea lions low-light vision. So, actually, a lot of the sea lion's training happens at night. … Recovering objects from the bottom of the ocean is really an amazing task that our sea lions do. It's pretty incredible because humans can't easily dive to depths much more than 100 feet, but sea lions can recover objects [at depths of] 500 feet. They are also able to do repetitive dives to those depths.

Sea lion training dummy—friend or foe?

SR: How long does it take to train an individual animal?

Clark: It depends on the task they are learning. Just like humans, they learn at different rates [depending] on how hard the task is. But they do start their training at a young age, and we start interacting with them right away, so they learn their basic husbandry behaviors. … Husbandry behaviors are behaviors that we teach them [in order] to better care for them. For example, we teach them how to open up their mouths so that we can look inside and check their teeth.

We use a method called "operant conditioning," which is the use of positive reinforcement. We reinforce the good behaviors and ignore the inappropriate behaviors.

SR: Do you train the sea lions differently from the dolphins?

Clark: Oh, very much. Since sea lions can walk on land they are very different [in the] way that you can interact with them. However, the basic principles of training—of operant conditioning—are the same whether it is a sea lion or a dolphin. It's all positive reinforcement.

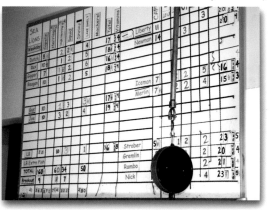

SR: Do they do any training on land?

Clark: Actually, they do quite a bit of training on land. A lot of their tasks [require] them to

Feeding regimes for "Reagan" and "Top Gun" platoon sea lions.

ride in boats to go from one place to another. Sometimes they [walk] up piers and onto the beaches. So, all that's done above the water.

SR: Do the sea lions ever get distracted by the noise?

Clark: That's actually one of the things we need to desensitize them to, since the sea lions are going to be traveling all around the world and working … in [a lot] of different situations with [a lot] of different noises. We want to them to get used to helicopters flying overhead and boats going by and different people around. We want to desensitize them to that.

SR: When the sea lions are going out and doing their operations, do they do it in groups or individually?

Clark: It really depends on what tasks they're doing. Sometimes the sea lions work in a team, and sometimes the sea lions work individually. The sea lions are very adaptable and very good at the job that they do. So, really, they can do it in any one of those circumstances.

SR: What exactly do the sea lions do?

Clark: There are two different projects that the sea lions focus their attention on. The first project is an object recovery project where they recover objects that the Navy has put down at the bottom of the ocean at [great] depths,

depths that are far too deep for [human] divers. So, the sea lions go down and attach a grabber to an object that's attached to a line. ... These are objects that otherwise, in the past, would be unrecoverable; they [would] go down to the bottom of the ocean and just stay there. The sea lions are very good at going down and picking up these objects from the bottom and attaching these recovery lines. The second project that the sea lions work on is a force protection project where the sea lions serve as sentries, as part of a security team, and go out and search for enemy swimmers or divers coming up to a pier. They protect piers and anchorage areas for U.S. Navy vessels.

SR: Have the enemy divers ever hurt the sea lions?

Clark: The sea lions are very good at their jobs and they are actually trained to ... detect a swimmer or diver without being detected themselves. So, they

go in, and they just let us know that somebody's there. A security team then goes in and takes care of the enemy swimmer or diver.

SR: Do you keep trained and wild sea lions apart? Would they be able to mate or play with each other?

Clark: Our sea lions live in water pens right here in San Diego Bay. The wild sea lions often do come up and take naps on our docks right

The pens housing the Navy sea lions.

next to our sea lions; so, they do get to see each other, as well as when they are out in the open ocean. Our sea lions sometimes interact with the wild sea lions.

SR: Were the sea lions ever used in the war with Iraq?

Clark: The sea lions were deployed in 2003 during Operation Enduring Freedom, and the sea lions were used to protect a pier where U.S. Navy sea vessels were kept. So, yes—the sea lions were used at that time.

SR: So, sea lions are used in the war that is going on? In what other ways are they used?

Clark: When [the sea lions] were deployed, they did a task where they would search out a pier area for enemy swimmers or divers. They did an excellent, excellent job at protecting U.S. Navy vessels and saving U.S. lives.

Bob Lynch

On a sunny and warm day, our group interviewed Bob Lynch on his boat at the San Diego Yacht Club. We sought him out because of his knowledge of San Diego Bay and his experience with ordnance recovery by sea lions. During World War II, Mr. Lynch enlisted in the U.S. Army and became a radio technician. Although he never saw combat, he remained in the armed services until just before the Korean War. After leaving the Army, he worked for General Dynamics. Throughout his career, Mr. Lynch had worked on several military aeronautical projects, the most famous of which was the Tomahawk cruise missile.

We didn't begin the interview until after Mr. Lynch had maneuvered his boat through the waters off the coast of Point Loma, where the naval base is located, and masterfully steered the vessel into its designated dock. The interview took place in the cabin of his boat, and though it lasted only a few minutes, the information we received was unique, exciting, and invaluable.

Mr. Lynch and students from High Tech High cruising the Bay on his boat prior to the interview.

Student Researcher (SR): What kind of industry are the sea lions living in San Diego Bay involved in?

Bob Lynch: Well, there [are a lot] of industries on San Diego Bay associated with the Bay, but one of the most interesting is the training of the sea lions—and that's done right out here, off Point Loma. They train them for all sorts of Naval duties: searching the harbor bottom for aliens, looking at the hulls of ships, and retrieving things from the bottom. Anyway, I had one experience... We were launching a missile out at San Clemente Island—and San Clemente Island is way out of San Diego—about 70 miles—and the missile did not work like we thought it should; and it dove in 1,000 feet of water, and boy—we wanted to get it back to figure out what happened. So, they got a sea lion out there, and they gave him a couple of nice fish and told him: "Go get that missile." They put a harness on his nose so that he dove down 1,000 feet and [clamped] the line onto the missile. In that way, we were able to recover the missile—and that probably saved us a couple million dollars. So, that's the kind of industry we have here in San Diego Bay.

Biology of the California Sea Lion

Consider the best characteristics of a beloved childhood pet or a hardworking drug-sniffing dog. The beneficial traits of these clever critters are rivaled by those found in the California sea lion (*Zalophus californianus*). Even their facial features resemble those of our canine companions. Showing lovable dog-like loyalty as well, sea lions have established themselves as allies with the U.S. Navy. Their ability to thrive in both marine and terrestrial environments makes them truly extraordinary creatures and provides their human associates with grounds for continued partnership and cooperation.

Sea lions are classified as pinnipeds, meaning "fin-footed." There are three genera in the pinniped family: *Phocidae* (true seals), *Odobenidae* (walruses), and *Otariidae* (sea lions). Grouped together with sea lions under the *Otariidae* genus are fur seals and eared seals. Sea lions can be distinguished from fur and eared seals by two of their unique physical features: they have an external ear flap, and their hind feet can rotate forward to help them with locomotion on land. There are five different species of sea lions that live in various locations around the world. These species are: the New Zealand sea lion, the Australian sea lion, the South American sea lion, the Stellar sea lion, and the California sea lion. (Bonner 1994) (Myers 2000) ("The Pinnipeds..." 2006)

The California sea lion has the greatest range of all sea lions, traveling from northern Baja Mexico to British Columbia and west to the Galápagos Islands and Japan. The California sea lion tends to reside where there is a lot of human activity and coastal construction. They live and breed near piers, buoys, jetties, and platforms. They can be seen near settlements everywhere from the Tres Marias Islands in Mexico to San Diego and San Francisco, California and Vancouver, Canada. Off Southern California, there are four main breeding places: San Miguel, San Nicolas, Santa Barbara, and San Clemente. Pupping season occurs during June and July, and pups stay with their mothers for six months or longer. ("Sea Lions" 1999)

California sea lions inhabit rocky shore and sandy beaches of coastal islands and the mainland. Adult males weigh up to 1,000 lbs. Females can weigh up to 220 lbs. Males have a dark brown coat with a lighter patch or mane on their heads. Females range from light to dark brown in color. As males mature, the tops of their heads get lighter. At the age of five, males develop a sagittal crest, a bony bump on the top of the skull that becomes more prominent with age.

California sea lions' diet consists of fish, lamprey, shellfish, and octopi. They will consume 9 to 31 lbs of fish daily. If properly nourished, they can live about 25 years. They have few predators, besides killer whales, great white sharks, and angry fishermen. The California sea lion is intelligent and well adapted, and many fishermen can relate stories of their mischievous nature. ("California Sea Lion" 2002) (Daugherty 1979)

Sea lions are very social animals that live in large groups. These groups often rest or float together on the ocean's surface, on "rafts," or on shore. While resting on rocks or the shoreline, sea lions point their noses skyward and are sometimes seen lying atop one another. They are also seen playing and leaping together on the surface while "rafting." ("California Sea Lions" 2006)

When they choose to walk on land, sea lions' short fur protects their skin as they traverse across rocks and other surfaces. Their top speed across smooth rocks may reach up to 15 mph, but can only be maintained for a few yards. Underwater, sea lions propel themselves through the water using their long front flippers. Their back flippers are not used much in actual swimming propulsion, but instead act as stabilizers. Their maximum speed underwater is about 25 mph. Their dives often reach depths of 800 feet, although most dives don't exceed 360 feet. ("San Diego Harbor..." 2006)

Sea lions use four different kinds of vocalizations when they get aggressive. There is the bark, squeal, belch, and growl. When two competing females are close together, their bark serves as a long-distance threat to other sea lions. Their squeal is made with a wide-open mouth that follows head-weaving behavior. The belch is somewhat more intense and is accompanied by forward thrusting of the head. The most intense vocal threat is a growl. The growl has a harsh quality and is often used during actual physical fighting.

Captive sea lions perform the tricks or specific tasks they need to survive. Training starts when they are young and may take up to ten years. Sea lions are trained to recognize hand gestures, numbers, and

letters. Vocalization, where the trainer says words like "ball" or "cube," is also used. During one series of experiments at the University of California's Long Marine Lab in Santa Cruz, a female sea lion learned how to respond to more than 20 hand gestures.

Sea lions have poor vision on land, and the range of their eyesight is very limited. Males can see up to 82 yards in daylight and 27

A bull sea lion displaying "belch" communication.

yards on a clear night. Females will become agitated if a creature approaches them within a few yards. When a strange object is near or approaching, a sea lion extends its neck and moves its head from side to side. But even though sea lions have poor vision, they can see shapes or outlines.

The great success in captive breeding programs within marine parks has made live capture for public display purposes unnecessary. Birthing takes place approximately 50 weeks after breeding. Pups weigh up to 16 pounds at birth and are nursed for at least five or six months— sometimes for over a year. During mating season, males guard their territories and bark almost continuously. Sea lions are very vocal and the pups have a bleat-like call. Mothers recognize their pups on crowded rafts or shore through smell, sight, and vocalizations. At an early stage pups also learn how to recognize their mother's vocalizations. ("California Sea Lion" 2002) ("San Diego Harbor…" 2006)

The biggest problem for these sea lions is weather conditions produced by El Niño, as during these events, warmer water causes the sea lions' prey to reside in deeper water. This forces sea lions to swim further from shore and dive to greater depths in order to feed. For younger, more inexperienced sea lions and pups this can cause problems. Many of these sea lions starve or can become separated from their mothers. (Rocca 1998) ("Stellar Sea Lions" 2006) (Kay 1998)

Hear the Wild

We are the life that brings
We are the ones that bark
Not the ones that sing
Not the ones that talk
And the water, that's what we need
But the docks, that's where we eat, sleep and breathe
That's where we lay until humans try and deceive
We play the side lines: watch, bark and retrieve
This is our nature
These are the things we do
You would do the same if someone tried to jeopardize you
We bark as strong as iron
The *Zalophus californianus*
A.k.a., the California Sea Lion

Moe Black

Dolphins

"The dolphins here are not tethered; it's our relationship with them that brings them home every day to this place where they feel comfortable and safe."

-Chris Harris

EVINRUDE

Surrounded by cynicism and disbelief, the U.S. Navy Marine Mammal Program (NMMP) began enlisting dolphins to their ranks. The Navy and collaborating civilian scientists recognized dolphins' innate traits that allow them to work with humans, and accomplish tasks in the deep depths of the oceans that their terrestrial human counterparts cannot do without being subjected to extreme danger. The NMMP soon began to train the dolphins to identify and locate underwater mines and "threat" swimmers.

Utilizing their natural sonar and deep-diving skills, dolphins work collaboratively with their trainers to save lives of American military personnel during warfare. After successful missions in the Vietnam War, Cold War, and Iraq War, the NMMP has become a thriving and indispensable part of the Navy. The dolphins in the San Diego area have more than earned their place in the ranks, and as part of the Department of Defense, they have established themselves as a welcome presence in the Bay and are here to stay for as long as the NMMP is in place.

Geography of the
Dolphins of the Bay

The Pacific bottlenose dolphin is commonly found just outside the surf zone off San Diego. Occasionally they venture into San Diego Bay and many dolphins work for the NMMP situated just off Point Loma. In the San Diego area, dolphins can also be found at SeaWorld San Diego.

History of the Dolphins of the Bay

     People have long known that dolphins are intelligent and good-natured animals, willing to help fellow creatures in need. Tales written by a wide range of authors reveal how the dolphin has achieved and maintained this positive image. In Aesop's fable, "The Lion and the Dolphin," we read one of the earliest examples of the dolphin's willingness to help another species. In this fable, the "king of the fishes" makes an alliance with a lion. The lion calls upon his ally in his time of need, but their pact is thwarted by the dolphin's immobility out of water. The lion attempts to accuse the dolphin of being traitorous; however, the dolphin's intelligence allows it to see where the real blame lies: with nature, for having been given sovereignty over the sea, but denied the ability to live on land. (Devine 1967)

     This fable is just one of countless stories that depict dolphins. There are also many nonfictional personal accounts of dolphins assisting humans. Such accounts of shipwrecked and drowning humans being saved by dolphins stretch back to the beginning of recorded history. The earliest known narrative was written by the Greek poet Arion in 600 BCE, and the thousands of years between then and now are filled with similar tales. One of the more recent accounts tells the enlightening story of Yvonne Bliss' encounter with a dolphin. In 1960, off the coast of Grand Bahama Island, Yvonne Bliss fell overboard from her boat.

> After many hours of being out of sight of land, exhausted from trying to swim in heavy currents, she became terrified in her awareness of a large animal close to her that she assumed to be a shark and kept moving away as it approached her. Realizing that it was in fact a dolphin, she noticed that it had 'pushed' her out of the strong currents and into a tidal stream carrying her towards shore. The dolphin kept with her guiding her to the beach. ("Synchronicity ... " 2006)

Stories like these are common, and are always filled with endless praise and gratitude toward dolphins. The majority of these stories tell of dolphins assisting humans stranded in the water, but there are also numerous accounts of dolphins helping boats navigate through treacherous waters or perilous storms. (Devine 1967) ("Synchronicity ... " 2006)

     In 1978, Kobus Stander and three other South African fishermen were lost in dense fog in dangerous waters with a visibility of about two meters. Suddenly, four dolphins surrounded them and began nudging the boat to the left. Realizing that the dolphins were helping them, Kobus steered the boat just in time to hear—and in a gap in the fog, see—waves crashing down on treacherous rocks; rocks that he had almost hit. The dolphins continued to guide the boat using gentle nudges for another hour and a half, after which they circled the boat to indicate to the fishermen to stop. When the fog lifted, the fishermen found themselves back at home in their bay. ("Synchronicity … " 2006)

"Kai" a Pacific bottlenose dolphin formerly of the NMMP now in retirement at SeaWorld San Antonio.

Although humans have been well acquainted with this sort of representation of dolphins for centuries, only in recent times has man truly begun to test the adaptability, kindness, and intelligence of these amazing creatures. Our current knowledge of these animals was first established with the first attempt to keep cetaceans, the group of marine mammals with teeth, including whales, porpoises and dolphins, in captivity. The first recorded attempt of cetacean captivity occurred when P.T. Barnum brought two beluga whales to New York in 1860. These saltwater animals died a few days after being put in a freshwater tank, and the attempt was deemed unsuccessful. Later, two belugas survived in the new saltwater tank, and became the first captive cetaceans to go on public display. They were featured in P.T. Barnum's circus alongside "human freaks" and other animals. ("History of Captivity" 2006) (Johnson 1990)

After P.T. Barnum's display of belugas in 1860, it was another half of a century before cetaceans were again seen in captivity. C.H. Townsend, the curator of the New York Aquarium, decided to exhibit dolphins in hope of attracting large crowds to the aquarium. In November 1913, five bottlenose dolphins were brought to New York to be put on display there. In June of the following year, Townsend wrote that there had never been a more successful exhibit in the 12 years of the aquarium's existence. In 1915, after 21 months in captivity, the last of the dolphins died from pneumonia. Even though the dolphin exhibit was a great success, it would be another 25 years before captive dolphins would be trained to do the sort of tricks we see today. ("History of Captivity" 2006) (Johnson 1990)

In 1938, Marine Studios was established in Florida and the same year, the oceanarium welcomed the facility's first bottlenose dolphins.

During feeding time, the dolphins at Marine Studios started jumping up to catch the fish that were thrown to them for food. This display always seemed to thoroughly entertain the public, as well as the keepers and curator of Marine Studios. In 1939, Cecil M. Walker, who was a member of the night staff managing its water purification pumps, observed a peculiar behavior. He noticed that one of the dolphins repeatedly brought a feather toward him. Walker decided to conduct an experiment; he took the feather and threw it back into the water. To his surprise, the dolphin brought the feather back again. The game continued with Walker experimenting with a variety of objects including a ball, a bicycle inner tube, small stones and other objects. As other dolphins began to join the game, it began to

SeaWorld San Diego in 1974.

resemble the act seen today at nearly every marine park in the world. ("History of Captivity" 2006) (Marine Mammal Program Video 2001)

With Walker's discovery came the birth of a new age in entertainment. It was not long before people all over the country began to flock to places like Marine Studios to watch performing dolphins. Along with the masses, scientists were also taken with this phenomenon. Soon, dolphins would become at the center of marine mammal research. Among those participating in these experiments was the U.S. Navy, which initially worked with dolphins to understand and develop the hydrodynamics of torpedoes and submarines. In 1959, at the Marineland of the Pacific, the Navy began work with a Pacific white-sided dolphin named Notty. They hoped that by studying the natural hydrodynamics of the dolphin, they would gain valuable knowledge for improving the Navy's torpedoes and submarines. (Wood 1973) (Shawn 1959)

Although this research did not bring up any new and valuable data in the area of hydrodynamics, the dolphin's amiability and cooperativeness left a definite impression on those participating in the project. Based on the information that had been collected, the objective of the project changed and the Navy began to look at two other unique dolphin traits. They looked at the dolphins' natural and highly developed sonar for ways to improve their own sonar techniques. The Navy also looked closely into dolphins' ability to dive and frequently return to depth without suffering from decompression sickness. The Navy realized dolphins, with their trainability and diving skills, could help it in its ventures: the idea for the U.S. Navy Marine Mammal Program (NMMP) was born. (Marine Mammal Program Video 2001)

At the time, the Navy was highly hardware oriented, and, not surprisingly, the idea of having dolphins do specialized work was often not taken seriously. Although supporters of the NMMP continued to demonstrate how the dolphins' highly powerful sonar, acute underwater hearing, and diving and swimming ability made them great candidates for undersea work, the idea was disregarded by the Navy's high command. Many felt the idea was interesting but believed that no valuable information or practical applications would come of it.

An NMMP dolphin and trainer.

Regardless, it was concluded that some marine mammal research was harmless. A fledgling marine mammal program set up their first station at Point Mugu near Los Angeles. This was also the location of the Pacific Missile Range facility and Naval Missile Center, which were also looking to undertake studies of marine life, including dolphins. As a result of these mutual interests, and eventual encouragement from the Office of Naval Research, the modest facility quickly began to grow. In 1963, the program got underway, expanding from their small location to a sand spit between Mugu Lagoon and the nearby ocean. (Wood 1973) (Naval Ocean Systems Center 1990)

The first open-ocean trained dolphin was a female Atlantic bottlenose dolphin from the Gulf of Mexico named Buzz-Buzz. She spent five months training at Port Hueneme, California before she was transferred to Point Mugu. Once at Point Mugu, she was trained for open-ocean work which, when completed, would be one of the biggest steps for the NMMP. Her training consisted of getting accustomed to working with a trainer in many different situations and always returning to a homing signal. After four months of training, Buzz-Buzz was transported to the open lagoon, where the first open-ocean work was successfully completed. This allowed the program to begin expanding and specializing its work. (Wood 1973)

Another dolphin that helped to revolutionize the program came to the Navy from an oceanside marine park in Santa Monica. When Tuf Guy, whose name would later be shortened to Tuffy, joined the program, he was quite the opposite of the everyday image of a bottlenose dolphin. He was uncooperative and filled with rage—and it was only when laboratory technician Deborah Duffield took an interest in Tuffy that he showed his true colors. Duffield trained Tuffy using a method, now the norm, called positive reinforcement. When a dolphin is trained, it is often given the freedom to demonstrate its capabilities. As the trainer's reactions depend on the dolphin's actions, a dolphin slowly but steadily achieves knowledge of basic tasks, gradually working towards more advanced tasks. In 1965, when the long and tedious process of training Tuffy was completed, he was employed to be a part of the first major military project, Sea Lab II. The project worked in the waters off La Jolla, which is where Tuffy completed this successful open-ocean experiment. He repeatedly dove 200 feet to the Sea Lab II installation, carrying mail and tools to Navy personnel, and was trained to guide lost divers to safety. (Schusterman 1936) (Weiss 1969) (Wood 1973)

The success of the Sea Lab II program was overwhelming. Dolphins could now be prepared for conflict. With the Vietnam War approaching, the Navy sent five dolphins to Cam Ranh Bay to perform underwater surveillance and guard military boats from enemy swimmers. From 1970–1971, the selected dolphins dutifully and successfully performed their tasks. This allowed the NMMP to further expand. ("The Story of Navy Dolphins" 2006)

In 1967, some of the Point Mugu personnel were relocated to the Point Loma area of San Diego. The new facilities and personnel came under the control of the recently established Naval Ocean Systems Center, later renamed Space and Naval Warfare Systems Center San Diego, or SSC San Diego. This was the beginning of the NMMP's involvement in San Diego Bay. The majority of the animals and trainers at Point Mugu moved to a new laboratory at the Marine Corps Air Station on Kāne'ohe Bay, Hawaii, while a small number of animals remained in San Diego as the program continued to flourish. ("The Story of Navy Dolphins" 2006)

Along with widening the variety of animals used, the program also began to acquire more animals. In 1986, Congress authorized the Navy to collect marine mammals for "national defense purposes." With an expanded budget and increased number of dolphins, the NMMP reached its peak. They would send their next amazing team of animals into the upcoming Gulf War. ("The Story … " 2006)

The Navy deployed six dolphins to the Persian Gulf, where they patrolled the harbor in Bahrain to protect U.S. flagships from enemy swimmers. With the end of the Cold War, the budget for the NMMP was drastically reduced, and all but one of its training centers was closed. In 1993, as the result of the Base Realignment and Closure process, the Hawaii lab was closed and the majority of the animals were moved to San Diego. Of the 103 dolphins remaining in the program, the Navy decided it needed only 70 to maintain its downsized operations. Much of the project was declassified to be able to respond to false claims by animal rights groups about use and abuse of the mammals. (Harris 2006) (Naval Ocean Systems Center 1990) (Marine Mammal Program Video 2001) ("The Story … " 2006)

When looking at San Diego Bay, rarely does anyone immediately think of the NMMP. Yet, although practically unheard of, the NMMP happens to be one of the most innovative and helpful programs based in the Bay. The program is still located in San Diego at SSC San Diego, and is home to about 70 bottlenose dolphins, a dozen or so California sea lions, and a beluga whale or two. The program is broken up into five teams. Each human-animal team is known in military jargon by a 'mark' number, or MK for short. The five teams are called 'MK 4,' 'MK 5,' 'MK 6,' 'MK 7,' and 'MK 8.' The MK 4, 7 and 8 teams use only dolphins, while the MK 5 uses only sea lions and the MK 6 uses both sea lions and dolphins. (Marine Mammal Program Video 2001) ("U.S. Navy Marine … " 2006)

The MK 4, 7, and 8 teams all use dolphins in relation to underwater mines, but each team utilizes dolphins' abilities for a slightly different purpose. MK 4 uses them to detect the location of tethered sea mines floating off the bottom; MK 7 dolphins are trained to detect and mark the location of mines on the sea floor or buried in sediment; and MK 8 dolphins are trained to swiftly identify safe corridors for the initial landing of troops on shore. During an operation, a dolphin awaits a cue from its handler before starting to search a specific area using its natural echolocation. The dolphin reports back to its handler, giving particular responses when a target object is detected. If a mine-like target is detected, the handler sends the dolphin to mark the location of the object, so it can be avoided by Navy vessels or neutralized by Navy divers. ("U.S. Navy Marine ... " 2006)

The MK 5 team is dedicated to the recovery of equipment that is fired from ships or dropped from planes into the ocean. This team uses California sea lions to locate and attach recovery hardware to underwater objects such as mines. In this role, they can out-perform human divers, who are restricted to short working times and limited diving. Finally, the MK 6 team uses dolphins and sea lions as sentries to protect harbor installations and ships against unauthorized human swimmers. Despite rumors, the animals are not trained to attack an enemy diver. They simply identify a foreign object, or swimmer, and report back to their trainer, who then takes the proper action. ("U.S. Navy Marine ... " 2006)

Despite the adversity the program has had to face over the years, the NMMP is still continuing to prove its success and value. Even during the controversial Iraq War, mine-clearance dolphins were deployed to the Persian Gulf in 2003. The Navy claims that these dolphins were effective in helping to clear more than 100 anti-ship mines and underwater booby traps from the port of Umm Qasr. Although this program is often the target of rumors and the wrath of animal activist groups, it is easy to see that they have only done good for our country. The Marine Mammal Program is simply further proof of the amazing capabilities of dolphins, and the limitless achievements they can accomplish while working in conjunction with humans. ("The Story ... " 2006) ("U.S. Navy Marine ... 2006)

Along with greatly expanding our knowledge about the biology and capability of these magnificent and intelligent creatures, the NMMP has worked to save lives. The dolphins' ability to dive to and from depths with ease, combined with their trainability, has enabled them to help specialists locate and disarm dangerous underwater bombs. By completing this daunting task, these dolphins have not only saved military lives, but civilian lives as well.

Without the capability to identify and disarm bombs, ships transporting troops would have to pass through potentially dangerous waters. Ships could be hit by hidden bombs and could sink or be severely damaged. Those onboard could face dire fates. Now with the teams of dolphins and their trainers, the ports, passages, bays, and all other routes for these ships are checked ahead of time.

In addition to saving countless lives, the NMMP and the dolphins that keep it running have had a substantial effect on the economy. By successfully identifying and clearing underwater mines, the dolphins and their trainers have saved our nation millions of dollars. For, every time a ship hits a mine, damage inevitably occurs. Whether the damage is the complete destruction of the ship or merely some minor problems, once a ship is damaged, it needs to be repaired or replaced. This costs our nation enormous sums of money. Taking this into account, it is easy to see how the dolphins of the NMMP are saving our country millions of dollars.

What's more, the program has helped our economy by reducing the cost of specialized deep-water divers. A dolphin can accomplish the work of several divers. At the minimum, the Navy would pay their divers the standard salary of about $3,600 a month (unmarried personnel), and an additional bonus as compensation for their strenuous work, or as an award for their diving capabilities. Considering that one dolphin could replace at least two divers, the Navy is saving many thousands of dollars a month. The NMMP has about 70 dolphins, which would bring the amount of money saved by the military up to several hundred thousand dollars a month. And, although the Navy still must pay for the dolphins' care, when combining the amount of money that our country saves between the number of ships not sunk and the divers they don't have to employ, it is easy to see how this program has had a beneficial effect.

The aircraft carrier USS Ronald Reagan heads out on its maiden voyage past the NMMP dolphin pens at Ballast Point.

Although it many not seem that such a small organization as the NMMP could have any affect on our lives, their program is consistently proving otherwise. In their work with the dolphins, the Navy has greatly expanded our knowledge of the physical and mental characteristics and abilities of these clever and unique animals. By helping and supporting this innovative and noteworthy program, our appreciation will likely grow and develop right alongside the NMMP, leading to great things.

1959
The Navy first begins to work with dolphins and study their hydrodynamics

1860
First cetaceans were placed in captivity when P.T. Barnum placed two beluga whales in his circus.

1915
The display at the New York Aquarium was closed after the last dolphin died of pneumonia

1913
The curator of the New York Aquarium placed five bottlenose dolphins on display

1935
Cecil M. Walker began the first experiment similar to common dolphin performances today

1993
Marine Mammal Program moves primarily to San Diego

1965 to 1975
Dolphins are used in the Navy for the first time during the Vietnam War

1965
The U.S. Navy Marine Mammal Program begins its first military project, Sea Lab II

NAVAL BASE POINT LOMA
PORT OPERATIONS

1987
Navy sends six dolphins to the Persian Gulf

1963
The U.S. Navy Marine Mammal Program begins

2003
Dolphins are deployed to Iraq

1986
The U.S. Navy Marine Mammal Program reaches its peak with over 100 trained dolphins

Jewyl Alderson

We set up our equipment along the western end of Shelter Island and awaited our first interviewee, Jewyl Alderson, a former member of the education department at SeaWorld San Diego. We sought out Ms. Alderson because, besides giving educational tours of the aquatic park, she also worked closely with dolphins, and consequently would be able to provide us with an insider's view of dolphin training. We began our interview with the Bay serving as a backdrop, and early on Ms. Alderson's knowledge of and love for dolphins and their capabilities was easily apparent. Her enthusiasm spurred us headfirst into the world of human-dolphin interaction.

Student Researcher (SR): Can you tell us why the dolphin is a good animal when it comes to training?

Jewyl Alderson: Dolphins respond well to positive reinforcement training techniques. … [Trainers] use positive reinforcement and are able to apply it [by having the dolphins] go and get something and bring it back, or go do a combination of behaviors that can be for entertainment or for other reasons. [Dolphins make] very good animals [for training]. Now, some animals don't respond as well such as cats and dogs—cats especially. They only respond to food a lot of the time. It's hard to do training with cats because you always have to have a treat for them.

A SeaWorld trainer uses positive reinforcement with fish.

With dolphins, they don't only like the primary reinforcement of fish and other food, but they like secondary reinforcements such as ice or play time or different kinds of toys. If the only reinforcement you can give is food, then there is a limit to how much training you can do. Because if the only thing that you're giving them is food then eventually, once they are full, then they will no longer respond. So, a dolphin enjoys a multitude of different reinforcements, and that really helps.

SR: You mentioned a combination; can you explain what that means?

Alderson: Well, dolphins have behaviors that you ask them to do and there's a way to train them. I can talk about that as well. Dolphins will do a number of behaviors so you can line them up and give them a few different reinforcements and ask them to do a few different behaviors through either visual or tactile means; so you can either visually tell them with the hand gesture or you can touch them so they'll do a certain kind of behavior. … You can ask them to do a few at a time, and when they're out in the middle of the pool— if you ever heard [trainers] use those whistles—that's a "bridge." You want to give them a positive reinforcement, but when they just

Taking cues from its trainers, a dolphin performs for the crowd.

did something and they're about to do something else or they just did something out in the pool, you want to reinforce immediately so that you actually use the whistle to say "You did a good job" and then they will come back and get their reinforcement.

SR: Can you explain some of the steps for training a dolphin?

Alderson: First you have to establish a relationship with the animal. … You can't really start training it until you have that relationship. Once you have that relationship, you can go up to the animal, you put your hand on their melon, you give them a fish—and you continue this "hand on the melon [forehead], and give it a fish." You're giving them a reinforcement by having your hand on their melon. Now, [you can] move your hand, and the animal [will realize] that every time your hand and their melon interact [with] each other, it's going to get a fish. So, if I put my hand over here, then the animal's going to come to my hand and target it, and it's going to get a fish.

Now, at the same time, you're using a whistle. … So, you keep your hand on its melon [and repeat the process]: fish, whistle, melon, fish, whistle—eventually the dolphin comes over [to your hand and] you tap its melon with your hand and you give it a fish—and now [the dolphin] associates the whistle with that reinforcement. Basically, the whistle actually just shows it that: "Yes, you just did the right thing. That's what we want you to do." That way, if it's in the middle of the pool and just did some large behavior, you whistle and [the dolphin] knows it did it right, and then it comes over to get its reinforcement.

Once I have it target trained, [the dolphin] will follow my hand in a circle—

and that's when it starts going in a circle and doing the "hula," and spinning around in the water. … Or maybe I want it to come over here, or over there—for that, my hand is a really important target tool. That's how you train the dolphin—use a target in order to get it to do what you want it to do. [For example, if you want it to do] a back flip while it's in the air; you move your hand backward. And that's how they learn to know what you want them to do.

Three dolphins and their trainer show off to the crowd.

SR: How long are they usually employed?

Alderson: The animals are used throughout their life; it really depends on their interactions. By the first year, they should be target trained and able to come to your hand. That's maybe [between] six months to a year … and then they start training a little bit. But for the first few months, [there is] really no trainer interaction at all—it's just the mom and the baby.

Now, as far as on the older side of things, it really depends on the animal—if it has a history of aggressive behavior, some kind of unexpected aggression by the animal during a training session or a show or something of that nature, then the animal will not be used with waterworks—waterworks is when the trainer is in the water with the animal. [Nonetheless], they may still be used for smaller acts in the show. But even when it's really old. … I mean, this is what it's been doing its whole life—it really doesn't know anything different—and it's good for it to keep up the exercise. Of course, the veterinarians are going to pull it if it's sick—then it won't be in a show and it is retired. But even a younger dolphin … it'll just be put in an area where there's no [crowd or] training interaction.

Chris Harris

Walking past armed guards onto the bayside campus of the Space and Naval Systems Center San Diego, we felt that we were constantly surrounded by tight security and watchful eyes. We felt very fortunate to have been able to get onto the base through the help of Tom Lapuzza, public affairs officer of Space and Naval Systems Command/SPAWAR, and we paid close attention as we were given a brief lecture about rules and regulations and red security badges that read "Visitor."

Once actually inside the base, we were greeted by biotechnician Chris Harris, who is a lead trainer in the NMMP and has traveled the world with Navy dolphins, and we proceeded down a long road laden down by our camera gear. We stopped at a grassy area in front of the dolphin pens. The Navy presence in the Bay at this spot was heavy, especially as the USS *Ronald Reagan* Carrier Strike Group was on its maiden voyage in the channel in front of us. As we conducted our interview with Mr. Harris, we soon realized the value of his information and discovered that the details he could give us concerning the NMMP were the link we had been missing in the story of the dolphins of San Diego Bay.

Student Researcher (SR): What types of dolphins do you use for the Navy Marine Mammal Program?

Chris Harris: The dolphins that are with our program are Atlantic and Pacific bottlenose dolphins. It's not uncommon to see Pacific bottlenose dolphins in [the San Diego] region. We tend to work with the Atlantic bottlenose dolphins for their affinity [with] working in shallow bays and estuaries. They're adept at going into very deep or very shallow water. ... The Atlantic

bottle-nosed dolphins that we have here are born here or they're flown here. Originally, they were flown here from the Gulf Coast many, many years ago, [but now] we have our own dolphins born here in San Diego.

SR: Can you tell us about how the dolphins are trained and at what age they enter your program?

Harris: All of the dolphins that we have here that are new to the training are born here at the NMMP or come to us from other facilities. We have an extensive breeding program and the dolphins start learning from the onset. So, from a very young age, one of the first tasks they learn is to develop a trust and relationship with their human counterparts and the learning process for the dolphin is a lifelong process. Dolphins continually will learn and we'll explore new avenues with them as we continue to learn more about their capabilities.

SR: Do you use the same methods to train dolphins as SeaWorld does to teach them tricks?

Harris: Yes. We do use the same methods that oceanariums use. It's positive reinforcement, or what we call operant conditioning, which reinforces those behaviors that we would like to see increased in frequency.

SR: Can you explain more about how you use operant conditioning?

Harris: Sure! Positive reinforcement, or the process of operant conditioning, is to basically dig the hole into which the behavior falls. We set the animals up to succeed in the direction we want to, or to create opportunities for the behavior to occur, and when it occurs we reward it. So, we would give the animals praise, or tactile reinforcement—a rub down, because they have very sensitive skin—and we also give food rewards.

Yo-yo, retired from the NMMP and now residing at SeaWorld San Antonio, turning in the water, making visible his ID brand.

SR: On the topic of dolphins in the military, can you describe how they were used in Iraq and other conflicts?

Harris: Well, the dolphins in the northern Arabian Gulf and the Persian Gulf conflict were used in two different capacities, one of which was to identify the presence of swimmers in and around U.S. Navy and coalition ships. Those dolphins would swim and, using their echolocation, identify the presence or absence of people that were not authorized to be there, and report that presence back to their human handlers—the Navy handlers—and then security forces could be dispatched to the area to make sure that the area was in fact secure. The other dolphins that we had on the northern Arabian Gulf were dolphins that look for man-made objects on the sea floor or in the water column. Now, those objects may be mine-like objects that may carry explosives that could damage U.S. civilian or coalition ships. So, the dolphins search the water column and report the presence of those mine-like objects, and then we have divers go down and verify that in fact it's a safe area to be in.

SR: Can you give us a summary of the process of training a dolphin to locate and recognize a bomb?

Harris: The process for training a dolphin to identify an object on the sea

floor, whether it's a swimmer or some other man-made object hidden on the sea floor, is to first give it samples of those objects or similar objects in a controlled environment. We show the animal the presence or absence of [those objects], and the animal is taught to report. The animal basically says "Yes, I see what you're showing me," and he'll come over and touch a small paddle. Then he'll get a reward, such as "Good girl," or "Good boy," or "Nicely done." Then we'll move that object around in different places, and basically it's a game of hide and seek. The dolphin is taught the game "Hide and Seek." When he spots the object he's been trained to see, he comes back and reports its presence.

An NMMP dolphin transport.

SR: How has this program increased our knowledge of dolphins?

Harris: Having these dolphins in our care has allowed us to explore how they interact with their environment, and it's led us to understanding more about dolphins and their natural history than at any time previously. The NMMP has contributed to that body of knowledge more than any other single entity in terms of publications and our understanding of dolphins, their needs, how they interact with their environment, and their capabilities. It's through this understanding that we learned that these animals' unique capability could be used to save lives and save money. The dolphins are extraordinarily good at doing their tasks and because they are so comfortable in that aquatic environment, it means that we don't have to have a diver who can get the bends, and who also gets cold working in a dark murky environment, and wouldn't be as effective.

So, it saves lives, and it saves money. It also contributes greatly to our understanding of not only our dolphins, but dolphins in wild population. There are a number of things that we consider any time we take a dolphin to a foreign location.

A Navy dolphin at "heel" in the Boat Channel of San Diego Bay.

We want to look at the water temperature; we want to look at currents. One of the first things we look at most closely is the overall water quality—is the environment polluted? We don't want to put our dolphins into harm's way, so we take careful samples of water. We have a crew go out before the dolphins are ever moved and do what's called a site inspection. When the dolphins travel, they travel with their own veterinary crew.

SR: Can you describe other ways in which this program benefited San Diego?

Harris: San Diego is certainly a hub for expertise in the care and welfare of marine mammals. We and our counterparts over at SeaWorld, the San Diego Zoo,

A dolphin performing for the crowd at SeaWorld San Diego. and the Scripps Institution of Oceanography make San Diego one of the premiere places to be to learn more about these animals. It's an exciting place to work. There are probably more marine mammals [and trainers] in San Diego than in any other city. A large part of our work with the dolphins here involves being freely released into the ocean every day. The dolphins are not tethered; it's our relationship with them that brings them home every day to this place that they feel comfortable with, and safe. And where their friends and relationships with their handlers are. That's one of the things that make us unique.

A dolphin uses its human-like imagination and intelligence to amuse itself by creating an intricate bubble-ring formation.

The Dolphin —*A Nature Reflection*

Gazing upon the horizon of the San Diego Bay, the different ways in which our Bay is now used are easily seen. A variety of ships pass through the Bay en route to fulfill the missions and desires of those aboard. To begin with, there are recreational ships that cruise along; enjoying all there is to offer. Then there are also military ships, which reign unquestionably over these waters, reminding us of our powerful and unique past. As well, commercial ships are fishing, gathering kelp, or tending to some other, similar task. All of them show me how valuable the Bay is to our economy.

Then, hidden amidst this common population of boats, I spy a smaller boat, less often seen. A dolphin and his trainer are cruising through the Bay on an unknown mission. As they fly by at top speed, I can see that the dolphin is suspended in some triangular device, a sort of canvas hammock, with his trainer glued to his side. Dolphins such as this one are often ignored, yet the power and capabilities of dolphins are truly amazing. As one who knows that they have saved the lives of thousands of our military men and women, I see them in a different light. They contribute more to our country than many people realize. Thinking about all that these animals do, their presence in the San Diego Bay doesn't seem insignificant. That small boat with the dolphin aboard has its own important place among all the other water traffic.

Jane Jensen

Dolphin Biology

Throughout generations, people have always felt some sort of connection to dolphins. Whether they see dolphins in a show, a holding pen, or roaming around out in the sea, people appear to be instantly attracted to these animals' intelligence, grace, and sociable personalities. Although the answer as to why we are so connected to dolphins may remain a mystery for many years to come, we can look toward the dolphin's biology to help us understand this question.

The Pacific bottlenose dolphin, *Tursiops gilli*, lives about 25–30 years. By and large, the females are about 360 lbs whereas the males may weigh upwards of 500 lbs. They are well known for their friendliness, and this tendency toward affability is closely reflected by their social structure, for they are typically found in small groups ranging between two and 15 animals. Much like humans, they prefer to be around members of their own kind and socialize, rather than be solitary creatures. Within these groups, dolphins, like humans, often separate into subgroups that are generally based on age, gender, family relationships and affiliations, and history for comfort and security. Dolphins are also similar to humans in terms of their mental capacity. They are the only other animals besides apes and

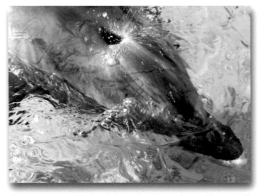

humans that possess a sense of self. This self-awareness helps to forge a firm connection between dolphins and human handlers or acquaintances. (Reynolds 2000)

Perhaps these similarities between our species and theirs, combined with dolphins' well-known tendency toward cooperation and friendliness, are what first attracted the Navy's attention. Regardless, these characteristics led to what started out as a hydrodynamics study to become today's full-blown underwater mine detection program. Dolphins' resistance to water pressures, loss of body heat, and decompression sickness make them suitable for diving to depths that are unsafe for their human counterparts. ("U.S. Navy Marine Mammal Program" 2006)

As an animal dives down into the water, it is constantly losing body heat to the surrounding water; as the depth increases, so does the amount of body heat lost. Dolphins, like any other warm-blooded animal, cannot properly function if their body temperature changes too drastically from their normal core temperature. Similar to other marine mammals, dolphins solve this problem through the use of blubber—a layer of fat surrounds the organs and the entire core of the animal to maintain a consistent body temperature. As body temperature decreases, the metabolism increases, raising blood flow, which in turn raises body temperature. (Reynolds 2000)

In most situations, the weight of a dolphin is directly related to its metabolic rate. Looking across a broad range of mammals with what is called "the mouse-to-elephant curve," one would think that either the dolphin would have to greatly increase its weight to achieve a metabolic rate sufficient to maintain its body temperature in deep-diving conditions, or that the dolphin's weight would limit its metabolic rate. However, dolphins are one of the few exceptions to this curve. Dolphins, and cetaceans in general, have a metabolic rate two or three times that of other animals. This enables them to keep their body temperature high in cold surroundings. They also have a large lung capacity, allowing them to take in significantly greater amounts of oxygen. These unique abilities allow them to dive to great depths as they can maintain a constant body temperature even in cold water far below the surface. Because of their increased lung capacity, they

can use a single breath for a longer amount of time. (Reynolds 2000)

In addition to the dolphins' exceptional diving abilities, their echolocation skills make them perfectly equipped for their jobs with the Navy. Echolocation (active sonar) is when an animal releases several supersonic "clicks" that go through the water and bounce off nearby objects. As the clicks bounce back to the dolphin as sound waves, their brain calculates, from the timing of each sound wave, the distance and approximate shape of the object. Thus, echolocation allows the dolphin to "see" objects that are obscured from human sight by murky water or turbulence. (Reynolds 2000)

The Navy's detailed research into the inner-workings of the dolphin mind, and more specifically sonar, have greatly shaped how we see the dolphin today. From a biological standpoint, through the Navy's involvement with this amazing creature, our knowledge about the anatomy, physiology, and lifestyle of the dolphin has greatly increased. We have learned more about how their sonar works and the dolphins' unique body shape that gives it great agility and speed. We have also learned much more about the dolphins' capabilities, which have allowed the Navy, among others, to depend on these animals for important and highly difficult tasks. Their unique physiology and social behavior has led to a fruitful partnership between both man and dolphin.

The Stranger

Plunging down into the deep water
Far down to the ocean's depths
Striving to protect my partners
From the danger fast approaching

Searching out I find the stranger
His desires dark as night
Marking him; I designate a target
Then the military men come and capture him

Joshua Washington

White
Seabass

"We saw a number of schools of white seabass of 50 or more fish swimming among the kelp. We each easily speared three fish."

-Bob Hetzler

White seabass, giants living in the Pacific coast kelp beds, are fish prized and respected by those who encounter them. These seabass are magnificent creatures; their metallic blue scales appear white when light reflects off them, and their tremendous size is nothing to scoff at. Furthermore, they are well renowned for their fierce fighting abilities. Fishermen of San Diego Bay have long sought after the white seabass.

Commercial fishing of the white seabass began along the California coast in the early 1920s. It continued in earnest for nearly three decades, but overfishing, spurred by continually improving fishing technology, caused a drastic drop in white seabass populations during the 1950s. As a result, there is currently no commercial fishing of white seabass permitted in the Bay, though sport fishermen are permitted to catch them—with restrictions, of course.

To combat the consequences of the careless overfishing that occurred in the past, nongovernmental organizations such as the Hubbs-SeaWorld Research Institute, the Port of San Diego and the San Diego Oceans Foundation are acting to repopulate San Diego Bay and the California coast with white seabass. Thanks to their tremendous efforts, populations of white seabass in San Diego Bay may soon be replenished, to the benefit of both the Bay and the humans who use it.

Geography of the White Seabass of the Bay

White seabass, once abundant in and around San Diego Bay, have declined in number. To combat this problem, the Hubbs-SeaWorld Research Institute (HSWRI) works to repopulate white seabass in the area. White seabass bred by HSWRI are released into the Bay at Grape Street Pier, a white seabass growout facility managed by the San Diego Oceans Foundation and run by volunteers. Every year since its establishment in 2003, the facility has released thousands of white seabass into the Bay. A smaller facility, using onshore tanks at the Southwestern Yacht Club, also releases white seabass bred by HSWRI.

History of the Seabass of the Bay

Though the human "ownership" of San Diego Bay has changed repeatedly over the years, for each group that dominated, the Bay has supplied a constant source of food. One large fish, the white seabass, was utilized by Native American tribes, Spaniards, Mexicans and Americans, and continues to be sought after right up to the present day. The combination of their unique traits—from fighting ability to delectability—has long made the white seabass a popular sport and commercial fish, resulting in great fluctuations in the species' population. (Rudolph 1995) (Thomas 1968) (Young 1973)

The first inhabitants of the San Diego Bay region were the Native Americans, who depended on the Bay, among other resources, for their survival. Fish, including the white seabass, played an important role in their diet. Kumeyaay who lived near the sea regularly caught fish of

Juvenile white seabass at the HSWRI hatchery in Carlsbad nearly ready to be transported to a growout facility.

different types, which no doubt included white seabass. They used tule rafts and plank canoes with paddles to transport themselves in the water. In addition to eating this "large palatable fish," the Native Americans also prized its ear bones, or otoliths. These unusual bones were considered "lucky stones." Such archeological evidence demonstrates that all parts of the fish, not just their flesh, were considered valuable. (Starr 1986) (Young 1973)

When the Spanish arrived in 1542, they first made contact with the Native Americans at Cabrillo Point, near the mouth of San Diego Bay. Accounts written by these explorers state that they traded beads and cloth for the fish caught by the Kumeyaay—fish that no doubt included seabass. The natives' consumption of the white seabass was continued by the subsequent inhabitants of San Diego and its Bay. During succeeding years, the Spanish diet may well have focused upon beef, given the importance of the local tanning industry during this time. However, fish were undoubtedly enjoyed—at least as a source of variety in diet during the Spanish period. Given the seabass' fine meat and taste, it might be concluded that this fish was a favorite of the new arrivals. (Starr 1986)

In 1822, Mexico gained independence from Spain and came into ownership of San Diego. Soon after, the city became the political center of California. A good descriptive account of San Diego under Mexican rule comes from Richard Henry Dana's *Two Years Before the Mast*. Dana arrived in San Diego in 1835 and described the area as beautiful, but isolated from the outside world. San Diego's main contact with the world came from its booming hide trade. Dana also noted San Diego's stunning Bay and busy port. From Dana's report of San Diego's dependence on the Bay, it can be assumed that fishing was present in the Mexican pueblo. Mexicans, like other people who lived near San Diego Bay, used its extensive resources, including the seabass, for their well-being. (Dana 1841) (Timeline of San Diego History 2006)

When the United States became the occupying power in San Diego after the Mexican-American War in 1848, new patterns in the utilization of the resources of San Diego Bay began to be documented. Whaling boomed in San Diego between the 1850s and 1870s. A fish catch record from 1889 shows 250,000 pounds of seabass, and 1904 marks the year in which more than 1 million pounds were caught. The recording of yearly landings began in 1916 and shows an interesting trend. In 1916, the seabass catch in California waters was about 475,000 pounds, with a low of 250,000 in 1944. The market skyrocketed to an astounding 3.4 million pounds in 1959, but again plummeted to 250,000 pounds in 1969, just ten years later. The heyday of white seabass came to a close in the 1950s, as the catch dwindled and afterward never fully recovered. A variety of factors caused this dramatic fluctuation, but these vast changes were all part of the complex story that is the seabass' existence in San Diego Bay. (Timeline of San Diego History 2006) (Thomas 1968) (Young 1973)

Soon enough, Americans began to take a scientific interest in the species contained in the area. The white seabass was first recorded as a species in 1860 by W.O. Ayres. Stewart states in his writing that there were many types of fish living in the Bay—including the seabass. These fish were generally caught using a rod and line since "reels were not plentiful in those days." For larger fish that put up a dangerous fight while being taken, a rifle was kept handy to shoot them as they came to the surface. After the installation of the 'sewage system' in 1888, which put raw sewage directly into the Bay, the fish population decreased considerably due to the pollution as well as other commercial activities. Though white seabass were once one of many types of fish that resided in San Diego Bay, increased fishing and pollution began to drive them out as early as the 1880s. Later decades showed an even greater decrease in the seabass population, though fishing for them remained popular for many years. (Stewart 1965)

Commercial fishing technology became a major factor in both the rise of fish catches and the eventual decline in the population of those same fish. At the dawn of the 20th century, when commercial fishing was new, boats equipped with gill nets were commonly used. According to a 1929 study, gill net boats provided approximately two-thirds of the total boat catch from 1918 to 1928. Gill net boats ranged in size from 24 feet to 40 feet in length. The smaller boats had to return to the market each day because they had no way of storing the fish. The larger boats could stay at sea for up to a week, while storing up to 6 tons of fish on ice below the deck. The gill nets used were large, about 150 feet in length, and had a seven-inch mesh. Each boat used between ten and 35 nets. The nets were either tied to rocks and attached to buoys and sunk, or placed between the fronds of kelp in a kelp bed. Most of the worthwhile fishing took place outside the Bay, such as around San Pedro and the nearby islands of Santa Catalina and San Clemente as well as along the coast to Dana Point. Nevertheless, fishing in the Bay did occur. (Whitehead 1929) (Young 1973)

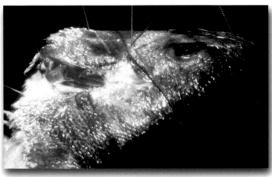

In the first decades of the 1900s, the price of white seabass was between seven cents and 15 cents a pound, with cleaned fish worth up to four cents a pound more. An interesting observation

A white seabass caught in a gill net.

about seabass prices involves the inverse correlation between value of the fish and number caught. In the early 1900s, desire for white seabass increased, yet the monthly boat catch steadily decreased. This time period begins to show the decline of the white seabass population in San Diego Bay. Though it began as a minor issue, it would soon grow to become a serious problem. (Whitehead 1929) (Young 1973)

With the departure of the white seabass came a call for regulations.

WHITE SEABASS CATCH IN CALIFORNIA

WEIGHT (KG)

4 M
3.5 M
3 M
2.5 M
2 M
1.5 M
1 M
.5 M
100,000
80,000
60,000
40,000
20,000

1922   1937   1959   1997   2000

A study was conducted from 1931 to 1964 in order to better manage the white seabass as a resource. This study found that the numbers of the white seabass were steadily decreasing. Consequently, in 1931 a closed fishing season was enacted, as well as a minimum length of 28 inches for white seabass catch. The new regulation was designed to stabilize the population, though some government studies argued that it was unnecessary. Nonetheless, despite a small spike in landed fish in the 1950s, the white seabass population continued to decline, revealing that the resource was not stabilized, despite the slight benefit from the 1958 Federal Aid to Fish Restoration projects. Starting in the 1950s, overfishing, paired with governmental indifference and increased pollution, caused the white seabass resource to be seriously depressed in San Diego Bay. (Thomas 1968)

The depletion of the white seabass was identified and acknowledged by California and federal government studies, but little was done about the problem until recently. The restocking of the white seabass in San Diego Bay is one of the most encouraging restoration projects of any fishery. Through the efforts of the Hubbs-SeaWorld Research Institute (HSWRI), California Department of Fish and Game, the San Diego Oceans Foundation, Harbour

Ocean Preservation Enhancement (HOPE), and volunteer groups, the population of white seabass is slowly increasing. HSWRI breeds juvenile seabass in their facility in Carlsbad and releases them into the Bay via the seabass net pens off the Grape Street Pier and a smaller facility using onshore tanks at the Southwestern Yacht Club. In addition, HSWRI also has a partnership with San Diego State University that has produced a number

of scientific publications regarding the biology of the white seabass. There are now a total of 15 white seabass growout facilities in Southern California. The most recent addition of white seabass to the pens off Grape Street Pier involved approximately 5,000 juveniles of about eight inches in length.

White seabass ready for release at the Grape Street Pier.

Their mortality rate has been relatively low, and nearly 4,000 of them were released from the pens into the Bay once they had reached approximately 12 inches in length. (Morris 2005)

The released fish are monitored to track their travel distance and biogeography. Small coded tags placed in the cheek of the young white seabass at the hatchery provide valuable information on the success of the program. Information campaigns alert fishermen to bring in the heads of caught seabass. The heads are scanned and if a tag is detected it is removed, and its data is extracted in order to determine how far the fish have traveled based on their release and capture locations. Though it is not known at present how much the population of white seabass has increased in San Diego Bay, the restocking project is intended to combat the declining population, and it is a good example of how the negative effects of humans can be reversed. (Buhr 2006) (Morris 2005)

One of the tagging devices used to monitor the white seabass released off Grape Street Pier.

Although there are numerous species of fish in the Bay that have helped to fill the gap left by the decline in seabass numbers, their reintroduction helps return the Bay to its natural balance. Pollution issues still remain, but a biological balance of species in the Bay is an important first step in its restoration. The success of the fish in the Bay is also an indicator of the improving water quality of the Bay itself. Thus, the efforts to restock white seabass in San Diego Bay and local waters play an important part in balancing the area's ecosystem. (Morris 2005)

Grape Street Pier growout pens.

Perhaps, more obvious than the biological transformation brought about by restocking efforts is the effect of this transformation on the people who love the fish. In the past, the greatest economic impact of the white seabass came from commercial fishing. Since there is no commercial fishing of the seabass in and around the Bay today, there is little immediate commercial benefit to the seabass restoration program. However, by adding more seabass to the Bay the fishery may someday be replenished enough to allow some commercial fishing. (Buhr 2006) (Morris 2005)

For now, recreational fishing has remained strong and brings economic benefits to the city. There is a limit on the number of seabass that can be caught by recreational fishermen, but nevertheless there is still a demand for the fish and anglers spend considerable funds in the sport of catching seabass. So, while fishing white seabass may never be the career option it once was, with an increase in seabass population, the economic impact of the fish has the potential to become greater on the local economy. (Buhr 2006) (Hetzler 2006) (Morris 2005)

1959
The number of pounds of white seabass caught in California reaches a peak of 3.4 million pounds

1931
Restrictions to white seabass fishing are enacted

1860

1860
White seabass is recognized as a species

1958
Federal Aid to Fish Restoration Project begins

1982
The Ocean Resources
Enhancement and
Hatchery Program
(ORHEP) is founded

2006

2003
The Grape Street
Pier growout facility
opens

1969
The number of pounds of
white seabass caught in
California reaches a low
of 250,000 pounds

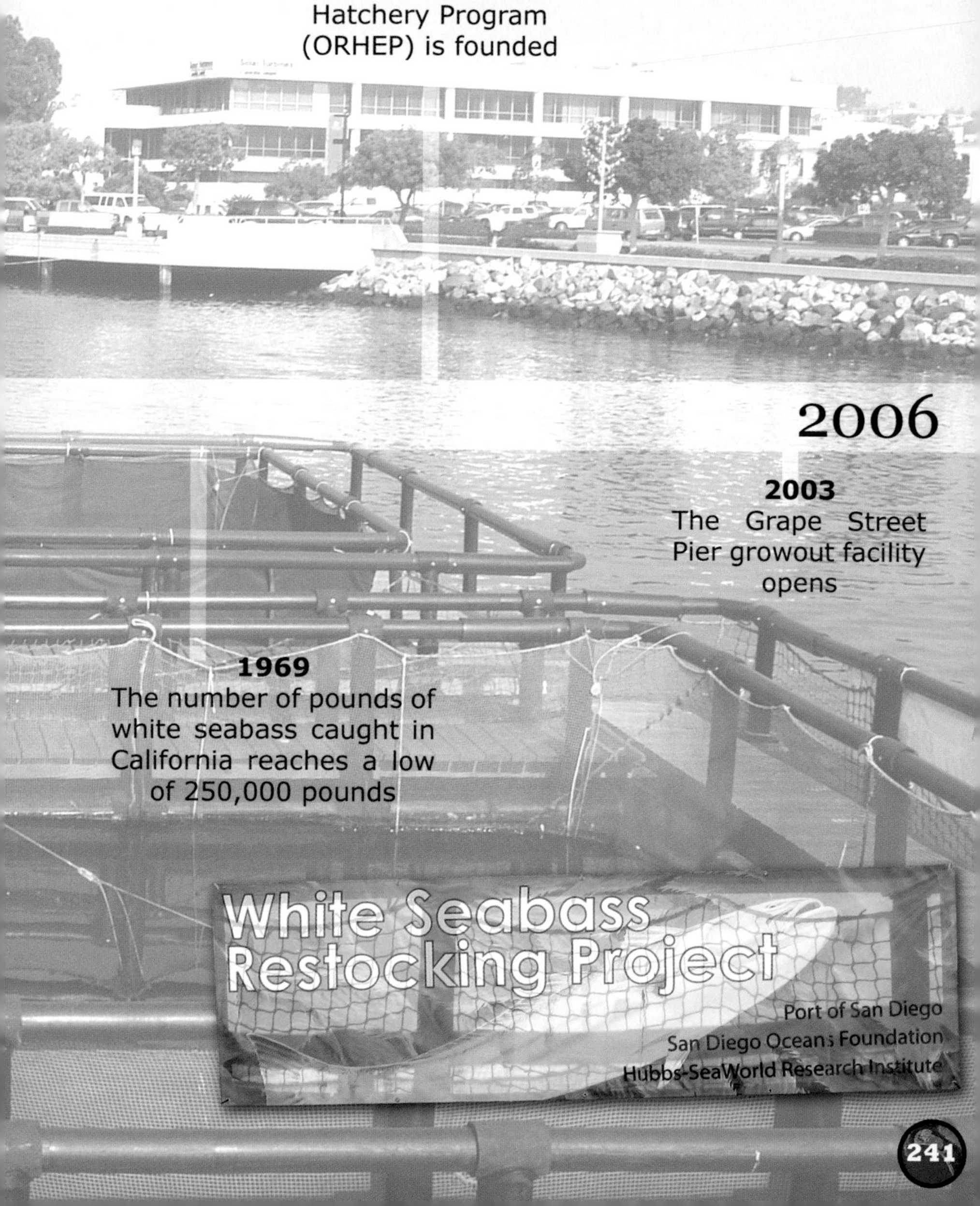

White Seabass
Restocking Project

Port of San Diego
San Diego Ocean Foundation
Hubbs-SeaWorld Research Institute

241

Gabe Buhr

We rolled up to the Carlsbad seabass hatchery's humble complex on a stormy afternoon. The dark interior of the main building was crowded with tanks, and it is there that we were met by Gabe Buhr. Mr. Buhr is a research biologist at the Hubbs-SeaWorld Research Institute (HSWRI) and is in charge of the transport and release of the fishes hatched at Carlsbad to the 15 white seabass growout facilities in Southern California that he coordinates for the Oceans Resources Enhancement Hatchery Program (OREHP). He led us on a tour of the facilities, which are set to release 300,000 white seabass a year. We conducted our interview in the laboratory section where Mr. Buhr told us about the HSWRI, as well as the specifics and successes of the restocking program. As expected, Mr. Buhr provided us with invaluable information concerning the technology behind the release of the white seabass, in addition to specifics of the hatching and growout process.

Student Researcher (SR): Why is it important to restock the white seabass?

Gabe Buhr: White seabass numbers … plummeted from over 50,000 fish caught per year back in the fifties and early sixties down to about 200 fish caught by recreational anglers per year in the late seventies and early eighties … that was one of the main reasons why white seabass were selected for this program. [They were also selected] because of their large size and their interest to both local recreational and commercial anglers, not to mention their contribution to our local kelp forest and reef communities. … I think it's important because we are definitely living in a world where the impact on our marine fisheries and marine ecology is [increasing] all the time. This program is one of the first steps in trying to take a proactive attempt to rehabilitate those fisheries or those ecosystems.

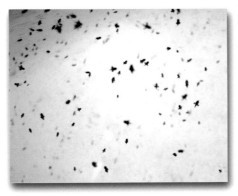

Juvenile white seabass.

Instead of just closing off an area and saying, "Let's shut this down and not let anyone go in there," we're trying to take a different stance and give the fishery a little boost on its way back to recovery. … I get to interact with a lot of people through different parts of our program volunteers, or [those who] just want to come up and say: "Hey, I've been fishing for white seabass for 30 years and I just caught my first white seabass ever last year. Thanks a lot for what you're doing!" So, it's kind of neat; I get to catch all of the rewards that come our way that a lot of the other guys stuck here all the time don't get. But [there are] definitely more white seabass around now than there were 15 years ago. You can ask anybody that!

SR: Do you think that the white seabass is an important resource to San Diego Bay and the California coast?

Buhr: They are a unique fish. They are the largest members of the croaker family here on the Pacific Coast. They are huge, you know. They get to be five feet long and weigh 80 pounds. It takes them a long time to get there. So, they are definitely a fishery that needs management and can easily be overfished, but their presence in our local kelp forest is very important. Not just to the kelp forest, but also in San Diego Bay as well.

SR: How did the marine finfish stock enhancement program and the facility get started?

Buhr: OREHP was started back in 1982 through a state legislative program run by the California Department of Fish and Game. In that capacity, they then contracted out to HSWRI because of our background with marine finfish culture. The goal of OREHP is to try to rehabilitate some of our depleted marine fisheries through fish raised in hatchery programs. It's a marine finfish stock enhancement program.

SR: When the program started, how did you get the initial stock of seabass?

Buhr: Well, when we first started this hatchery back in 1995, we obviously didn't have any brood stock on site, and that was when seabass

Juvenile white seabass from HSWRI in the research lab of Dr. Sue Lowery, USD.

were pretty hard to come by, too. So, we had a really big cooperative effort between local recreational fishermen and commercial fishermen to try to get us some brood stock from the wild that would be healthy and viable members for our program. It was a learning curve, because we didn't really know a lot about white seabass and [things like] transporting them from the open ocean to the tanks here to see how they adapted to captivity. It definitely took some time, but now we have a full stock—200 fish here onsite and another 100 fish offsite as a part of our program, and those fish have been doing well now for a couple of years.

SR: Do you continue to add seabass from the wild to your brood stock or do you just use hatched fish from the facility?

Buhr: No, all of the brood stock we have onsite are captured in the wild. We don't use any fish that's raised in our facilities for brood stock. And to maintain a really strong genetic variability, we are continually swapping fish in our program. Every year, we try to at least switch out 5% of the fish here in our facility. All of our fish are tagged individually so that we can identify them, find out [things like] who's been here the longest, and who's been contributing to the program, [so that we can] make some decisions on which fish we need to remove. ... Our program is trying to rehabilitate the white seabass fishery, not hurt it ... so we [do everything] possible to maintain genetic variability and make sure the fish we release aren't diseased.

SR: Can you explain just what happens to the fish in this facility and how the restocking process works?

Buhr: We have brood stock onsite—those fish spawn in tanks on their own without [handling] other than changes in temperature and photo period. Once the fish spawn, we can harvest the eggs and set them up in incubators and they hatch pretty quickly, in just a day or two. ... We raise the larvae from that stage on, and we take them through all of their metamorphosis here. We give them a beginning diet of live feed and then wean them on to a pelleted feed that we distribute to them throughout their time in the program. Onsite, we raise them to

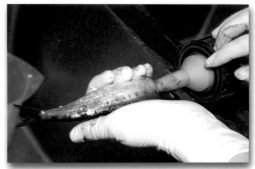
Nutritional supplements being injected into food source for adult white seabass at the HSWRI hatchery in Carlsbad.

Seabass tagging device.

a size of about three or four inches, at which time we tag every single fish with a coded wire. We move them to our growout facilities where we maintain them for another four to six months until they are about 10–12 inches long. At this point, we release them. The growout facilities are a great addition to our program because instead of releasing three or four inch [seabass] that would probably be [eaten by] lots of other mouths ... waiting to gobble them up, we get fish that are 10–12 inches long that have a better chance of surviving. They are a great benefit to our program, and they also give us a greater growout capacity. So, instead of being able to raise x amount of fish because [we only have] so much room, we [instead] have all of this extra [facility] space up and down the coast. These are all run by volunteer groups, so we are able to have this huge culture capacity without having to incur all of the costs of a full-staff operation.

SR: How do you record captured fish after they leave the fishery?

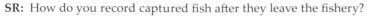

Buhr: We try to get everyone that captures a white seabass to turn in its head. Once we get the head, we can use a wand to scan it and determine if there is a tag or not. If there is a tag, we can dig that tag out of the fish and get that really important information from the tag and find out if it's one of ours. So, that's an important part on the adult side of the fish- ery. It takes a fish that we've released about three to four years at least, or maybe five years, to recruit into the adult fishery. To fill in that kind of gap, we have our own onshore gill-netting program where we target sub-adult and juvenile fish. … White seabass don't really have an affin-

Gabe Buhr holding a frozen seabass head.

ity for their release habitat like a salmon or steelhead. Instead, when we release them, they just take off and they don't send postcards! We never hear from them again, so we have to actively go out and find them on our own. It's a real important part of our program because it definitely justifies what we are doing and it lets us know that we are being successful … that our fish are out there and they are coming back.

SR: From what you've seen so far, how successful are your restocking ef- forts?

Buhr: Well, I'd like to think that they are very successful, but I also think that we are on the cusp of really finding that out. In the early years of this program no one was really doing anything with white seabass so we had to learn a lot of this on our own … on the fly. So, the first few years of the program had pretty low production. The last five years of this program we have released over 700,000 fish, so that's over two-thirds of the production in the whole history of the program. And, those fish are going to recruit into that adult fishery starting now. I think that over the next five years is when we may either make the grade—or won't—and I think things look good. We get more fish back all the time—older fish. Last year we got a fish that was released ten years ago in Santa Barbara, and it was caught offshore at the Cortez Bank 100 miles off the coast of San Diego. Our fish are out there, and they are a part of the wild fishery, which is even more important because not only are they out there, but they are out there reproducing with the wild fish. I think our restocking efforts are doing well, but to get a number on it, it's a little premature. We're going to have to watch the tags over the next few years and get a handle on where things go from there.

Noelle Morris

It was an overcast morning in December when we arrived at the Grape Street Pier on San Diego Bay to interview Noelle Morris regarding the white seabass restocking program. The pier represents one of the most successful of the white seabass growout facilities along the coast of Southern California. With the assistance of volunteers, the facility raises white seabass from the Hubbs Hatchery in Carlsbad and releases them into the Bay. Ms. Morris, runs the facility in addition to being the executive director of the San Diego Oceans Foundation (SDOF).

When met with Ms. Morris, we passed the locked gate that blocks the pier off from the general public and set up our equipment overlooking the two growout pens along the pier. Her extensive knowledge and experience helped us shape our story and her insights into the current work of the SDOF and the Hubbs-SeaWorld Research Institute (HSWRI) have helped us understand the extent of human participation on which the restocking of the white seabass depends.

Student Researcher (SR): What is the importance of the Grape Street Pier where we are today?

Noelle Morris: Today we're here at our San Diego Bay growout facility where we actually raise and release white seabass back into the wild with volunteer help. This facility is capable of holding 14,000 fish at one time and can annually re-introduce 42,000 white seabass back into the wild.

Volunteers release white seabass from Grape Street Pier into San Diego Bay on December 7, 2006.

SR: When did the restocking program start?

Morris: The program started back in 1983 through the California Department of Fish and Games' Oceans Resources Enhancement Hatchery Program (OREHP). As part of the state's OREHP program, the Hubbs-SeaWorld Research Institute built an experimental marine fish hatchery in Agua Hedionda Lagoon in Carlsbad, California in 1995. The hatchery represents a unique facility that blends mariculture with scientific research toward the goal of not only improving the depleted fishery in Southern California, but also of increasing our knowledge of the species and its life history. At the hatchery, they are breeding young white seabass

fingerlings from egg stage to a few inches long. Once the cultured white seabass reach 3 inches, they are tagged and transported to one of 15 grow-out facilities located up and down the California coastline.

Aerial view of Grape Street Pier, far right.

SR: How did the SDOF get involved with HSWRI?

Morris: The SDOF became involved with HSWRI's white seabass restocking program back in 1996. At that time, HSWRI was rearing fish at the marine fish hatchery in Carlsbad and releasing them directly into the Agua Hedionda Lagoon. Wanting to expand, HSWRI asked us to become a volunteer partner. Within a year, we designed and installed our own growout facility in Mission Bay. We expanded our program to San Diego Bay in 2003.

SR: Can you give us an overview of the things that are done at this facility?

Morris: We raise and release white seabass back into San Diego Bay. The program is managed by the San Diego Oceans Foundation completely through volunteers. These volunteers feed the fish on a daily basis while making observations about their health and activity. These data are recorded onto log sheets that help HSWRI further plan and design their program.

SR: What sort of technology is installed at this facility?

Morris: The facility utilizes solar panels, which runs four automatic feeders and two winch systems.

SR: What is the diet of white seabass at the Hatchery?

Morris: Before white seabass are transported this facility, they are weaned onto artificial pellets at the hatchery. The diet of a white seabass needs to be high in protein, so their food is infused with vitamins. This food is the best

Seabass milling about in one of the Grape Street Pier pens.

available on the market today, although many of the volunteers complain of its stinky smell! Once the fish are released into the wild, white seabass will eat crabs, sardines, shrimp … basically anything smaller than themselves.

SR: How big do the fish get before they are released?

Morris: The fish are raised in this pen for approximately three to four months or until they reach 12 inches in length. At 12 inches, we release them into the Bay. HSWRI conducts tracking studies to determine the migration patterns of the white seabass. These studies have shown that the fish are able to find their way out of the Bay and into the open ocean within three days of being released.

SR: What impact does this facility have on the San Diego community?

Morris: This white seabass restocking facility is important to the community because it successfully blends marine technology, science education, and community participation. These volunteers are helping to restore a fishery that has been depleted. They ensure that the fish are fed every day, which provides them with a sense of "connectivity" to the ocean.

SR: Are there plans to expand any of the growout facilities?

Morris: Our plans to expand the growout facilities are quickly approaching. We were just contacted by the Port of San Diego with the possibility of doubling the size of this facility so that it would be actually 40 feet by 40 feet instead of 20 feet by 20 feet, and our capacity would go from 50,000 to 100,000 fish annually.

My Buddy Chester

When I feel lonely
I like to venture outside where
I know Chester my fish
A friendly white seabass
Is always by my side

Skidding around down below
Chester's in his pool
Always going, going with the flow

He makes me giddy
When I'm down
He turns my frown upside-down.

Chester will soon leave his pool
To travel down to Mexico
Hope he doesn't get caught
Or worse

I hope he lasts longer
Than all the other fish,
And I certainly don't
Want him to end up
On someone's dinner dish

Hilary Dufour

Bob Hetzler

As our group searched for a fisherman from the glory days of white seabass, we came across Bob Hetzler, who has definitely been one of the most interesting people we've encountered in this project. After growing up in San Diego and learning the art of spearfishing from the likes of the Bottom Scratchers, a free-dive club, Mr. Hetzler worked for a number of years in the tuna industry.

Currently, Mr. Hetzler is president of HOPE (Harbour Ocean Preservation Enhancement), a tax exempt corporation that runs a white seabass grow-out facility in Huntington Beach, California. Not only is he well versed in regards to the current and past events surrounding the restoration of the white seabass, but he also has had first-hand experiences spearfishing white seabass in San Diego during his younger years.

Student Researcher (SR): When and how did you start spearfishing?

Robert Hetzler: We free dived mostly from [La Jolla's] Casa beach, [which is protected by the sea wall]. The 'Bottom Scratchers' also used the Casa as their beach to spear fish. We got to know them and learned how they were able to spear and land the huge black seabass weighing up to 500 pounds. The black seabass came to this area every year in September to spawn. We were able to purchase Bottom Scratchers' home-made spear guns with three to four surgical cords. These give the power to shoot a fish from 15 to 20 feet and still pierce the fish—such spear guns were not available at the sport shops at that time. This was about 1950.

SR: When did you start catching white seabass?

Hetzler: I used to go on the sportfishing boats when I was 14, and we would catch seabass as well as a lot of other fish. In 1950, we started to spear

white seabass with the spear guns we acquired. Up to that time, there was no spear gun that was available with the capacity to spear seabass and yellowtail [tuna].

SR: What was a typical day of spearfishing like?

Hetzler: When we started spearfishing, the wetsuit had just been developed, but we could not afford the new suits. We used our surfboards to paddle out to the outer kelp beds, tie up the board to a kelp frond, and start diving among the kelp forest. The white seabass liked to lie under the kelp fronds or, at times, would be swimming in schools among the kelp. It was beautiful diving since the kelp is like a big underwater forest. One of the key developments the Bottom Scratchers made was adding breakaway gear to their spear guns. When you spear a large white seabass, it will head for the bottom and then tangle around the kelp. While swimming, the fish will pull you underwater. The breakaway gear allowed you the line to get back up to the surface to get another breath of air [before diving down again] to remove the fish from the bottom of the kelp. We usually dove in water up to 50 feet, which is nearing the depth limit of the kelp.

SR: Can you describe a particular fishing incident?

Hetzler: In about 1957, a friend of mine [said] that he heard the white seabass were in good numbers off La Jolla. I was working for the Inter-American Tropical Tuna Commission then. We arranged to go diving after work about five in the afternoon. We used his skiff through the La Jolla Shores surf. I believe it was an "El Niño" year with quite warm water. We saw a number of schools of 50 or more white seabass swimming among the kelp. We each easily speared three fish. When we ran his boat toward the beach, we spied a large area of floating squid. We noticed big boils through the squid made by big white seabass. By now it was dark out, but the water was phosphorescent and the fish looked like torpedoes going through the water. We went home and got our rod and reels and came back to the area in his boat. We had no bait, but used only bone jigs (the metal jigs were not available then). We would jig our lure up and down, which would make a small glow. Then we would see the torpedo glow of the fish

Bob Hetzler with a freshly speared yellowtail during the glory days of spearfishing in San Diego.

head for our lure, and we would be on with [a fish of 50 pounds or more]. Hammerhead sharks got into the feeding, and at times we would only wind in the head of a fish.

SR: Did your early experience as a fisherman influence your career in the tuna industry?

Hetzler: Yes. I planned to go into marine biology or fishery biology. Actually, I started to work part-time at the Tuna Commission in my junior year in college. I was married then, and we made ends meet [through] part-time jobs and what I caught fishing. We had abalone, lobster, and all kinds of fish.

SR: Did you notice any trends in the white seabass population?

Hetzler: Yes, the prevalence of white seabass became less and less starting in the late sixties. The annual sport catch went from 50,000 to 60,000 fish to less than 2,000 fish by the late eighties. The removal of the commercial gill-net fishery in the late eighties allowed the fishery to slowly recover. It wasn't until the late nineties that the catch began to increase. Although the California Fish and Game consider the seabass fishery fully recovered, it still isn't at the level of the fifties and sixties.

SR: When did you first hear about the Ocean Resources Enhancement Hatchery Program [OREHP]?

Hetzler: The program started in the mid- to late eighties based on [the ability of the] HSWRI to spawn white seabass in the laboratory. ... OREHP is made up of a number of groups including the Department of California Fish and Game, United Anglers, San Diego Electric and recreation groups to use mitigation funds from the electric company to build a hatchery and manage the program. There are now [many] growout pens located from San Diego to Santa Barbara, including Catalina Island. Last year, the one-millionth fish was released.

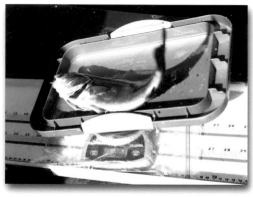

A white seabass being weighed prior to being released into the Bay.

SR: How did you get involved in the effort?

Hetzler: In the early nineties, I became a director of the United Anglers, which was trying to expand the growout pens. I was also active in two fishing clubs in Huntington Harbour. These were the Harbour Rod & Reel Club and the Huntington Harbour Anglers. I was able to get both clubs and the Bolsa Chica Conservancy (an environmental group) to put up some seed money to build a pen. That was in 1994.

SR: What do you do at HOPE (Harbour Ocean Preservation Enhancement)?

Hetzler: I am president of HOPE. I arrange for the voluntary staff to run the pen, coordinate with the hatchery for delivery, growth and release of the fish, and I'm the one that prepares the final release report showing mortality levels, feed levels and growth levels. I also have the responsibility for the pen maintenance and to have the annual tax return prepared. Lastly, I am part of the White Seabass Committee that reviews the hatchery operation, governmental permit problems and a forum for all the growout pens to compare operation difference, success, and problems.

SR: Can you describe your growout facility?

Hetzler: There are basically two types of pens. One is a fiber glass raceway 16 feet in length, eight feet wide and four-and-a-half feet deep. The other type of pen is a net pen that has a predator net outside (for seals and birds) and a smaller mesh inner net. Both seem to work equally well. ... Since our facility is some distance from the harbor entrance, our water tends to be warmer and have lower oxygen content than the other pens. Our pen showed that the seabass can survive in higher water temperatures and lower oxygen levels than thought possible. With the higher temperature, the growth rate of our fish is one of the highest of all the pens. In 2004, we had one of the first released fish returned, having grown from about ten inches to about 32 inches. The following year, we had another fish out nine years that grew to 42 inches. This was from fish we were just learning how to raise. Another interesting aspect of the hatchery-raised fish is that they are fed a pellet-type food, yet, they quickly adapt to eating live bait. We have small smelt enter our pen through the screens that cannot get out. The smelt are seen in the pen until the seabass reach about eight inches when, suddenly, the smelt disappear.

Gentle Giant

Stoic mammoth of the rocky sea
Commands respect by all does he

Deep gray flesh
with white gold
meat
Heaving a final
breath, he perishes at
the fisher's feet

But returning once more to his
watery home
Another rises once again from the tumultuous foam

Amelia Pludow

Biology of the White Seabass

The white seabass, *Atractoscion nobilis*, is a unique creature. Formerly known as *Cynoscian nobilis*, the seabass are a member of the *Sciaenidae* ("Croaker") family and are considered one of the "noble" fishes due to their size and difficulty to capture. The term "croaker" comes from

the sound males make. By vibrating their swim bladders a croaking sound is emitted that attracts mates.

These seabass have been found as far north as Juneau, Alaska and as far south as Magdalena Bay, Baja California. They spawn between April and August in shallow water. During the juvenile stage, seabass can be found near kelp beds, in bays or near sand beaches. Juvenile white seabass can be up to two feet in length and have yellow fins with between three and six darker bars on either side of their body. ("White Seabass" 2006)

The appearance of mature white seabass is striking. The scales along their back are a sharp metallic blue or gray. Their stomachs are white. Generally, there are dark specks on their bodies as well and, as they

mature, white seabass develop a dark spot at the base of their pectoral fin, which serves as an important marking point for spearfishermen to easily recognize that they are of legal size. (Eschmeyer 1999)

White seabass live in schools and are found on the bottom of the ocean in rocky areas or in the kelp beds, where they are near the top of the food chain. Mature seabass can grow to five feet in length and come to weigh 80 pounds, though in recent years seabass this large are rarely

Sardines.

seen. Their diet includes smaller fish, especially anchovies, sardines and squid. Seabass are a relatively long-lived fish, and they can survive up to 20 years in the wild. (Eschmeyer 1999)

Community—*A Nature Reflection*

As I sit here, my thoughts take me beneath the Bay's glassy surface, to the levels of life hidden from view. Contained within the Bay and its surrounding ocean are noble white seabass. Visually appealing, these huge fish can cut through the water effortlessly. However, it is for a different reason that they are prized by humans. Though they cannot see them, I know that the ubiquitous fishermen along the shore of the Bay and the fishing vessels that dot the body of water would all be pleased to find a seabass on the end of their lines. They would thrill at the fight the fish would present and would later enjoy the delicate taste of seabass meat. I assume the white seabass is gently circling somewhere beneath the water I stare at, yet, it is impossible to know for certain.

Whether you are sitting on a rock in the San Diego Boat Channel, crouching in the dirt at the Chula Vista Nature Center, or overlooking the Bay near the Grape Street Pier, the connection between the Bay and its city is always present. Although various people are constantly using this human-encroached but beautiful body of water, you can always find a sense of peace and calm here. Water swells and ripples while light shifts over its dark expanse. The Bay can be empty and uninhabited by humans, leaving you to your thoughts. Birds glide across the sparkling water appearing to fly so low as to brush it with their wings. Over the many years, numerous different species have made this place their home. San Diego Bay is a community, between the sea and the land, between human and fish.

Hilary Dufour

"Our success at The Abalone Farm hit the newspapers and within a couple of years other groups saw the promise of red abalone culture."

-David Leighton

Abalone

Over the centuries, abalone have played an important part in the diets of the people living along the coast of California. Native Americans ate abalone meat and used the abalone shells to create tools and decorations long before Europeans arrived in North America. In the mid-1800s, many Chinese arrived in San Diego and began harvesting abalone from shallow waters for shipment to China and elsewhere in the United States. However, by the early 1900s, the Chinese had moved on to other industries where they were less pressured by anti-Chinese legislation. The Japanese succeeded the Chinese, harvesting abalone in deeper waters using improved diving equipment.

The modern commercial abalone fishery in San Diego began in the mid-nineteenth century and peaked in 1957. Throughout California, about 4 million pounds of abalone were harvested annually until 1969, when a severe decline in the abalone population began. In some places, commercial abalone fisheries disappeared entirely. When wetsuits, diving equipment, privately owned boats and charter dive boats became readily available, recreational interest in diving for abalone led to a further scarcity of the animal in many places along the coast of California.

The state of the abalone population today is a cause of concern for many groups. Restoration efforts are underway to restock the abalone colonies along the Point Loma kelp beds using animals cultured in San Diego Bay under the direction of the Space and Naval Warfare Systems Center (SPAWAR). However, the commercial demand for abalone remains high, and as the still scarce wild abalone are under strict federal protection, abalone meat for sale commercially in California must be produced exclusively through farming, or imported from Mexico or the South Pacific. Only recently have abalone farms begun to produce enough to meet the commercial demand.

Geography of the
Abalone of the Bay

SPAWAR
Abalone Culture

Point Loma
Kelp Beds

For countless years, abalone have been an important resource in the Bay. However, the decline of the abalone populations in and around San Diego Bay has made it necessary for active restoration programs to take place. One such program has been taking place under the direction of the SPAWAR base in San Diego. The program works to restore abalone poulations along the Point Loma kelp beds.

History of the Abalone of the Bay

The first people known to harvest abalone along the western coast of North America were the Native Americans. Experience taught the Native Americans that unlike other shellfish that they ate, abalone could be harvested at any time during the year without posing danger from poisoning. During that time, abalone were abundant because there had been limited encroachment by humans. Native Americans could gather abalone by waiting for low tide, when they could walk out along the shore and gather up any abalone that came within reach. The primary species collected by these early inhabitants included the green and black abalone. This light harvesting most likely gave the abalone plenty of time to grow and replenish their numbers, preserving their abundance and providing the Native Americans with an almost unlimited supply of abalone. (Gallegos 1998) (Howorth 1978)

Later on, the Spaniards reached the Western Coast of North America, looking for new places to claim. They established a series of settlements and missions to substantiate their claim to the land they found. However, these new settlements did not provide enough food to ensure the settlers' survival and prosperity. Noting this, the generous Native Americans in the area showed the Spaniards how to utilize the diverse resources in the ocean, including the harvesting of abalone and other shelled creatures. The Native Americans warned the Spaniards that most of these creatures were poisonous during certain times of the year, but in spite of this counsel the Spaniards still attempted to eat the poisonous shellfish, and several Spaniards got sick and died. This bad experience caused the Spaniards to stop harvesting all shellfish, including abalone— shellfish that were safe to eat all year long. However, despite the Spanish aversion towards eating abalone, they would eventually come to be eaten once again by later generations of settlers. (Lundy 1997)

As North America began to become more developed, many immigrants journeyed to California looking for a fresh start. Among them were large numbers of Chinese. Abalone had already been a valued food commodity in China for hundreds of years, and when the immigrants discovered that there were enormous stores of untapped abalone in California waters, they wasted no time in starting their own abalone trade. The Chinese harvested abalone between the tides using metal bars to pry them from the rocks. They then stripped the shells and dried the meat, shipping much of their haul to China where the demand for abalone was high and sale of the mollusk fetched good prices. The Chinese also sold the shells of the harvested abalone to people in the United States for several cents each. (Lapota 1982)

As gathering abalone was such a sure way to make a good living, the Chinese fishermen soon established themselves in many places along the coast of California where abalone were plentiful at this time. One such area where the Chinese set up a robust abalone fishery was San Diego. There were several areas around San Diego Bay that were fished for abalone, and the city itself also served as a base for setting off for Mexico, where the fishermen could harvest large amounts of abalone and bring them back to the United States. Initially, the Mexican government allowed the Chinese free movement through their waters, but soon Mexico applied a $60 tax to any boats harvesting in Mexican waters. (Culver 1997)

The initial deceleration of the Chinese abalone industry came with the Chinese Exclusion Act in 1882, which made it much harder for the fishermen to leave the United States for Mexico or to sail anywhere. The blow that permanently destroyed the Chinese industry came in the form of the 1888 Scott Act, which made it completely illegal for the Chinese to return to the United States as citizens after fishing outside American waters, which by that time was where much of the harvest of the Chinese fishery existed.

The fall of the Chinese fishing industry paved the way for another ethnic group to take control—the Japanese. (Lundy 1997)

Since they were not yet hindered by the same crippling laws as the Chinese, the Japanese were able to take up the business with no problems. Japanese dominance over the industry brought new and improved equipment and methods for gathering abalone. Initially, the Japanese used a method known as Sake Barrel diving. They used empty sake barrels as platforms upon which they could catch their breath between dives to the bottom. This gave them a distinct advantage over old harvesting techniques since the abalone stocks were still abundant below the low-tide line. Very soon though, the Japanese started using diving suits and air pumps so that they could stay down longer and maximize their harvests. In this way, the industry gained strength until the drying of abalone became illegal in

1915, which eliminated the fishermen's main source of income and many boats went out of service. However, the lull in the demand for abalone only lasted for a short time due to new developments in their consumption in the United States. (Howorth 1978)

Ernest Doelter, nicknamed Pop Ernest, first opened his restaurant Café Ernest in Monterey, California in 1907, and it was there that he perfected his recipe for making abalone steaks. His small restaurant attracted locals and people from all around the area. His patrons included several well known California writers of the time, including Mary Austin and George Sterling. His success led him to move to San Francisco in 1914 where he introduced his abalone steaks to a local restaurant during the 1915 Panama Pacific Exhibition. The dish was wildly popular with patrons and soon upscale restaurants all over San Francisco were serving their own versions. The secret to Pop Ernest's recipe was in pounding out the abalone steak before cooking it to make sure it was soft enough to eat—taking care not to pound it too much and make the meat mushy. This recipe single-handedly helped the abalone fishery to survive in California and created a huge demand that the Japanese divers were happy to fill. The Japanese fishermen enjoyed a large increase in business up until WWII, when all of the Japanese in California were interned in camps and consequently lost their livelihoods. This loss provided another new group of people the opportunity to dominate the abalone harvesting industry. (Lapota 1982)

With the Japanese in internment camps, European Americans began to take over the abalone trade. They used the most up-to-date methods including new suits and motorized air pumps. Aside from

Red abalone epipodium (lateral foot lobe) and sensory tentacles extending below shells.

abalone harvesting many of these fishermen also harvested seaweed. The abalone fishery really took off during the 1950s when the price increased constantly and catches were above 4 million pounds per year. One innovation that helped to contribute to this success was the adoption of the "dry suit," which allowed them to dive to colder water depths and stay down longer, therefore maximizing their catches. However, just because fishermen were experiencing record abalone harvests didn't mean that the abalone populations were at healthy levels—to the contrary, abalone numbers were being depleted at a fast pace. Besides the large numbers of divers hunting for abalone, there was also the problem of roaming sea otters. Whatever the divers didn't get, the sea otters would eat. Also, around this time there was a lot of development going on up and down the coast. This construction boom led to pollution flowing into the ocean— seriously affecting the abalone's ability to reproduce.

A final blow to the abalone population was the rise of sport diving. Many people were starting to dive for recreation, and the adoption of the SCUBA system only made diving easier. Many of these sport divers knew about abalone and wanted to collect them to eat or sell to a local store. All of these factors contributed to the large decrease in abalone numbers. (Lundy 1997)

Annual Catch of California Abalone

*The colored lines on the above graph represent red, green and black abalone harvest data.
SDHS Union-Tribune Collection.*

Around this time, San Diego was a relatively insignificant port for abalone fishermen. The Bay had become so sandy that it did not support a shellfish population very well. There were only a few abalone fishermen working locally. Those with seaworthy vessels went to San Clemente Island, returning to San Diego with large amounts of abalone on a regular basis. All along the coast of California the abalone populations were being devastated. The first clear evidence of this was from the 1950s when the total catch of green abalone, which had been seriously overfished during the early 1900s, was only a small fraction of the total number of abalone caught. (Culver 1997)

The problems with the fishery stocks increased until finally in 1997 the California Department of Fish and Game decided to close the California abalone fishery to both commercial and sport divers. Even

Abalone grown at Carlsbad Aquafarm.

though many fishermen claimed that there were adequate supplies of abalone, it was evident that the abalone populations were suffering. Catches had fallen to record lows, and even though more ships were setting out to harvest abalone the total haul didn't increase, showing that there simply weren't any more to be caught. (Hobday 2000)

Some people had seen the enormous demand for abalone and realized that it could be very profitable if they could find an efficient way to farm them. The original attempts in the 1960s were hampered by the fact that they could not figure out how to get the abalone to spawn reliably. A breakthrough came in 1977 when Dr. Daniel Morse, at UC Santa Barbara, published a paper in *Science* detailing how abalone could be tricked into spawning through the addition of hydrogen peroxide to their water. This provided abalone farms the additional boost they needed to make large-scale abalone farming feasible. (Howorth 1978) (Leighton 2000) (Morse 1977)

There were plenty of other problems that the farmers ran into while trying to grow abalone. One was that it took several years for the abalone to become large enough for consumption. Another problem was that the farmers couldn't always induce the abalone larvae to start their bottom-dwelling lives. This problem was also solved by Dr. Morse when he discovered that gamma-amino butyric acid (GABA) is a key to getting abalone to settle. If given a trace of this chemical cue, the larvae would quickly swim to the bottom and start growing. Interestingly, GABA has been found in abundance in the red coralline algae—a natural food source of young juvenile abalone. The first successfully farmed abalones were produced in the 1970s. Farmed abalone is now featured in restaurants throughout California. (Lundy 1997) (Leighton 2000) (Morse 1979)

A final major problem that abalone farmers have faced is the assault of invasive species or diseases. These can devastate entire groups of abalone and cost the farmers years of work and financial losses. Researchers with funding from California Sea Grant worked between 1994 and 1999 to combat one such disease—a non-native sabellid worm that infected the shells of cultured abalone. An alternative host of the worm was identified as the black turban snail, and over a million of the species were removed from the infested area, effectively preventing the worm's establishment in the wild. (Culver 1997)

A message of hope in this molluscan tragedy comes from the restoration work done by SPAWAR Systems Center on San Diego Bay. One of their main goals is to create and maintain reproductive nodes within the outplant site. Abalone have great biotic potential due to their massive spawning events. Abalone from the Navy "farm" are housed temporarily in plastic "condos" and transported to the outplant site in insulated coolers. Recent restocking efforts have survival rates of approximately 50 percent following six months of outplanting. The approach, developed by David Lapota and others with SPAWAR, appears to be very promising. (Lapota 2006)

Abalone tanks at SPAWAR Systems Center, San Diego.

Ron Burton from Scripps Institution of Oceanography has also been working to aid in the restocking efforts. He, along with California Sea Grant Trainee Kristen Gruenthal, examined the reproductive connectivity of red and black abalone. They found that the mobility of red abalone was such that a few well-placed outplant sites could greatly contribute towards restocking this species of abalone in the wild. Black abalone, however, being less mobile, would require many smaller reserves in order to boost their native populations. (Burton 2005)

Abalone are seemingly dull creatures, but they have a lively past and an uncertain future that needs to be protected. They have been passed from one cultural group to another and their meat has been prepared in different ways by each. What started out as an obscure food only popular outside the United States has turned into one of the most expensive seafood delicacies on our menus. Many controversies over the laws regarding the collection of these valuable creatures have arisen. However, the abalone population was almost completely destroyed in a period of only 50 years

1882
Dominance over the abalone fishing industry shifts from the Chinese to the Japanese with the passage of the Chinese Exclusion Act

1700

1849
Chinese fishermen begin harvesting abalone with techniques used in China

1942
Japanese lose their jobs in the abalone industry in WWII. They are replaced by European Americans

1997
The California Department of Fish and Game closes the abalone fishery to both commercial and recreational fishing due to low abalone populations

2000

1915
Abalone steaks grow in popularity among consumers

1977
Dr. Daniel Morse discovers how to make abalone spawn with force, allowing aquafarmers to increase their populations

MUSSELS CLAMS OYSTERS
CARLSBAD
AQUAFARM
Grown in the pristine waters
of the Rancho Agua Lagoon
San Diego, California
ABALONE RED SEAWEED

David Lapota

David Lapota is a biologist and oceanographer working for Space and Naval Warfare (SPAWAR) Systems Center, San Diego. Dr. Lapota has worked with abalone since 1977. Among his many findings, he has studied the effects of environmental parameters upon abalone population growth. Dr. Lapota was also involved in helping a Taiwan-based abalone growing company, which hoped to become established in Carlsbad.

When we interviewed Dr. Lapota, we were surprised and pleased by the range of scientific insight he could provide. His understanding of the environmental factors that help produce a thriving abalone population have paved the way for abalone farms. These farms might one day provide a commercial supply of abalone and provide a basis for their repopulation in the wild.

Student Researcher (SR): What do you think is the single largest danger to the abalone population today?

David Lapota: Man's poaching of the remaining abalone populations.

SR: What impact has the lack of abalone had on the environment?

Lapota: The depletion of abalone has decreased biodiversity within coastal areas.

SR: Have you been involved in any abalone farming projects? What was your job?

Lapota: I was involved in a Hubbs-SeaWorld Research Institute project for temperature studies. I was also involved, in a limited function, in trying to help a Taiwan-based company become established in Carlsbad growing abalone. This was a two-year project from 1978–1980. We changed the zoning in Agua Hedionda Lagoon to allow for aquaculture activities. I was actually a [point of contact] for local agencies dealing with the company, [California Aquaculture]. However, the Taiwan-based company left because of stringent water quality discharge standards.

SR: What are the ideal conditions for growing abalone?

Lapota: Temperature and availability to appropriate supplies of algae is paramount to any success. For red abalone, seawater temperature should be about 16–18°C. Green [abalone] can handle temperatures up to 21°C. The Laminaria-type kelps provide superior food for sustained growth, although Macrocystis is more readily available.

SR: What is the biggest danger abalone face once they are transplanted into the wild?

Lapota: Finding a suitable place to call home, [that is] not too exposed to [predators such as] crabs and octopi, yet [leaves them] able to snare drift kelp floating by. Snoopy sport divers are also a hazard and hard to control even though a ban [on abalone fishing] is in effect.

SR: Is San Diego an ideal place to grow abalone?

Lapota: San Diego is certainly an ideal place because of the physical environment. San Clemente Island would also provide a good habitat for growing populations. I believe there are too many stresses up in the Los Angeles area for outplanting activities to be successful.

SR: Is your abalone project successful?

Lapota: We are considered a "clean" facility within the state, [meaning] that we can engage in outplanting. … Just recently, we have had good survival among the abalones four inches in size that we outplanted eight months ago. Divers counted [a survival rate of] more than 50 percent, which is very good.

SR: What is the U.S. Navy's role in your restoration project?

Lapota: The U.S. Navy has been instrumental in permitting us to establish this project within the laboratory's role of environmental science. They recognize that the Navy can be a good steward of the marine environment.

SR: Do you believe that the California Department of Fish and Game should allow both a sport fishery and a commercial fishery at the same time?

Lapota: No, I think it would be a poor idea. Let's try to restore the resource first—*then* we can begin to think about that. I *do* think the only abalone re-

Outplanted green abalone in cinder block refuge system.

source for a fishery will be from land-based private-owned abalone farms. Coastal farming (in situ) is difficult to protect, and marine waters can be polluted only a few times of the year to kill your growing herd.

SR: Will commercial fishing of abalone be possible anytime soon off San Diego's shores?

Lapota: The fishery is gone and will remain so for decades.

SR: How important to the restoration of the abalone population is awareness or ignorance?

Lapota: I believe if people realized just how long it takes for an abalone to reach legal size (seven to nine years), it just may make them think a little longer about removing every abalone they see in our coastal waters. Even for the best-run farms, it takes approximately four years to rear a four inch red abalone for export overseas.

Steve Le Page

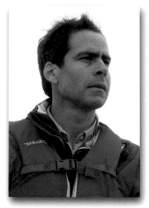

We drove up the coast to Carlsbad Aquafarm to conduct an interview with Steve Le Page. It was pouring rain—which actually seemed rather fitting as we were visiting an "aqua" farm. Once we'd arrived, we were first given a tour to see the complete operation of mussel culture and harvest then we conducted our interviews. Mr. Le Page provided us with lots of information on mussel and abalone farming methods and techniques. He has an M.S. in biology and is the principal investigator representing Carlsbad Aquafarm, Inc. in a study of fecal coliform pollution in local San Diego lagoons. Mr. Le Page is also a research biologist for the reestablishment of abalone (*Haliotis*) into the Point Loma area. We were excited to learning more about the farming of abalone from such a knowledgeable person.

Student Researcher (SR): Can you describe the life cycle of an abalone in captivity?

Steve Le Page: Well, the life cycle of abalone in captivity versus the life cycle of abalone in the wild is about the same, [except] instead of being free floating in the ocean, we keep them in tanks. Generally, their life cycle starts off [with them] as little planktonic larvae. During this [stage of their development], they're growing and getting ready to metamorphose and change into juvenile abalone, and they settle out onto the substrate or rocks or on the side of the tank. From there, the juvenile abalone are fed kelp and seaweed—different types of seaweed—and they grow up into adults. [After two years] they become reproductively viable, and we can spawn them and start the cycle all over again.

SR: What stage of their development is the most problematic?

Le Page: The [post-larvae] form. When they're in [the post-larval stage], they require a lot of intensive care. They need to be fed all the time and we need to watch out for any sort of bacterial contamination that might be in the water, so that's where we experience the greatest amount of mortality.

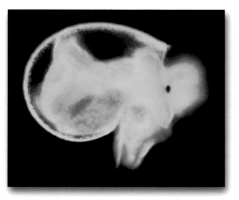

Planktonic veliger (larva) of red abalone.

SR: Do you believe that the first aim of aquafarms should be to replenish the natural population of abalone?

Le Page: Well, there are two aspects to [abalone] aquaculture. One, of course, is to provide the marketplace with a food product. The other is to help take the pressure off the natural environment. The biggest thing that we have is by supplying the food market with abalone we [satisfy somewhat the demand and reduce] the pressure on the fisheries. The current status of the abalone fishery is that it is closed. So, as of right now, the only way

An abalone tank at Carlsbad Aquafarm.

you can get abalone is through an aquaculture facility [or by importing wild abalone from another country]. There is no pressure on the environment. The reason why there is no fishery is because the population in the natural environment has been depleted to such low levels. ... If we could, it would be great to be able to start restocking the natural environment.

SR: Once the abalone are transplanted into the wild, what is the biggest danger they would face?

Le Page: Predation is the biggest danger that they would face. This comes in many forms—all the way from other types of larger invertebrates ... to fish.

SR: How long do you think it will be before the abalone numbers are large enough to sustain harvesting?

Le Page: That's a million dollar question right there. The sustainability of our ocean is dependent on so many different factors, one is the fisheries; another is disease. Currently, there are two potential diseases that are still in the abalone population. One is called the withering foot disease—the foot being what abalone use to hold onto the rocks. This disease weakens the foot and makes [the abalone] very susceptible to predation. Another one is a sabellid worm that infests [their shells]. It makes it hard for them to grow, and [will also] eventually kill them. So, we've got two hurdles to get over. First of all, we have to be able to make sure the disease isn't in our environment anymore. [Second, we need to] be able to get enough abalone back out there for the natural population to replenish itself. We could be 15–20 years off.

SR: Do you believe that they should allow a sports fishery and a commercial fishery at the same time?

Le Page: Sportfishing and commercial fishing pressure on the abalone population can be handled if the numbers are great enough. Obviously, sport fishermen would take far fewer abalone than a commercial fisherman, so you would almost expect that the California Fish and Game [Commission] would open up sportfishing before they would open up commercial fishing. But really, it's a numbers game. As long as the number [of abalone can] sustain the fisheries, be they both commercial and sport, [it could] make sense to open it up to both. But if the numbers can't support it, then you can't do that.

SR: Do you think any commercial fishing will be possible anytime soon off the San Diego coast?

Le Page: Well, again, it all depends on how we're going to be dealing with the disease issues and the numbers [issue]. These animals are relatively slow growing, so we might be able to open it up sometime in the near future, but I personally feel we're still 10–15 years off—if it ever gets reopened at all.

Hidden Treasure

Tucked away
Within a tiny crack
Or lying atop a small rock
There lies a hidden treasure
Who few seem to mock
What is this treasure? you may wonder
Your thoughts cast asunder
Well, some people refer to it as the "Jewel of the Sea"
Others know it simply as the shell of an abalone
It leaves many filled with astonishment and awe
But with its iridescent crimsons, blues and greens
It can be no surprise that the abalone
Is the hidden treasure of the sea

Brooke Castro

David Leighton

We read about the pioneering work of David Leighton on abalone farming along the Pacific Coast, and his work led us to seek him out so that we could hear for ourselves the challenges and successes of abalone aquaculture. After developing culture methods for red abalone at The Abalone Farm in Cayucos, California, Dr. Leighton came back to La Jolla for a postdoctoral position and continued to work with abalone—chiefly with the warm-water tolerant and faster-growing green abalone, *Haliotis fulgens*. Dr. Leighton's research has been conducted with funding from the California Sea Grant College Program, the Ocean Studies Institute, World Research, Inc. and as an adjunct professor at San Diego State University (SDSU). We contacted him for our interview at the SDSU Marine Lab established at Agua Hedionda Lagoon.

Student Researcher (SR): How did you first get started in the field?

David Leighton: As I neared the last steps in my doctoral program I was joined by two others (nonbiologists) to start The Abalone Farm in Cayucos. This was quite a challenge since it was the first attempt to grow abalone to adult sizes in tanks on land! Even in Japan, where abalone seed production had been in progress for about ten years, no group had completed the life cycle in captivity.

A friend of mine, Buzz Owen had successfully spawned abalone and reared their young to about one to two inches in an oyster hatchery at Pigeon Point, near San Francisco, beginning in 1965. He was eventually able to spawn most of the California abalone species. In addition to recording the natural occurrence of abalone hybrids, he crossed many of them in the lab. He was the first to show hybrid abalone could be produced artificially. We at the abalone farm built a seawater system and hatchery with homemade tanks, but little progress was made culturing red abalone until later that first year (1968). [At the end of the year we] had about 60 baby abs! The next year it was quite different. We had thousands. Our successes hit the news-papers and within a couple of years

A green and red hybrid abalone grown at Carlsbad Aquafarm.

other groups, including the California Fish and Game, saw the promise of

red abalone culture. By 1980, about ten "abalone farms" were registered in the state.

SR: What do you think is the single largest danger to the abalone population today?

Leighton: Regarding natural abalone resources, throughout most of the world where abalone exist and have been fished, populations are showing marked declines. The principal cause of decline has been over-fishing. There are many other factors, however, that dictate the success or failure of abalone populations. First, few had realized abalones grow slowly, and as relatively sedentary organisms living on limited areas of rocky substrate, they were easily picked off. There are many natural predators that limit abalone abundances, but now disease has been recognized as a factor. Mass mortalities in abalone populations were unknown a couple of decades ago. Abalone were thought to have effective natural defense mechanisms against bacteria and other pathogens. Since about 1980, diseases of several forms have stricken abalone populations in many parts of the world. Habitat alteration and pollution are also part of the complex equation.

SR: What are the largest difficulties in farming abalone and how can these problems be overcome?

Leighton: Abalone culture, regardless of the species and part of the world involved, would appear to be an inefficient process. The greatest mortality rate is experienced during a brief post-set period when the larvae have settled, begun to metamorphose, and are about two to eight weeks old. Seldom do more than about 5 percent of settling post-larvae survive to advanced juvenile stages (about one centimeter). … Juveniles [more than] one centimeter are entirely vigorous and will continue to grow if given appropriate care. I should add that post-larval attrition in culture is a common observation, whether it be a clam, mussel, oyster, scallop or abalone. So, aquaculturists compensate by stacking the numbers in favor of mass culture. Abalone may produce millions of larvae.

SR: What types of resources does it take to start an abalone farm?

Leighton: We started when permits were not a problem for either construction along the seashore or the activity of our farm. Now perhaps funding and permitting costs are the greatest obstacles. For abalone, food—[such as] fresh kelp or costly artificial food—is necessary. There is a period of two to five years before first harvest after beginning operations. But for a fruit orchard, you have to expect a few years of tree growth before any significant harvest, right? So, patience, care and money are the three basic requirements.

SR: Do you believe that the aim of these farms should be to first replenish the natural population, and only then supply restaurants? Or vice versa?

Leighton: Efforts to seed abalone for the benefit of ecology, or for the fishery, would have to be funded by the government or, say, a fishery association. The private sector is interested in controlled crop production for near term promise and long-term profits.

SR: Once abalones are transplanted into the wild, what is the biggest danger they face?

Leighton: As some naive investigators have found, juvenile abalone can't just be spread on the

Juvenile green abalone with the green shells produced after they are fed Egregia.

bottom. Predators make quick work of tender juvenile abalone. They must be housed in some sort of protective shelter until they are acclimatized. One day is sufficient, generally. ... Juvenile abalone, if mistreated in transit from hatchery to release site, release compounds attractive to crabs, starfish, lobster, octopus and finfish.

It may take another decade for the greater portion of the abalone populations to return by natural processes. Years ago I developed the liming method to control sea urchins in potential kelp bed areas. Abalone had essentially disappeared off Point Loma in the early 1960s, but when we spread lime and removed the bulk of the urchins, the kelp came back vigorously, and larval recruitment of red and pink abalones was highly successful. This was done in 1963–1964; tiny red abalone were again abundant and growing rapidly by 1965. Many reached seven inches by 1970—that's fast growth for red abalone. With that experience, we can be a bit more hopeful that, under the right circumstances, a fishery could recover within a decade. Ideally, since adult red abalone may reproduce at an early age of five years or so, and more productively in succeeding years, perhaps 15 years is a reasonable time to expect the population will be self-sustaining.

Howard Stacklin

Howard Stacklin's career with the U.S. Navy led him to live in many different locations around the world. One such location was Japan, where he first became interested in diving for abalone. Upon his return to the United States in the 1950s, he became an avid abalone diver. At this time, the abalone populations in and around San Diego Bay were still bountiful, and the abalone fisheries open to the public.

As students researching San Diego Bay's abalone restoration program, we knew that Mr. Stacklin's experiences would give much needed insight and information on abalone diving and the decline of the abalone population. We sought out an interview with Mr. Stacklin, and when we arrived at his home, we found him well versed in abalone matters, including the current restoration efforts and other events concerning abalone. In addition, we found his memory of his past personal experiences while diving for abalone to be impeccable.

Student Researcher (SR): Could you tell us a little about yourself?

Howard Stacklin: As far as diving goes … along the coast of San Diego County [my diving buddy and I] went looking for abalone when it was in season. … You would find [abalone at] various depths, between 30–50 feet of water, and maybe [between rocks] at low tide. To take an abalone, a person was required to have some type of [measuring] device [typically a tool called an "ab iron"] for removing it from the rocks. When you did that, you were required to measure the abalone to make sure that it was properly sized for the [species] of abalone that it was.

After that, we would go ahead and use the measuring device [ab iron] to pry the abalone from the rock face. Then we would take it home and start processing it, using the [ab iron] to help pry the abalone out of its shell. Or we could use a very stiff knife. Once you got the abalone out of its shell, you could go ahead and clean it off and trim some of the edges of the abalone and prepare it by cutting very thin slices, or thicker slices for tenderizing. In that case, you could fry it to cook it up. A lot of abalone meat by itself is tough and chewy. The abalone today is very expensive.

SR: What would you compare the taste to?

Stacklin: Maybe squid is the closest thing. You have to tenderize [the abalone meat].

SR: You said that when you came back to the United States you started diving for abalone. When did you come back to the United States and where in San Diego did you dive for abalone?

Stacklin: We arrived in San Diego about March 1957. Back then we would go just about every weekend to look for abalone. We had our air tanks and we could dive down for an hour. After that we would go down with snorkels. You have to make sure that when you go down to get abalone [they are in season]. … Police would look through their binoculars and catch [people who dove illegally] and arrest them. At that time there were quite a few abalone in various sizes. You could easily get your limit. When you dove down with snorkel you could get about three. I would put them under my wetsuit. Once, I dropped one but put the other two in my float. Then, I went back down to get the other one, and I saw something shooting through the water … the abalone was getting thrown around, [but] then I noticed that it was an eel that was trying to get the abalone. I had no argument with that. I could have done without.

A Life Worth Living

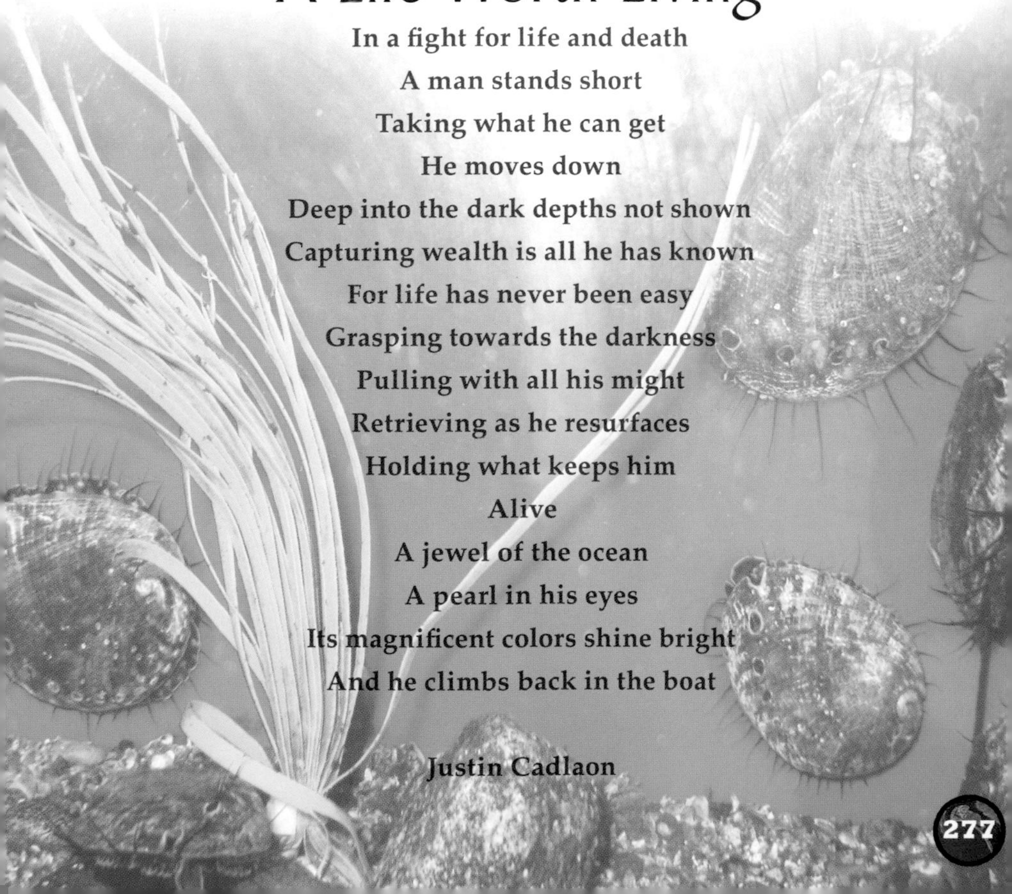

In a fight for life and death

A man stands short

Taking what he can get

He moves down

Deep into the dark depths not shown

Capturing wealth is all he has known

For life has never been easy

Grasping towards the darkness

Pulling with all his might

Retrieving as he resurfaces

Holding what keeps him

Alive

A jewel of the ocean

A pearl in his eyes

Its magnificent colors shine bright

And he climbs back in the boat

Justin Cadlaon

Abalone Biology

Abalone are relatively slow-moving mollusks that look like flattened, snail-like creatures, and are capable of growing to nearly the size of a dinner plate. As adults they may be restricted to a single reef or kelp bed, yet their microscopic larvae are planktonic and capable of traveling great distances during a seven- to ten-day odyssey drifting on the currents. The larval stage of abalone is somewhat distinct since they are lecithotrophic (yolk feeding). After approximately a week, they metamorphose into juvenile form. The metamorphosis can be induced in a laboratory setting by exposing the larva to extracts from red coralline algae or the mucus tracks of adult abalone. Mature abalone are partial to living in crevices and under rocks, making it hard for their predators to spot them. Their shells have respiratory pores, and they possess a suction foot to grip onto rocks with such force that at times their predators, humans included, are unable to pry them off. (Hahn 1989) (Morris 1980)

Abalone belong to the family Haliotidae and the genus *Haliotis*, which means "sea ear," referring to the flattened shape of abalone shells. There are a total of 100 to 130 different species, including hybrids, of *Haliotis* worldwide. Red abalone, green abalone, pink abalone, and black abalone are four common abalone types that thrive in the waters around San Diego Bay. (Hahn 1989) (Morris 1980)

Red Abalone
Haliotis rufescens

Red abalone have traditionally been the most popular and commercially important of all the abalone species in California. They can be found in the low intertidal zone where there are rocky headlands and promontories with heavy surf. Red abalone can grow up to 30 cm. They flourish in depths between 6 and 17 m, though they can still be found offshore in depths of over 180 m. They prefer to live in water with temperatures ranging from 7–16º C. (Hahn 1989) (Morris 1980)

The outer surface of red abalone shells are red, and often the inside edge of their shells are red as well. Their shell exteriors are rough, and have shell holes that are oval with raised rims. Three or four of the shell holes usually remain open. The interior of their shells are iridescent and smooth, and their foot areas are black, while the sole of the foot ranges from tan to grey. The surfaces of their epipodia (i.e., the lateral lobes of their foot) are smooth and broadly scalloped along the edge. (Hahn 1989) (Morris 1980)

Green Abalone
Haliotis fulgens

Green abalone are usually found in rocky areas, at a low intertidal zone up to 10 m in depth. Near depths of 18 m the green abalone population becomes scarce. On the other hand, green abalone are plentiful at 2–3 m, where they hide in deep crevices and are exposed to strong waves. Green abalone are often found in crevices where algae cover is dense, for they feed exclusively on large, drifting algae. They can grow to be about 25 cm in length, but they are usually less than 20 cm. Adult green abalone are relatively sedentary, though they move about somewhat more than pink and red abalone. (Hahn 1989) (Morris 1980)

Their tentacles are olive-green, and their shell exteriors are also olive-green—often with fine spiral ribs. Their shell holes are circular and slightly elevated. Five to seven of these shell holes usually remain open. The interior of green abalone shells are iridescent and range in color from dark green and blue to lavender and copper, with a gleaming muscle scar. When compared to other California abalone, green abalone are considered to have the most beautiful shell. The epipodia of green abalone are a mottled cream and brown, with tubercles scattered on their surface and a

frilly edge. (Hahn 1989) (Morris 1980)

Pink Abalone
Haliotis corrugata

Pink abalone are uncommon in the low intertidal zone, and are mostly located on rock surfaces from 6–60 m in depth. They usually range from 15–17 cm in length, but can reach 25 cm. Pink abalone occupy more sheltered waters than green abalone, and they seldom settle or thrive in waters cooler than 14° C. They feed on pieces of drifting algae that they capture with their foot. (Hahn 1989) (Morris 1980)

Their shells are round, usually with a greenish and reddish brown scalloped margin, and irregular diagonal rows of wavy corrugations. Their shell holes have raised rims and two to four remain open. Their shell interiors are strikingly iridescent and mainly pink and green in color. Their tentacles are black while their foot ranges from yellow to light orange. They have a mottled black and white epipodium with many tubercles on the surface and a lacy edge.

Black Abalone
Haliotis cracherodii

Out of all the species of local abalone, black abalone live the closest to shore. They are not a preferred food due to their dark meat color and inferior flavor, but black abalone were a prime yield for the Chinese fishermen who harvested them in the intertidal waters of San Diego and Southern California. Black abalone are usually found living under large rocks or hiding in crevices—crowded together and sometimes stacked two to three animals high. They are most abundant intertidally, though some are located in depths of up to 6 m, preferring water temperatures in the 7–24° C range. Like all abalone, black abalone graze on kelp and other seaweeds. However, unlike other abalone species, they sometimes graze on algae from the shells of other organisms, since the intertidal zone they inhabit often lacks seaweed. Smaller black abalone feed on diatom films and coralline algae and larger ones graze on loose pieces of algae. (Hahn 1989) (Morris 1980)

The maximum length of their shells is around 20 cm. The exterior is smooth and can be dark blue, dark green, or nearly black in color. The outer dark edge of their shells extends beyond the nacreous (iridescent) area and forms a narrow dark band when seen from below. The shell holes of black abalone have rims, but are not elevated above the surface of their shell. Five to seven shell holes usually remain open. The interior of black abalone shells are pearly, with pink and green iridescence. Their tentacles are black. Black abalone have black and smooth epipodia. Their shells usually lack encrusting marine growth. (Hahn 1989) (Morris 1980)

The Shell—*A Nature Reflection*

The interior of the shell gleams with a polished sheen, and its iridescence causes it to change colors as it is tilted from side to side. Looking into the abalone shell while feeling its rough exterior reminds me of all the things we have learned about abalone. Only a short while ago, I knew next to nothing; but now I am a veritable abalone encyclopedia. As I look into the shell, I begin to imagine what it must have been like in the early days of abalone harvesting around San Diego.

The Chinese fishermen, for example, would probably wake up early in the morning, long before sunrise, to gather abalone in the San Diego Bay or outside its shores even down to the Mexican waters. I imagine that when they return, they'll go through the long, arduous process of drying the abalone meat. Undoubtedly, the smell would permeate the area nearby. Then they would probably ship the processed abalone back home to China.

I find myself continuing to look at the opalescent hues of the shiny shell, and suddenly in my mind the reign of the Chinese fishermen over the abalone industry in San Diego ends, and the Japanese take over with the abalone harvesting using their more sophisticated equipment. I can even imagine a Japanese boat floating in tranquil waters, waiting to be loaded down with freshly caught abalone. Suddenly, a loud splash upsets the calm water around the boat. The instigator, a Japanese abalone diver, sinks quickly to the ocean floor and begins to pry some of the plentiful abalone off the nearby rocks. Above the diver, his partner pumps air to him through tubes to keep him alive. I can picture the diver's feeling of satisfaction as he gathers the abalone, thinking of all the money they will bring to his loved ones.

However, upon the onset of World War II, I am reminded that the Japanese were forced into internment camps and the Americans rapidly came to dominate the abalone industry. Their numerous fishing boats scour the ocean for the shelled delicacy that they find makes them more money by the day. Once again, I steal a quick glance into the shell I hold in my hand, and am reminded of the mouthwatering smell an abalone exudes as it is being served in restaurants and homes.

Yet, as I flip the abalone shell over in my hand and turn my sight away from its iridescence to the tough exterior of the shell, I find myself envisioning the disbelief of the Twentieth Century abalone harvester as they are told that they have been destroying the very source of their livelihood. Some of them become angry when they learn that they aren't allowed to harvest abalone any more, but many others realize that it is necessary if there are to be any abalone left at all.

In my hand I hold only one small abalone shell. However, it is through this shell that I can perceive the multifaceted history of abalone harvesting here in San Diego Bay and in our local waters.

Brooke Castro

"We use mussels as a key species to mark the general health of our waters."
                              -Bonnie J. Becker

Mussels

Mussels live in sheltered bays and intertidal areas along coasts around the world. They are sophisticated bivalves that supply wildlife and humans alike with a nutritious source of protein. Along San Diego Bay, the bay mussel (*Mytilus galloprovincialis*) is among the most common shellfish. These mussels attach themselves to any surface that will support their unique lifestyle, and they can be seen clinging to cliffs, piers and all sorts of rocky surfaces.

In 1990, about 30 miles north of the Bay, Carlsbad Aquafarm set up a successful commercial model for domestication and farming of mussels. This operation takes advantage of the sheltered Agua Hedionda Lagoon to cultivate mussels for public consumption. There are locations along San Diego Bay that also hold potential for mussel farming. Unfortunately, although significant successes have been made in cleaning up the Bay, the San Diego County Department of Environmental Health still posts warnings regarding the consumption of shellfish from the Bay. However, should the ongoing clean-up efforts continue, it might be possible to establish productive mussel aquaculture right here in San Diego Bay.

Geography of the Mussels of the Bay

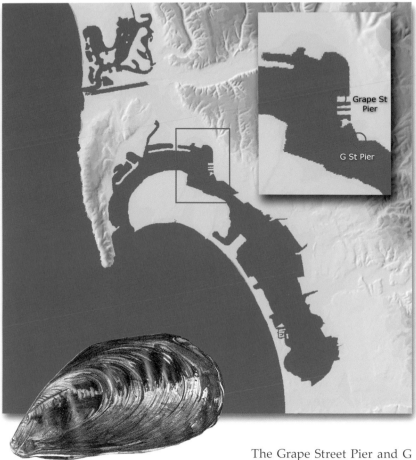

Grape St Pier

G St Pier

The Grape Street Pier and G Street Pier are both locations in downtown San Diego along San Diego Bay where mussels are raised as indicators of the Bay's health. The number and size of the mussels grown from the two sites paints a picture of how close the Bay is to being capable of supporting a mussel farming industry.

History of Mussels on the Bay

The bay mussel (*Mytilus galloprovincialis*) is one of the most common marine mollusks on the U.S. West Coast. It performs many important tasks and is vital to the ecology of the enclosed bays and protected shorelines.

 The bay mussel is also nutritious and good to eat, and its sedentary lifestyle makes it very easy to farm. Although mussel aquaculture is highly profitable, the spread of mussel farming is greatly hindered by the lack of unpolluted bays in which to establish a farm. San Diego Bay, with its calm and chilly waters, is potentially a perfect location for mussel aquaculture. However, the growth of mussels for consumption is not possible at this time despite the efforts of many local agencies to reduce pollution. By looking into the past, it is possible for us to uncover the reasons for the Bay's pollution, and how this came to affect its mussel population. (Korringa 1976)

In San Diego, the first people to consume mussels were the San Dieguito Native Americans, who harvested them from the Bay as early as 7500 BCE. Lacking any domestic animals such as cows or pigs, mussels were an important source of dietary protein for these earliest inhabitants. Later on, when the Kumeyaay natives replaced the San Dieguito Native Americans, they continued the trend of harvesting and consuming mussels—right up until the arrival of the Spanish missionaries in 1769. The missionaries founded their first mission on Presidio Hill, fairly close to the Bay and overlooking modern-day Mission Valley. Padre Junípero Serra reported that the missionaries consumed bay mussels that were given to them by the local natives. "They brought fish and mollusks to us, going out in their canoes just to fish for our benefit." (Dario 1964)

Despite such cordial beginnings, relations between the Spaniards and Native Americans eventually soured and armed conflict took place. The Spaniards had an advantage because of their guns and horses, plus the introduction of European diseases that resulted in many Native American deaths. The Kumeyaay moved inland, away from San Diego and the Bay, marking the end of the consumption of mussels by Native Americans. (James 1905)

On the other hand, the victorious Spaniards continued to consume local mussels until 1821, when Mexico won its independence from Spain and San Diego came under Mexican rule. Over the next quarter century little changed, until after the 1846–1848 Mexican-American War, when San Diego became part of the United States. The new influx of Americans into San Diego following this change in ownership drastically altered the way San Diego and its Bay were used. (James 1905)

From written records, we can attest that the Americans—like the Spaniards and Native Americans before them—collected and consumed mussels, which became an important part of life. Occasionally it was made into a social event, recollected with nostalgia in the memoirs of San Diegans: "The big fun was the mussel boil" (Stewart p. 47). The Americans had no qualms about consuming mussels. "After the mussels were well boiled, they would open, the water would be poured off, and the mussels passed around to the sitting picnickers" (Stewart p. 48). This consumption of mussels continued until the fateful year of 1888. (Stewart 1965)

San Diego was home to multiple ethnicities that, for the most part, learned to accept one another. Under this social setting, and with the onset of fresh economic opportunity, the number of local inhabitants gradually began to increase. "The population of San Diego in 1870 including Old Town, was approximately 2,300 and in 1880 it was ... slightly over 2,600" (Stewart p. 5). The arrival of many immigrants, merchants and travelers caused massive destructive changes in San Diego, as the sudden influx of people created a new set of environmental problems. In 1888, the San Diego City Council created a sewer system that brought with it as many problems

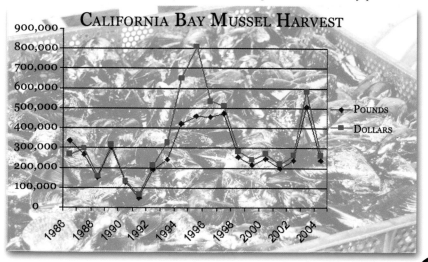

CALIFORNIA BAY MUSSEL HARVEST

as it solved. "When the city sewer system was originally installed in 1888, fish [abounded] … [but later] chlorines, detergents, and other disinfectants [were passed through the sewage system]" (Stewart p. 120). The system discharged millions of gallons of raw sewage containing dangerous heavy metals and chemicals, lead and chlorine that made the consumption of mussels and most marine life in San Diego Bay dangerous. "The odors at times were almost unbearable … For a distance of a quarter to half a mile from the Bay" (Kelly p. 1). San Diego Bay has yet to fully recover from the construction of the sewage system, even though its outfall was moved to discharge off Point Loma in 1963. (Kelly 1888) (Stewart 1965)

To this day, the Port of San Diego will not allow the Bay to be used for aquaculture because of the pollution. Even so, wild mussels still grow in the Bay and serve as natural biological indicators of its health. Mussels are filter feeders, and when they filter the Bay's water for food, they inadvertently collect impurities from the water as well—especially heavy metals and chemicals. The State Mussel Watch Program developed by NOAA's Center for Coastal Monitoring and Assessment has been monitoring chemical contaminants in mussels since 1986. This program collects mussels from more than 200 sites in the United States, including San Diego. The

program has concluded that: in the future, with the right resources and proper implementation, certain sections of the Bay could be used for mussel aquaculture similar to the Carlsbad operation. (Korringa 1976)

Though current global focus lies elsewhere, it is still necessary to continue using what resources we have available. Developing nations with huge populations to feed, show a need for aquaculture, because ever-shrinking ocean fisheries cannot meet demand. Aquaculture could feed the masses without tying up valuable land or destroying the environment.

Though salmon, oyster and bass currently hold a large portion of the aquaculture market, mussel aquaculture will have a place. Mussels will no longer be a meal affordable only to the rich and will become a source of food for many people around the world. China, in its bid for self-sufficiency, has become the largest world producer of various mussel species (more than 400,000 metric tons annually) used mainly to feed its own people. Already, the Chinese are feeling the advantages of diversifying their diet: they are more robust, healthier and happier. It has been found that societies with less malnutrition have stronger economies, more efficient workforces, commit fewer crimes and have superior armed forces. (Korringa 1976) (Trevelyan 1991)

Mussel aquaculture enjoys several advantages over traditional farming and fish aquaculture. Mussel farmers don't have to worry about droughts, wars, locusts, predators or fires affecting their harvests, for their mussels are raised in stable environments. The only weak spot for mussel cultivation is  finding locations with good water quality; something which is especially difficult in California. Regardless, some aspiring and innovative mussel farmers like John Davis of Carlsbad Aquafarm have refused to be hampered by technicalities. The Carlsbad Aquafarm, for example, uses a "depuration" system to clean their mussels. After harvest, Davis' mussels soak in tanks for as long as 48 hours in purified water to purge their tissues of any impurities. Davis thinks the cost of the depuration system is warranted because "the last thing in the world I want is for someone to get sick from my product." (Davis 2006) (O'Connor 1995) (Trevelyan 1991)

In order for a mussel aquaculture venture to be successful, three important factors must be considered: their diet, their growth rate and the ease of their collection. Diet is a very important factor—especially when cost is considered. However, the efficient siphoning of plankton for food is not a major issue in areas with incoming tides or in controlled environments, as these waters contain all the plankton the mussels require.

Additionally, the growth rate of the bay mussel is fast, taking only about 12 to 14 months to reach market quality. Bay mussels are also easily harvested and will grow on any hard surface. This includes ropes, which can be pulled up, and their mussels removed and sold. (Diamond 1999) (Korringa 1976)

Locally, mussels are important in California because of the positive effect they have on the economy. Around 500,000 pounds of farmed California mussels are sold each year at the average price of $1.75 per pound, providing a return of $875,000. Although the California mussel industry is expanding, if production is not stepped up, New England, Spanish, Chilean and Chinese mussel farmers can and will out-compete West Coast companies through mass production and low prices.

Mussels growing on ropes at Carlsbad Aquafarm.

Currently, mussels sell for 90 cents per pound on the East Coast. (Trevelyan 1991)

While mass expansion of California mussel aquaculture might lead to oversupply and dramatic price drops, with the right marketing and support from the Food and Agriculture Organization of the United Nations, such oversupply could open new markets in protein-deprived developing countries. The diets of Africans and Asians could be supplemented by low-cost, tasty, and nourishing mussels. Eventually, cities that seek tax revenues from aquaculture farming would be forced to clean up their bays and inlets. (Trevelyan 1991)

Although restoring San Diego Bay to its pre-1888 state is impossible, the possibility of sectioning off certain areas of the Bay for commercial mussel aquaculture is not. If prospective areas are kept away from pollutants and given enough water flow, it is possible that San Diegans may once again be able to eat native bay mussels. (O'Connor 1995)

Dinner

I wonder what will be served for a meal

Will it be whale? Will it be shark? Will it be seal?

I sit and wait impatiently, nothing else to do

I notice as I've been sitting my hunger grew

I see him, dressed in white and as perfect as can be

"Hooray" I shout, it's the waiter coming to serve me

Bowl in his hands; can't tell what's inside

I know it will be scrumptious and take my taste buds for a ride

He sets the bowl in front of me and away he hustles

I look down, and to my dismay, a bowl filled with mussels!

My heart sinks, my eyes well up with tears, drop upon my food

I stare in utter disbelief; to the mussels my eyes are glued

Of all the things they could've served, why'd they have to pick this one?

They're slimy, salty, black and smell, and have just ruined all my fun

Then an idea comes rushing to my head, and cheers me up a bit

It has to do with the candle on my table—for it is lit

I take the mussels in the bowl, and heat them over the flame

I know that thankfully, once they're cooked, they will never taste the same

Once they're done, I take a bite, and to my surprise …

They still taste as horrible as can be and bring tears to my eyes

Celeste Byers

1769 CE
Missionaries'
meals include
mussels from
the Bay

7500 BCE
(Before Common Era)

7500 BCE
Native Americans at Ballast
Point incorporate mussels
into their diet

1888 CE
San Diego installs a sewer system that pollutes San Diego Bay, causing the consumption of locally grown mussels to cease

2000
(Common Era)

1990 CE
Carlsbad Aquafarm, a shellfish aquaculture business, is established

1850 CE
"Mussel Boils," a social event involving massive amounts of mussels from San Diego Bay, become popular

MUSSELS CLAMS OYSTERS
CARLSBAD
AQUAFARM
Grown in the pristine waters
of the Rancho Agua Lagoon
San Diego, California
ABALONE RED SEAWEED

Bonnie J. Becker

In order to interview Bonnie J. Becker, we traveled to the Cabrillo National Monument. As we unloaded our equipment, we introduced ourselves to Dr. Becker, who was just leaving the research station at the park. Dr. Becker's interest in marine biology began when she was a little girl who loved to sail on her father's boat where she became fascinated with what she called "sea critters." She attended Harvard University and majored in biology as an undergraduate. For her graduate studies she attended SUNY Stony Brook and finished her Ph.D. at Scripps Institution of Oceanography in La Jolla.

We were very excited to meet her—not only was she our first interviewee, but Dr. Becker is a real expert on mussels. Dr. Becker has worked in many different locations and aquariums such as the New England Aquarium in Boston, Seacamp in the Florida Keys, marine stations in Madagascar, SUNY Stony Brook, a private marine biology consulting firm in Santa Cruz and, at the time of this interview, at the Cabrillo National Monument. We were looking for a good spot to film, so she took us to a viewpoint with a spectacular vista of all of San Diego Bay. She stood tall in her ranger outfit and as the wind blew her hair, she shared her knowledge with us, telling us a great deal about her mussel studies.

Student Researcher (SR): How does the bay mussel reproduce?

Bonnie J. Becker: It reproduces in a [fashion similar to] other marine invertebrates. The male and female mussels release their eggs and sperm into the water and [the eggs are] fertilized in the water. Then you have planktonic larvae that are like little microscopic bugs that float around for about two to four weeks before finding their way back to adult mussels. Then [the larvae] will land on adult mussels and metamorphose into juveniles.

SR: How do mussels travel?

Becker: Mussels travel during the dispersal phase. Some adult mussels can move if they get dislodged and conditions are right for resettlement. But for the most part, in order to travel any great distance, [the mussel needs to do so] during its larval transport phase.

SR: What creatures are mussels related to?

Becker: Mussels are bivalves so, bay mussels are related to other species [of mollusks] like clams and oysters, and more [distantly related mollusks] such as snails and octopi.

SR: Where do mussels stand on the food chain in San Diego Bay?

Becker: Mussels are filter feeders—they take in little microscopic plants and animals and filter them out—so, really they are primary consumers. … They will also eat some zooplankton if it is small enough to make it through their filtration system so, they are on a few different trophic levels.

SR: Why are mussels important to us?

Becker: Mussels are important for a variety of reasons; here at Cabrillo, we use mussels as a key species to mark the general health … of our tide pool, [which serves] as home to over 300 other species and animals. So, [mussels] are important ecologically. They are also eaten by people, as they are a great-tasting source of protein.

SR: In what type of environment do mussels prefer to live?

Becker: It depends on the mussel. Here in San Diego, we have bay mussels and California mussels. California mussels have to settle on the open coast. They need a lot of waves and they also need to settle on the rocks. Bay mussels are a little more [tolerant]. They will also only settle on hard things like rocks, [and both species] will also settle on ropes and things like that. [But only] the bay mussel will settle in either the Bay or along the coast.

SR: Do bay mussels prefer to live in deep or shallow water?

Becker: For the most part you can find them in shallower water. I know California mussels can grow fairly deep, but you tend to find mussels in the first few meters of water.

SR: Are there specific surfaces on which bay mussels prefer to live?

Becker: Bay mussels cannot grow in sand or mud so, they have to grow on something solid like rocks. Basically, they will grow on anything that will support them.

SR: Do you know how they are collected?

Becker: Mussels are very easy to collect; they don't move so, you can just go down to the shoreline and grab them off the rocks.

SR: Are there any prime locations for mussel growth in the Bay?

Becker: Bay mussels tend to be more on the outer [areas] of the Bay like Shelter and Harbor Islands. I have searched for them along [parts] of Chula Vista, but I haven't had any luck finding them. Perhaps it's because there aren't any hard substrates for them to land on as it is very muddy down there.

SR: How do bay mussels help determine the health of the Bay?

Becker: They have been used in a program called Mussel Watch. In Mussel

Watch you collect mussels from an environment and analyze them for pollution. There are a few reasons [why] we use mussels; first, they can tolerate fairly nasty conditions in places where there is a fair amount of pollution. If you went out to the Bay and analyzed a scoop of water, all you would know is what the water looked like in a specific place [and time]. But the water is very

variable. Mussels are constantly taking in water, and looking at the mussels you get a larger view of what animals are exposed to in terms of pollutants in the Bay.

SR: Does this have anything to do with why people stopped consuming mussels in the Bay?

Becker: Yes, there has been a lot of publicity about mussels and how you are not supposed to eat them in certain places. They take in certain algae that grow in the summer and could be toxic because they [retain that algae in] their flesh. The Bay is a slightly different situation because there are a fair number of pollutants and [the mussels] might not be so good for human consumption. That's something that would need to be tested.

SR: What do you know about the Carlsbad mussel farm?

Becker: From my understanding, they hang ropes out into the middle of the lagoon and the mussels … attach themselves to the ropes. So, there is a high level of settlement in that lagoon. [Because of the power plant that takes] in water constantly, there are more mussel larvae attaching onto the ropes.

SR: Are there any negative consequences about mussel aquaculture?

Becker: [There are] some negative consequences. Mussel farms have a large number of animals that produce waste, and there can be a lot of waste near a mussel farm. I have an understanding that as long as you aren't ruining any habitats there really isn't much damage done.

SR: Are there any other things we should know about the bay mussel?

Becker: West Coast ecology started with a species called *Mytilus edulis*— what we used to think was the bay mussel. In the late 1980s, there was a genetic study that showed that there weren't any *Mytilus edulis* on this coast at all and that 50 years of research on *Mytilus edulis* was actually on the species *Mytilus trossulus*. There are two species of Bay Mussels on the West Coast: *Mytilus trossulus* [in the north], and *Mytilus galloprovencialis* in the south. Throughout the nineties they discovered that *Mytilus trossulus* can be found in some places in the south so, we have both species in San Diego Bay and they can interbreed. *Mytilus galloprovencialis* is not native—it's from the Mediterranean so, in the forties, [the species] must have [invaded and overtaken] *Mytilus trossulus*. … They're basically identical and Scripps [Institution of Oceanography] found a new mussel on their pier that was identified as *galloprovencialis*. The species is one of three different bay mussels—*trossulus*, *edulis*, and *galloprovencialis*—none of which are truly native to San Diego.

John Davis

S hortly after we arrived at Carlsbad Aquafarm, a barge came to the nearby docks bringing extremely muddy oyster and mussel lines from the lagoon. John Davis, owner of the aquafarm, was on the barge, carrying a large pile of seaweed for disposal. We found out later that seaweed tangles up the lines and has to be removed. After consulting with Steve Le Page (interviewed in the abalone chapter, p. 270), Mr. Davis graciously agreed to be interviewed by us. We set up our equipment at a spot near the docks and shortly afterward started filming. After we had completed our interview with Mr. Davis, we were encouraged by the belief that there was still hope for our local mussels. For, even though the Bay isn't completely pollution-free, with a little more cleaning up mussels can still live, thrive, and even be eaten. Perhaps, mussels are like the "canary in the coal mine." They remind us that we must clean up our act, or face the consequences.

Student Researcher (SR): What are some of the difficulties in managing the farm?

John Davis: When you are in the aquafarming business, growing live animals in the ocean and in the lagoons and various waterways, the difficulties are dealing with Mother Nature; we can't control what takes place in the ocean or the lagoon. All we can do is our very best and plant our oyster and mussel seeds and hope that Mother Nature provides the nutrients and [clean water], and we don't get too many red tides [or] too many days where pollution has damaged or killed some of our animals. We have the water, but if it doesn't have the nutrients or is not clean enough we lose our crops.

SR: What kind of quality control methods do you implement?

Davis: You all saw us come in, and we were pretty muddy. That's because we were harvesting in the mud and in the water of the lagoon. Once [the mud on them is] washed off, the mussels and the oysters and the clams are taken into our depuration facility. They are immersed in tanks of sterile salt water ... and kept there for 48 hours—or longer, if necessary. They're washed in the tanks daily and before they are sold to the marketplace, we run a laboratory test to make sure that there is no bacterium inside our shellfish. And this is done on every batch that comes out of the aquafarm. So, we have the freshest and the safest shellfish that you can possibly buy today. When shellfish are flown in from other parts of the world, they are maybe two to four days post-harvest before they actually get to the marketplace.

SR: How did you get into this business?

Davis: It was an opportunity to give back. The ocean has always been there for me as a diver, as a fisherman, and for many years I had tried to figure out what I can do to give back all the bounty that it has provided me for so many years. Then the opportunity came for me to establish this farm and to actually grow shellfish and not harvest them from the wild. ... If you think about it a little bit, every mussel, every oyster that we grow here at the farm is just one more mussel or oyster that doesn't have to be taken from the ocean. We are pretty pleased and proud of that and this is one of the reasons that I got into the business.

SR: What model did you use as a base for your business?

Davis: There are no books for [aquaculture]. There are no guidelines. There are a lot of books but they deal with the academics. The actual operation of the aquafarm is dependent on the location, the water [depth and volume], current, temperature and limitations of the area.

Delivering mussels from Carlsbad Aquafarm.

Also, in the business you always have to be careful when you select a species to grow because if you're going to grow something that [needs] the very warm water of the South Pacific and try to do that in the cold water of California, it just won't work. You have to select a particular species and make sure that it is compatible with your area... It's a trial-and-error operation as far as the growing goes. As far as the business goes, keeping track of your sales and money is just one simple, basic part of the business.

SR: What do you enjoy about your job?

Davis: I like having the opportunity to create, and I particularly like the opportunity to pursue aquaculture with no horizons. Whatever you can dream about, think about, is what you can accomplish. ... A good percentage of seafood is going to be grown through aquaculture, because ... the demand [for all species] is tremendous, and the ocean is not going to be able to sustain that demand. You will find that we are taking animals out of the ocean that we have never consumed before—mainly because of the shortages and the overharvesting and overconsumption. ... Aquaculture is a way that we can help.

SR: What are your opinions on the environmental issues in San Diego Bay?

Davis: That's a pretty big question. You cannot grow any filter-feeding animals for human consumption there, and you probably wouldn't want to even attempt seaweeds and other things. Many of the fish are contaminated with PCB metals and other products. I think the agencies working in San Diego Bay are doing a pretty good job. ... There is a lot of work being done with dredging, and I know the Coast Guard and some environmental groups are working on the copper oxide coming off the boats hulls. They are developing new paints for the bottom of the boats and the shipyards are collecting all of the waste from the repainting of their ships. The Harbor Police Department is moving a lot of derelict vessels [that often leach] something that we don't want in the water. The more of them that can be removed from San Diego Bay, the better opportunity we will have to clean it up. It has improved enormously, and you can test the Bay yourself by just going down there and looking around. If you can find barnacles or mussels growing on the pilings or underneath the docks, you know that the pollution-control measures are making progress.

A mussel raft.

SR: Do you have any advice for people who want to start a mussel farm?

Davis: Don't. I say don't. I love it, and I have been doing it for a long time … getting a great deal of satisfaction from it, but it is extremely difficult. We have regulations. I have 11 agencies that regulate me and it's hard enough to operate a business with the restrictions of even one regulatory agency. We get almost no help in aquaculture from the U.S. government, whereas Canadian products come subsidized by their government. This is a very unfortunate situation because our competition comes from Canada, Korea, Russia, Japan, all over the world. I have to sell in the same market place as a Canadian and there's a differential in the dollar value and the subsidized issues it makes it very difficult to compete. However, we can, we will, and we are. That's one of the reasons why I would advise [any] prospective mussel farmers to think twice. I might add that we are short of ideal aquaculture sites. Ninety-five percent of our wetlands have been turned into marinas or housing developments in California alone, and that's why this is such a unique place. The water being shared by the power plant hopefully will be shared by the desalinization facilities. … If this power plant wasn't here, there wouldn't be any lagoon. It would be a sandflat swamp but the plant keeps it open by dredging it each year. So, we have the water to grow all of the aquaculture and that's really a significant thing. At the far end of this lagoon is a sanctuary for birds and some of the endangered gobies. So, we have aquaculture on one end and a sanctuary on the other end.

SR: Is there any thing that makes Carlsbad Aquafarm stand out from other aquafarms?

Davis: Most definitely. We grow the *galloprovincialis* mussel, the Mediterranean Bay Mussel, which is the sweetest, nicest-tasting mussel you can get. We

Mussel depuration system.

depurate, which means we purify the mussels, guaranteeing you that [there will be no] bacteria in the mussels when you eat them. Nobody else is doing that. The purification process removes the sand and anything else that is in the shell. We also do state testing, which includes testing for PSP [paralytic shellfish poisoning] and any other bad diseases that are associated with shellfish. [So, you purchase] clean, safe shellfish [from us] that's very fresh; right out of the tank, right out of the water … that's why we are significant.

The Biology of the Bay Mussels

Bay Mussel
Mytilus galloprovincialis

The bay mussel is one of the most populous animals that live in and around San Diego Bay. The mussels growing in large clumps on rocks, docks, pilings, floats and gravel are an accustomed sight along the San Diego waterfront. April is the first month of their spawning season when they spawn by discharging gametes. Fertilization of the eggs occurs shortly afterwards. ("*Mytilus trossulus...*" 2006)

Bay mussels begin life as planktonic, defenseless larvae that are carried by the ocean currents across vast distances. Even at this early stage, they have a foot, which is tongue-like in shape with a groove on the ventral surface, and is continuous with their byssus pit. From this pit a viscous secretion pours out, entering the groove and gradually hardening after coming into contact with sea water. This process forms an extremely tough byssal thread that carries the mussels through the currents. After enduring several weeks of this dispersal method, they settle on a bed with this tough, wiry, and iridescent byssal thread serving as an anchor to keep them from being ripped off their substrate by storms and predators. After about nine or ten months the mussels reach their maturity size of about six to ten cm. (Cowles 2006) ("*Mytilus trossulus...*" 2006)

Bay mussels have triangular-shaped brownish-blue tinted shells that are comprised of two valves. These shells protect them from predators and the sun, and require the consumption of massive amounts of plankton for their growth. Mussels are filter-feeders. They eat plankton and in the process inadvertently consume pathogens and other pollutants. They feed by continually drawing water through a siphon; the water is then brought into the branchial chamber where detritus particles and plankton are trapped by mucus sheets moving over the gills. The filtered water exits through the siphon and labial palps funnel the food

into the mussel's mouth where it gets fully digested. ("Common Mussel …
" 2006)

For a long time there has been some confusion as to the species of
mussel that is truly native to San Diego Bay. The Blue mussel (*Mytilus edulis*),
is very similar to the bay mussel and was once thought to be indigenous.
However, it has been determined that the blue mussel is almost exclusively
found on the Atlantic Coast. Genetic studies show that a percentage of
what we know as bay mussels are not actually *M. galloprovincialis* but a
sympatric species, the Mediterranean mussel (*M. trossulus*), named because
it originated in the Mediterranean. The Mediterranean mussel is believed
to have been introduced to the San Diego area by Spanish ships during
the conquest of the New World. The Mediterranean mussel is physically
almost indistinguishable from the bay mussel, and the two species have
been known to crossbreed. (Cowles 2006) (Morris 1980)

Growing Mussels in the Bay

Mytilus galloprovincialis, also known as the bay mussel, is one of
the most common marine mollusks along the San Diego coast. This mussel
performs many important tasks and is vital to the ecology of the area.
Increasingly, California aquaculture businesses are incorporating mussel
production into their operations, and production doubled in less than two
years from 236,457 pounds in 2002, to 508,416 pounds in 2004, resulting in
a net income of $1,525,248. World populations are constantly increasing,
and as fisheries continue to be overexploited, aquaculture will be relied on
to meet demand.

We students at High Tech High understood this, and wanted to see if aquaculture (more specifically, mussel aquaculture) in San Diego Bay was at all feasible. In order to grapple with this problem, we began by researching different methods used in mussel aquaculture in other areas, and we found that the bare rope for natural mussel "sets" employed by Carlsbad Aquafarm would be the most efficient method for us to use.

We cut six-foot lengths of nylon rope and marked these with a zip-tie every foot so that we could observe if water depth and mussel concentration had any correlation. Then, in order to weigh the rope down and give the mussels a stable growing environment, we placed 16 ounces of beach sand in two ziplock bags and tied them to the ends of the ropes.

We tested this mussel rope design at the Grape Street Pier on December 15, 2005. Grape Street Pier is a private, gated pier regulated by the Port of San Diego, and provided an ideal location for preventing the public from tampering with the mussel lines. We attached 30 lines along the dock at three-foot intervals. On April 20, 2006, we returned to Grape Street Pier to observe the lines and record how many mussels had taken hold during our four-month absence. We recorded the results on a simple chart, writing in the number of mussels we counted along each foot-long interval of the six-foot ropes.

Our findings suggested that while San Diego Bay, with its calm protected waters, would be perfect for mussel aquaculture, the current water quality is too poor. The consumption of mussels from the Bay is not feasible because of pollution. However, in the future, certain sections of the Bay could be used for mussel aquaculture if conditions improve.

Results

On our last field trip to the Boat Channel, they occasionally smashed beneath our feet; at the wharf along the San Diego Bay, they clung along the wharf's support columns. At the Chula Vista Nature Center, they fastened themselves to rocks and pieces of discarded junk. No matter where we went, mussels seemed to be everywhere.

Now, as I walk down to the dock where the mussels we are growing are kept, a gust of salty wind and boat exhaust greets me. Everyone around me has noticed it too—this mixture of natural scents combined with the less natural odor exuding from the crowded urban San Diego boat scene. Once we arrive at the growing station, we begin to pull up the long cords that months ago we anchored beneath a dock floating on the eastern side of the Bay. I immediately observe how the mussels on the ropes are steadily settling and proliferating along the entire rope. They're the ones in charge here. If they could, I bet they would kick all the other organisms out. They would establish themselves as the dominant species. I sigh as I then think about their predicament; they are trapped and lodged tightly on our suspended cords.

Nevertheless, we count their numbers boldly, proudly—like jewelers counting their cache of diamonds. Our movements remind me of an eccentric, pillaging army. Though instead of being soldiers, we are scientists; and in place of loot, we take data. But, like all effective armies, we will move off—if only to strike again when the data are ripe.

Celeste Byers

Diamond Reflection

Shawn Teeter

Throughout our year-long study of San Diego Bay, biogeographer Jared Diamond's insights into human cultural transformations and interactions with the environment were used to guide our work. Since the earliest recorded instance of its habitation by humans, San Diego Bay has undergone many natural and human-induced changes. With the arrival of each new group of people, new resources were sought, and different products were harvested. Even the very depths and contours of the Bay have been changed to suit human need for food, transportation and commerce.

Through the course of this study, we have presented twelve themes—twelve different ways in which the Bay has been used. Each of these topics presents a different approach or story, and each topic has resulted in a different set of outcomes and consequences. We have looked at a diverse group of individuals, inhabitants and interests in the Bay: Native Americans, Chinese fishermen, waterfowl hunters, the tuna and salt industries, the conversion of kelp for gunpowder and additives, the domestication of sea lions and dolphins, and the cultivation of white seabass, abalone, and mussels.

Using the activities and examples detailed in Diamond's Pulitzer-prize winning book, *Guns, Germs, and Steel*, we explored parallel examples of exploitation and restoration taking place in the Bay. We looked to Diamond's messages for inspiration and guidance in understanding the interconnections between our twelve stories. In Diamond's broad sweep of history, many tales of similar human exploits, social conflicts and environmental challenges are recounted and explained. We used these tales, stories and examples to gain an understanding of what might be taking place in our own backyard.

We sought to apply Diamond's work to each of our themes in order to achieve greater perspective. By doing so, we hoped to show the concerned reader how San Diego Bay and comparable metropolitan waterways can be maintained, restored, and continued as valuable resources for their inhabitants—human and otherwise. We attempted to point out what problems remain with the health of the Bay and, by using Diamond's ideas, to make suggestions about improvements.

Guns, Germs, and Steel starts with an important question: "Why do certain people have more worldly possessions than others?" Diamond recounts his experience with an Indonesian native politician named Yali. Yali and Diamond discussed the concept of material wealth, or materialism, using the term "cargo." (In this study, we have used the term "cargo" for the human acquisition of material possessions.) Yali asked: "Why do certain people in the world have more cargo than others?" This fundamental question inspired Diamond to look at a variety of historical biogeographical case studies to try to determine the answer.

Diamond suggests an answer lies at the heart of civilization's replacement of hunter-gatherer societies. This transformation from living off the land's bounty to agriculture and pastoral activities brought about the desire for cargo and with it exploitation of the environment, frequently to the point of obliteration. In many cases, the negative effects of exploitation are not apparent for an extended period of time. However, as can be evidenced by the myriad of destructive forces now at play in our environment today, short-term gain is often followed by long-term loss. In addition, and at far greater cost, the sometimes voracious quest for cargo can lead to attacking, killing or enslaving other humans. This is evident throughout Diamond's comprehensive odyssey of biogeography and human history.

The issue of "cargo" can be clearly seen during the clash between Native Americans and Spaniards in early San Diego history. The earliest inhabitants of San Diego Bay and its surroundings did not exploit their land to the utmost because, as hunter-gatherers, they had no use or wish for more cargo. In addition, biogeographers tell us that the local environment during this time was very rich in edible flora and fauna. Some exploitation by Native Americans did occur as they did controlled burns of chaparral habitat, planted oak trees and redirected water flow for their benefit. These earliest inhabitants of the region displayed the beginnings of agricultural development—activities that were unknown to many. However, when the Spaniards arrived, they exploited the land and the people whenever possible. The Spaniards' desire for cargo and material gain motivated their explorations and subsequent colonization of the New World. Their love for cargo overrode humanitarian considerations. Diamond's understanding of cargo's role in motivating conflict between people also relates to the story of the Chinese fishermen, another topic in our book.

There are parallels but some important differences in the struggles and cultural conflicts experienced by Chinese fishermen and Native Americans. While Native Americans were primarily using the land for survival, and not for cargo, Chinese fishermen came to San Diego looking for a way to support their families and acquire cargo. Generally speaking, the Chinese fished the seas for profit rather than subsistence. This key motivation separates Chinese fishermen from Native Americans, who interacted with their environment at a pure survival level. It can be argued that Chinese fishermen's desire for cargo led to the initial destruction of San Diego Bay and its surrounding environs, with the depletion of stocks of finfish and abalone. The desire for cargo *alone* did not lead to the environmental issues we now face. The desire to protect and keep cargo has turned men to war. Thus, war, which results from mankind's unquenchable lust for material possessions, would contribute to and compound the problem.

In recent wars, superior technology and the supplies necessary to support them have become essential. One such element is the supply of munitions. The use of kelp for gunpowder, presented in our book, is illustrative. Potash, which has long been a key ingredient of gunpowder, was in short supply in WWI as the Allies' enemy, Germany, controlled its source. With the discovery of potassium salts in local seaweed and the development of efficient extraction methods, the United States was able to overcome this shortage. Thus, humans used a San Diego resource for war purposes and, in a greater sense, the acquirement of more cargo.

In more recent years, kelp has been used for additives, leading to additional problems for the coastal environment. From the early 1920s to the late 1980s, kelp harvesters were quite plentiful in and around San Diego Bay. Unfortunately, even though kelp growth is fast, the demand outweighed production, and thus, environmental restrictions were placed on kelp harvesting. Two main reasons for the termination of kelp harvesting were the rising costs of cleaning up wastes and related environmental taxation regulations. Thus, ironically, the love for one cargo, taxes, eventually drove out love for another cargo, kelp.

Up to this point, San Diego Bay and its surrounding environment had been used by both "cargo" and "noncargo" peoples solely as a place from which products (finfish, abalone, kelp) could be taken from nature's bounty. With the depletion of many of these resources by the early 1900s, users of the Bay would be forced to take a different approach. They would take the next step Diamond sees in the development of civilization: the domestication of plants and animals. Recently, some measures have been undertaken to cultivate giant kelp in order to maintain productive kelp beds. There have also been other programs involved in its rehabilitation and protection. For instance, limits have been placed on kelp harvesting, and divers have tried various means of removing or destroying its prime predator, sea urchins. A variety of chemical solutions have been dumped on urchin colonies, and pipes were once used to suck them up. Years after this approach was implemented, Craig Barilotti, while working at Kelco, produced a report that halted the practice of destroying or removing sea urchins to regulate kelp growth. With protective measures, the kelp forest seems to be recovering, albeit slowly. A more interesting example in the movement toward recovery rests with the white seabass.

Currently, Hubbs-SeaWorld Research Institute has been restocking the Bay and surrounding coastal waters of Southern California with white seabass. White seabass were over-fished and therefore, could not continue to provide cargo. Interestingly enough, not everyone who once exploited the white seabass did so for cargo. Seabass fishing is also an activity don purely for pleasure or prestige. Sports fishermen today may choose to pursue the species that bring the most acclaim as trophies or the thrill of the hunt, rather than those that provide the most meat, fur, or other resource. Thus, the highly acclaimed reputation of the seabass, combined with its great taste, has made it important cargo.

With an important and socially valued cargo, we become aware, even sensitized, to its potential loss. However, with the increased awareness of "at risk" species, the flip side of the argument can be made. People now return trophy fish, including seabass, to the sea after enjoying a good fight rather than keeping it for food. Restocking the seabass allows many objectives to be satisfied: we will not lose our cargo, we can enjoy fishing, and we can return it to the sea in noble fashion. The seabass is not alone in our efforts to restore what we have taken. Many other animals have been over-harvested in San Diego Bay, and are now being restocked or are the subject of farming efforts.

Examples of these animals are discussed in two other chapters in our book—abalone and mussels. Abalone were pushed to the brink because of their ease of harvesting and delectability. A few years ago, the white abalone was given endangered species status, making it the first marine invertebrate on the list. Several decades ago, black abalone covered the shoreline and were easily picked up by local residents but this is no longer the case. Because of this, several private organizations are currently seeking funding alternatives for replenishing former abalone populations. While abalone farms that produce a smaller size abalone for harvest have achieved some success, wild abalone replenishment efforts are still in their infancy and meeting severe challenges.

While mussels were never pushed close to extinction, they do

Students from High Tech High grew mussels on rope lines off the Grape Street Pier in San Diego Bay.

represent a cargo-related problem. Mussels grown in the Bay can no longer be eaten because of water pollution. Mussels have natural water filters that can tell us a great deal about the health of San Diego Bay so it would be progress indeed if we could one day eat mussels grown there. Presently, mussels are produced in aquaculture farms north of San Diego in Carlsbad, where the water is much cleaner. The sea "farmer" must be cautionary and realize that aquaculture can lead to de-oxygenation of nearby water, and vast amounts of fecal matter are expelled ıto the surrounding waters. The desire for mussels leads to aquaculture, which in turn leads to pollution created as a byproduct of the initial desire. This cycle leads us to pose the question: "Have we lost sight of the 'natural' state?"

We are still a cargo-loving people, who have resorted to the farming and restoration of local species in order to maintain our supply of cargo at all costs. This fundamental desire has led to a unique adaptation of an old idea. While horses, elephants, and camels have been used to military advantage in the past, we now use dolphins and sea lions. The domestication of animals for harvesting has transformed into the domestication of animals for our national defense.

Both dolphins and sea lions have been used by the military in San Diego Bay. These animals have performed many different functions including reconnaissance, mine-disabling, apprehending invaders, and protection of personnel and property. They have been used since World War II in every major conflict involving the United States because they can be domesticated. Diamond states the requirements of domestication are: diet, growth rate, captive breeding, disposition, tendency to panic, and social structure. Dolphins and sea lions satisfy all of these: they eat fish, grow relatively fast (growing several feet per year), gain weight readily, breed easily in captivity, are not aggressive towards humans, and are comfortable dwelling close together in relatively small spaces. Thus, we have captured wild animals and domesticated them in order to protect our cargo. In doing so, while we may treat these animals humanely, we are still exploiting them.

When considered in light of Diamond's work, our last three topics provide different but complete tales of the human theme of exploitation. The first is waterfowl hunting that used to be a popular recreational activity in and around San Diego Bay. Wild ducks and geese were often hunted at Hog Ranch Point, at the southern end of the Bay, and duck hunting was in style in an area known as "Duckville" for its abundance of waterfowl. But with the arrival of more people to San Diego, the marshes—natural habitat of the waterfowl—were drained, and commercial development took their place, bringing about the destruction of wetlands. Moreover, with increases in human population, more regulations were passed and enforced—among them, a city law to prohibit the discharge of any firearms within city limits. Together, these factors served to halt all waterfowl hunting in San Diego. Ironically enough, waterfowl hunters did not endanger the birds they hunted as much as many would tend to think. In fact, duck hunters have turned out to be among the most active and dedicated conservationists. They work to preserve the wetlands that house the birds they hunt—habitat that others have destroyed. Due to their efforts, the very people blamed for the birds' demise are actually the people responsible for their restoration.

Salt has an interesting story of transformation too. It is a natural mineral, harvested from the Bay since 1870. There is anecdotal evidence of Native Americans harvesting salt, but it was done in a primitive fashion. The transformation of the South Bay Salt Works (SBSW) in present day San Diego relates to a unique group of avian fauna. Many rare and endangered birds migrate or stay there. Normally, these birds would nest and congregate on sandy beaches. However, urban sprawl has forced the birds to seek alternatives. One excellent alternative is the soft, sandy levees dividing up the SBSW. Thus, though the facility provides cargo, it has been transformed into a sanctuary for wildlife. The SBSW provides an interesting example of an activity initiated to produce cargo transformed into a restoration project for wildlife.

The story of tuna brings all of Diamond's lessons into a final consideration. Presently, tuna are seen by many as endlessly bountiful, just as the seabass, mussels, abalone, and kelp once were. In fact, some experts say there are still plenty of tuna around. Others disagree and say the harvesting of tuna must be controlled and still others argue that tuna are already in critical decline and that conservation measures will not be enough to save the species.

By examining the "exploitation cycle" developed in the tuna chapter, many considerations concerning their fate are brought to light. The cycle proposes: 1) humans voraciously exploit an animal population; 2) humans attempt to control the exploitation; 3) humans realize after the population is near extinction that a restoration project must ensue; and, finally 4) the arrival at a sustainable harvest.

It should be noted that such a state of equilibrium is seldom achieved. Aquaculture and recreational activities, such as pole fishing and duck-bagging limits, which control excessive exploitation *does* point to the possibility of sustainable harvests

Of course, exploitation always came with its share of risks.

in tightly closed systems. While it might be argued that we are only at the first stage of exploitation with tuna (i.e., the voracious collection of bountiful species), this is by no means certain. The debate here concerns a conflict between the views that tuna may either be migrating in widely differing patterns or they may be disappearing completely. The state of tuna is uncertain. One reason: Because they are warm-blooded fishes, their migration patterns are more difficult to predict than those of cold-blooded fishes, which swim in water dictated by their temperature.

If we take a closer look at the exploitation cycle of tuna in local waters, we have already moved from free-for-all exploitation to the restriction and controlled use of a limited resource. We need only to look off our coast to see that the tuna are mostly gone. Regulations are in place to protect them. Concerning our local tuna we can now ask, "Will it be enough, or are the tuna gone forever?" While wild tuna are held in pens at sea and might be considered to be undergoing a process of domestication, larger pressing questions concerning tuna remain. "Will such pens provide adequate protection for the species? And, will any limited and local attempts at restoration be possible for a species with such a wide-ranging, even global habitat?"

The chapters on Native Americans and Chinese fishermen have shown us two quite different approaches to cargo acquisition and utilization of Bay resources. Native Americans were able to keep the environment sound and healthy, while surviving for thousands of years. Subsequent heavy restoration was unnecessary, as the environment had not been too deeply impacted. However, as soon as cargo came into the picture, the environment was exploited and the infamous cycle began. In another story, we found kelp was used for gunpowder and additives, and an unfettered approach to harvesting led to its virtual elimination. While kelp is to some degree restored, it remains protected at the end of an exploitation cycle: a sustainable harvest commodity.

The cycle continues with the story of abalone, mussels, ducks, and white seabass, all of which are currently the subject of restoration efforts. These efforts are costly, artificial, and have not yet reached the possibility of a natural and sustainable harvest. We might conclude from these chapters that it is always more efficient to harvest in

Maiden voyage of the tuna clipper Stella di Genova.

a controlled fashion rather than to over-exploit and then backpedal to try to save the species. Instead, we are engaging in a tragic cycle of exploitation that, even if it does reach the point of restoration, may only yield results that are artificial and create unforeseen consequences.

While SBSW has been transformed into a sanctuary for rare and endangered birds, it is in fact an example of restoration taken to the most extreme, and may be an impossible-to-sustain situation. The SBSW operation is saving some birds, but we must ask: "At what larger costs to the environment?" It addresses a species-based restoration problem of protecting certain birds, instead of addressing the larger picture of urban sprawl all along the coast, which caused the decline in the first place.

It is not clear at this point whether or not tuna will need restoring in the future. Given our track record with species restoration, such an endeavor may not even be possible, since tuna are distributed world-wide. We are at the point of shifting from simple species restoration projects to the rehabilitation of the oceans themselves.

Black stilts feeding along the shore of the evaporation ponds of South Bay Salt Works.

As recently established in the Northern Hawaiian Islands and in areas as nearby as the Channel Islands, Marine Protected Areas (MPAs) that stop exploitation in the first place may be the best solution. Thus, the creation of MPAs short-circuits the exploitation cycle. Without exploiting, harvesting, or in any way interfering with an endangered species, we can be assured of its protection.

Only when humans realize the great problem of a declining environment, and learn to manage their love for cargo, will humankind be able to live in harmony with the environment. Humanity cannot survive by simply doing spot-checks on individual species or issues. We need to address the bigger picture and integrate restoration solutions effectively to truly save the environment. San Diego Bay will continue to be utilized, exploited, and restored for many years to come. Only when we realize that all the pieces of the bigger picture we call nature must be considered, will we be capable of sustainably using the Bay, and the rest of the world's environment, to its fullest potential.

Bibliography

H History **T** Timeline
B Biology **G** Graph

Native Americans

H Bouscaren, Steven. *Personal Interview*. Dec. 2005.

H Carrico, Richard L. "Sociopolitical Aspects of the 1775 Revolt at Mission San Diego de Alcala: an Ethnohistorical Approach." *The Journal of San Diego History*. Volume 43, Summer 1997: Number 3. 15 Dec. 2006. <http://www.sandiego-history.org/journal/97summer/missionrevolt.htm>.

H —. *Strangers in a Stolen Land: American Indians in San Diego 1850–1880*. Newcastle, CA: Sierra Oaks Publishing Company, 1987.

G T B H Gallegos, Dennis and Carolyn Kyle. *Archives of California Prehistory, Five Thousand Years of Maritime Subsistence at CA-SDI-48, on Ballast Point, San Diego County, California*. Salinas, CA: Coyote Press, 1998.

H Guassac, Louis. *Personal Interview*. Dec. 2005.

H Heizer, Robert F., and Albert B. Elsasser. *The Natural World of the California Indians*. London: The University of California Press, 1980.

H Johnson, William Henry. *Pioneer Spaniards in North America*. Boston: Little, Brown, and Company, 1903.

H Jordan, Winthrop D., et al. *The Americans*. Geneva, IL: McDougal, Littell & Company, 1985.

H Masters, Patricia. *Personal Interview*. May 2006.

T May, Ron. *Personal Interview*. May 2006.

H McKeever, Michael. *A Short History of San Diego*. San Francisco: Lexicos, 1985.

B Morris, Robert H., Donald P. Abbott, and Eugene C. Haderlie. *Intertidal Invertebrates of California*. 1st ed. Stanford: Stanford University Press, 1980.

G H Showley, Roger M. *San Diego: Perfecting Paradise*. Carlsbad, CA: Heritage Media Corp., 1999.

Chinese Fishermen

B "Abbreviated Life History of California Sheephead (*Semicossyphus pulcher*)." 2003. *State of California*. 29 Oct. 2006. <http://www.dfg.ca.gov/mrd/rockfish/sheep-head.html>.

B "*Caulolatilus princeps*." *Fishbase*. 11 Oct. 2006. <http://www.fishbase.org/Summary/speciesSummary.php?ID=3539&genusname=Caulolatilus&speciesname=princeps>.

(T) (H) Chen, Jack. *The Chinese of America.* San Francisco: Harper and Row, 1980.

(G) (H) "Chinese Fishers." *San Diego Union.* 1 Sept. 1887, page 3.

(H) Bentz, Linda. "Redwood, Bamboo and Ironwood: Chinese Junks of San Diego." *Mains'l Haul.* Volume 35, Summer 1999: Number 4.

(B) Eschmeyer, William N. and Earl S. Herald. *Pacific Coast Fishes.* New York: Houghton Mifflin Company, 1999.

(B) (H) "The Fishes of San Diego Bay." *San Diego Union.* 14 Jan. 1880, page 4.

(H) Harris, Jeffrey Todd. "The Abalones of San Diego: A Problem in Resource Management." Master's Thesis, San Diego State University, 1974.

(H) Kelly, Roger, and Ronald May. *Shadows of the Past.* National Park Service, 2001. 21 Dec. 2006. <http://www.cr.nps.gov/history/online_books/cabr4/index.htm>.

(T) (H) Lee, Murray K. *Personal Interview.* Dec. 2005.

(H) —. "A History of Chinese Immigration to America." Aug. 1993.

(G) (T) (H) —. "The Chinese Fishing Industry of San Diego." *Mains'l Haul.* Volume 35, Summer 1999: Numbers 2 and 3.

(T) (H) —. "In Search of Gold Mountain." 2000.

(T) (H) Liu, Judith. "Celestials in the Golden Mountain: The Chinese in One California City, San Diego, 1870–1900." Master's Thesis, San Diego State University, 1977.

(H) May, Ron. *Personal Interview.* May 2006.

(T) McCunn, Ruthanne Lum. *An Illustrated History of the Chinese in America.* San Francisco: Design Enterprises, 1979.

(G) (H) McEvoy, Arthur F. "In Places Men Reject Chinese Fishermen at San Diego, 1870–1893." *The Journal of San Diego History.* Volume 23, Fall 1977: Number 4. 11 Oct. 2006. <http://www.sandiegohistory.org/journal/77fall/chinese.htm>.

(T) (H) —. *The Fishermen's Problem—Ecology and Law in the California Fisheries 1850–1980.* New York: Cambridge University Press, 1986.

(B) "*Mugil cephalus.*" *Fishbase.* <http://www.fishbase.org/Summary/speciesSummary. php?ID=785&genusname=Mugil&speciesname=cephalus>.

(B) *Ocean Biogeographic Information System.* 11 Oct. 2006. < http://www.iobis.org/>.

(H) Richardson, William Clyde. "The Fishermen of San Diego." Master's Thesis, San Diego State University, 1981.

(B) "*Scomber japonicus.*" *Fishbase.* 11 Oct. 2006. <http://www.fishbase.org/Summary/species-Summary.php?ID=117&genusname=Scomber&speciesname=japonicus>.

(B) "*Semicossyphus pulcher.*" *Fishbase.* 11 Oct. 2006. <http://www.fishbase.org/Summary/speciesSummary.php?ID=3671&genusname=Semicossyphus&speciesname=pulcher>.

(B) "*Sphyraena argentea.*" *Fishbase.* 11 Oct. 2006. <http://www.fishbase.org/Summary/speciesSummary.php?ID=3678&genusname=Sphyraena&speciesname=argentea>.

(B) (H) Stewart, Don M. *Frontier Port: A Chapter in San Diego's History.* Los Angeles: Ward Ritchie Press, 1965.

(H) Van Tilburg, Hans Konrad. "Vessels of Exchange: the Global Shipwright in the Pacific." *Seascapes, Littoral Cultures, and Trans-Oceanic Exchanges.* 12 Feb. 2003. Library of Congress, Washington D.C. 11 Oct. 2006. <http://www.historyco-operative.org/proceedings/seascapes/tilburg.html>.

Waterfowl Hunting

🅗 Brown, Jim. *Personal Interview.* Dec. 2005.

🅗 Diamond, Jared. *Guns, Germs, and Steel.* New York: W.W. Norton & Company, 1999.

🅗 Ducks Unlimited. *Ducks Unlimited, Inc.* 31 Oct. 2006. < http://www.ducks.org/>.

🅑 Ehrlich, Paul R., David S. Dobkin, and Darryl Wheye. "Dabblers vs. Divers." 1998. *Stanford University.* 23 Oct. 2006. <http://www.stanford.edu/group/stanford-birds/text/essays/Dabblers_vs._Divers.html>.

🅗 "The Federal Duck Stamp Program: U.S. Fish and Wildlife Service." *U.S. Fish and Wildlife Service.* 11 Oct. 2006. <http://www.fws.gov/duckstamps/Info/Stamps/stampinfo.htm>.

🅗 Hagerbaumer, David. *Personal Interview.* May 2006.

🅗 —. *Waterfowling These Past Fifty Years.* Amity, OR: Sand Lake Press, 1998.

🅗 Heather, Jim. *Personal Interview.* Apr. 2006.

🅗 Hooper, Frances. "Indian Ways and Traditions Recalled." *Churchill County Museum Association.* 30 Oct. 2006. <http://www.ccmuseum.org/Hooper/hooper3.htm>.

🅗 "Point Loma—Environmental Management of Pre-Contact Kumeyaay." *Kumeyaay Nation.* 11 Oct. 2006. <http://www.kumeyaay.com/history/article_detail.html?id=22>.

🅗 Scharff, Robert. *Complete Duck Shooter's Handbook.* New York, NY: Putnam Publishing Group, 1957.

🅑 Unitt, Philip. *San Diego County Bird Atlas.* San Diego: Ibis Publishing Company, 2004.

🅑 🅗 Vavra, Ron. *Personal Interview.* Nov. 2005.

🅖 "Waterfowl Hunt Results for State Operated Hunting Areas." 6 Oct. 2006. *California Department of Fish and Game.* 2 Dec. 2006. <http://www.dfg.ca.gov/shoot/shoot.html>.

🅗 Winterhald, Bruce. *Hunter-Gatherer Foraging Strategies: Ethnographic and Archaeological Analyses.* Chicago: University of Chicago Press, 1981.

Tuna

🅗 *ABD-Infofish Global Industry Update.* Kuala Lumpur, Malaysia, 1991.

🅗 "All Things Considered, September 7, 1998." *NPR.* 15 Mar. 2006. <http://www.npr.org/templates/story/story.php?storyId=1033491>.

🅗 "Annual Landings Query." National Oceanic and Atmospheric Administration. 14 June 2006. <http://www.st.nmfs.gov/st1/commercial/landings/annual_landings.html>.

🅗 Bonarno, Alessandro and Douglas Constance. *Caught in the Net: The Global Tuna Industry, Environment, and the State.* Lawrence, KS: University Press of Kansas, 1996.

Bruni, Guy. *Personal Interview*. May 2006.

Cary, Harold F. *Statement of the American Tunaboat Association on the Effect of Imports on the Domestic Tuna Industries Before the United States Tariff Commission in Accordance with a Resolution of the Committee on Finance*. Washington, D.C.: 1957.

Gibbs, Elizabeth. "Tuna." *Rhode Island Sea Grant*. 5 May 2006. <http://seagrant.gso.uri.edu/factsheets/tuna.html>.

Immenschuh, Jean. *Personal Interview*. June 2006.

Pourade, Richard F. *Rising Tide*. 1967. *San Diego Historical Society*. Jan. 2007. <http://www.sandiegohistory.org/books/pourade/rising/rising.htm>.

—. "The History of San Diego Chronology." *San Diego Historical Society*. 15 May 2006. <http://sandiegohistory.org/books/pourade/dream/dreamchrono.htm>.

Richardson, William Clyde. "The Fishermen of San Diego." Master's Thesis, San Diego State University, 1981.

Rockland, Steven. "An Analysis of the San Diego Tuna Industry and its Impact on the Local Economy." Master's Thesis, San Diego State University, 1976.

Schoell, Mark. "The Marine Mammal Protection Act and its Role in the Decline of San Diego's Tuna Fishing Industry." *The Journal of San Diego History*. Volume 45, Winter 1999: Number 1. 11 Oct. 2006. <http://sandiegohistory.org/journal/99winter/tuna.htm>.

Soltez, Edward S. "Pole Fishing for Tuna." 2004. *San Diego Historical Society*. 11 Oct. 2006. <http://www.sandiegohistory.org/videos/tuna.htm>.

"*Thunnus albacares*." *Fishbase*. 11 Oct. 2006. <http://www.fishbase.org/Summary/SpeciesSummary.php?id=143>.

"Transient Tropical Tuna Status of the Fishing Industry." *Course Proceedings*. San Diego State University, July 1978.

"Tuna Species Datasheet." *Atuna*. 2004. 5 May 2006. <http://www.atuna.com/species/species_datasheets.htm>.

"Types of Tuna." *Fine Living*. 5 May 2006. <http://www.fineliving.com/fine/favorite_things_essentials/article/0,1663,FINE_1426_1712410,00.html>.

Vetter, Russ. *Personal Interview*. Jan. 2006.

Wolf, Thomas. *In Pursuit of Tuna: The Expansion of a Fishing Industry and its International Ramifications*. Phoenix: Arizona University Press, 1980.

Salt

"About the Salt Industry." 22 June 2005. Salt Institute Online. 8 Mar. 2006. <http://www.saltinstitute.org/4.html>.

"Black Skimmer." *United States Geological Survey*. 9 May 2006 <http://www.pwrc.usgs.gov/bioeco/bskimmer.htm>.

"Brine Fly." *Bugbios*. 9 May 2006 <http://www.insects.org/entophiles/diptera/dipt_002.html>.

"Brown Pelican." *Natureworks*. 9 May 2006 <http://www.nhptv.org/natureworks/brownpelican.htm>.

(H) "Guerrero Negro." 22 Feb. 2006. Tours and Information. 10 Mar. 2006. <http://www.san-
      bachs.net/cgi-bin/mexico/mexico2.cgi/ City=GUB&Airport=Guerrero+Negro>.

(T)(B)(H) Jones, Allen. *Personal Interview.* Dec. 2005.

(H) Lovejoy, Paul. *Salt of the Desert Sun: A History of Salt Production and Trade in the
      Central Sudan.* New York: Cambridge University Press, 1986.

(H) "San Diego Bay National Wildlife Refuge Article." U.S. Fish and Wildlife Service, 2006.

(H) Stadtlander, Doreen and John Konecny. *Avifauna of South San Diego Bay: the Western
      Salt Works 1993–1994.* Carlsbad: Coastal Ecosystem Program, U.S. Fish and
      Wildlife Service, 1994.

(G)(T)(H) Strahl, Tracy. *Personal Interview.* Dec. 2005.

(B)(H) Touchstone, Victoria. *Personal Interview.* Jan. 2006.

(B) Unitt, Philip. *San Diego County Bird Atlas.* San Diego: Ibis Publishing Company, 2004.

(H) "What is Salt?" 29 June 2005. *Salt Institute.* 11 Oct. 2006. <http://www.saltinstitute.
      org/15.html>.

Kelp Additives

(B)(H) Barilotti, Craig. *Personal Interview.* Jan. 2006.

(B) Bushing, William W. "Giant Bladder Kelp (*Macrocystis pyrifera*)." 21 Dec. 2006.
      <http://www.startthrower.org/research/kelpmisc/kelp_mp.htm>.

(H) Carmignani, Karyl. *Amber Forests of the Sea.* Blue Planet Quarterly. Volume 4, Issue
      3, Winter 2005.

(H) "CP Kelco | San Diego." *CP Kelco.* 20 Nov. 2006. <http://www.cpkelco.com/com-
      pany/manufacturing/sandiego/>.

(H) Currie, Andrew. *Phone Conversation.* Nov. 2006.

(H) Glantz, Dale, and Ronald McPeak. "Harvesting California Kelp Forests." San
      Diego: Kelco, 1984.

(B)(H) Limbaugh, Conrad. *Fish Life in the Kelp Beds and the Effects of Kelp Harvesting.* San
      Diego: Final résumé from Kelco Company. Fellowship Grant. 1955.

(H) McMahon, Shannon. "Goodbye to a Sea Giant." 10 June 2005. *The San Diego Union-
      Tribune.* 2 Oct. 2006. <http://www.rain.org/pipermail/cinms-advisory-l/2005-
      June/000760.html>.

(B)(H) McPeak, Ronald H., Dale A. Glantz, and Carole R. Shaw. *The Amber Forest:
      Beauty and Biology of California's Submarine Forests.* San Diego: Aqua Quest
      Publications. 1988.

(B)(H) North, Wheeler J. *The Biology of Giant Kelp Beds (Macrosystis) in California.* Lehre,
      Germany: Verlay von J. Cramer. 1971.

Kelp to Gunpowder

"A Wonderful Industry in Actual Operation." *Los Angeles Times.* 1 Jan. 1914.

Bedford, Dennis. "Annual Status of the Fisheries Report." 2003. California Department of Fish and Game. 21 Dec. 2006. <http://www.dfg.ca.gov/mrd/status/report2003/giantkelp.pdf>.

Brown, Werner C. and Alexander F. Giacco. "Hercules Incorporated: a Study in Creative Chemistry." New York: Newcomen Society, 1977.

Diamond, Jared. *Guns, Germs, and Steel.* New York: W.W. Norton & Company, 1999.

Dyer, Davis and David B. Sicilia. *Labors of a Modern Day Hercules: The Evolution of a Chemical Company.* Boston: Harvard Business School Press. 1990.

"History of Gun Powder Point." *History of NIC and GPP.* Chula Vista Nature Center Publication, 1997.

Kelly, Jack. *Gunpowder: Alchemy, Bombards, and Pyrotechnics: The History of the Explosive That Changed the World.* New York: Basic Books, 2004.

McMahon, Shannon. "Sea Turtles Making Waves in Bay." *The San Diego Union-Tribune.* 30 May 2006.

Mondragon, Jennifer and Jeff Mondragon. *Seaweeds of the Pacific Coast.* Monterey: Sea Challengers, 2003.

Moore, Barbara. *Personal Interview.* Dec. 2005.

Neushul, Peter. "Seaweed For War: California's World War I Kelp Industry." *Technology and Culture.* Volume 30, Number 3. pp. 561–583. July 1989.

—. "The Hercules Powder Company." Chula Vista: Chula Vista Historical Society, 2005.

Sherwood, Frank. *Personal Interview.* Dec. 2005.

Unitt, Philip. *San Diego County Bird Atlas.* San Diego: Ibis Publishing Company, 2004.

Sea Lions

Bonner, Nigel. *Seals and Sea Lions of the World*. New York: Facts on File, Inc., 1994.

"California Sea Lion." *The Marine Mammal Center*. 2002. 14 Oct. 2006. <http://www.tmmc.org/learning/education/pinnipeds/casealion.asp>.

"California Sea Lions." *British Columbia Adventure*. 14 Oct 2006. <http://www.fishbc.com/adventure/wilderness/animals/sealion.htm>.

Clark, Druann. *Personal Interview*. 2006.

Coy, Bonnie. *Assessing the Impact of Modern Environmental Stresses on California Sea Lions* (Zalophus califorianus) *using Fluctuating Asymmetry*. Washington D.C.: American University, 2002.

Daugherty, Anita. *Marine Mammals of California*. Sacramento: Department of Fish and Game, 1979.

Folkens, Peter C. "California Sea Lion." 2001. *International Marine Mammal Association*. 1 June 2006. <http://www.imma.org/pinnipeds/Californiasealn.htm>.

Gordon, David. *Seals and Sea Lions*. Monterey, California: Monterey Bay Aquarium, 1994.

Lefebvre, Kathi A., et al. "Detection of Domoic Acid in Northern Anchovies and California Sea Lions Associated with an Unusual Mortality Event." *Natural Toxins*. Volume 7, Issue 3. 1999.

Lynch, Bob. *Personal Interview*. Jan. 2006.

"Marine Mammal Protection Act." 1994. *U.S. Department of Energy*. 7 Nov. 2006. <http://www.eh.doe.gov/oepa/laws/mmpa.html>.

Martin, Beth. "The Good News about DDT." 1996. Science Notes. 1 June 2006. <http://scicom.ucsc.edu/SciNotes/9601/SeaLion/00Intro.html>.

Moore, Emma. "Seals at La Jolla Beach Threatened." *Upwelling*, Apr. 2006. 1 June 2006. <http://www.farallones.org/e_newsletter/2006-04/LaJollaSeals.htm>.

Myers, P. "Otariidae." 2000. Animal Diversity Web. 14 Oct. 2006. <http://animaldiversity.ummz.umich.edu/site/accounts/information/Otariidae.html>.

"The Pinnipeds: Seals, Sea Lions, and Walruses." *The Marine Mammal Center*. 21 Dec. 2006. <http://www.marinemammalcenter.org/learning/education/pinnipeds/pinnipeds.asp>.

Rocca, Benyamin. *El Niño Kills off our Sea Lions*. University of California, Irvine. 1998. 1 June 2006. <http://www.dbc.uci.edu/~sustain/global/sensem/rocca98.html>.

Rogers, Terry. "Lifeguards Watching for More Sharks Near Beach." 2003. SignOnSanDiego. 1 June 2006. <http://www.signonsandiego.com/news/metro/20030831-9999_2m31sharks.html>.

"San Diego Harbor Cruises on Hornblower." 14 Oct. 2006. <http://www.sandiego-harbortours.com/>.

"Sea Lion Arena." Saint Louis Zoo. 15 Mar. 2006. <http://www.stlzoo.org/yourvisit/thingstoseeanddo/historichill/sealionarena.htm>.

"Sea Lions." 1999. Campuserve.com. 1 June 2006. <http://ourworld.compuserve.com/homepages/jaap/sealion1.htm#california>.

Smith, Chuck. "California's Native People—The Northwest Region." 23 Aug. 1999. *California's Native People.* 14 Oct. 2006. <http://www.cabrillo.edu/~crsmith/anth6_nwcoast_subsist.html>.

"Steller Sea Lions." *Seal Conservation Society.* 1 June 2006. <http://www.pinnipeds.org/species/steller.htm>.

Thomas-Anderson, Melissa. "Domoic Acid Sickens Sea Mammals." 21 May 2003. *Daily Nexus.* 14 Oct. 2006. <http://www.ucsbdailynexus.com/science/2003/5335.html>

"U.S. Navy Marine Mammal Program." *SPAWAR Systems Center San Diego.* 14 Oct. 2006. <http://www.spawar.navy.mil/sandiego/technology/mammals/>.

Dolphins

Alderson, Jewyl. *Personal Interview.* Dec. 2006.

Devine, Eleanore and Martha Clark. *The Dolphin Smile.* New York: Macmillan and Company, 1967.

Harris, Chris. *Personal Interview.* Jan. 2006.

"History of Captivity." *Whale and Dolphin Conservation Society.* 21 Oct. 2006. <http://www.wdcs.org/dan/publishing.nsf/allweb/281C1D97F10E9573802568DD00306F2C>.

Johnson, William. "The Dolphin Circus." 1990. *Iridescent Publishing.* 21 Dec. 2006. <http://www.iridescent-publishing.com/rtm/ch1p6.htm>.

Marine Mammal Program Video. 2001.

Naval Ocean Systems Center. *Fifty Years of Research and Development on Point Loma: 1940–1990.* San Diego: Naval Ocean Systems Center, 1990.

Reynolds, John E. III, Randall S. Wells, and Samantha D. Eide. *The Bottlenose Dolphin: Biology and Conservation.* Gainesville, FL: University Press of Florida, 2000.

Schusterman, Ronald J., Jeanette A. Thomas, and Forrest G. Wood. *Dolphin Cognition and Behavior: A Comparative Approach.* London: Lawrence Erlbaum Associate Publishers, 1936.

Shawn, W.M. *Sea Animals and Torpedos.* China Lake, CA: Weapons Planning Group, 1959.

"The Story of Navy Dolphins." *Frontline.* 14 Oct. 2006. <http://www.pbs.org/wgbh/pages/frontline/shows/whales/etc/navycron.html>.

"Synchronicity: The Dance of the Dolphins." *Dolphin Synergy.* 14 Oct. 2006 <http://www.dolphinsynergy.com/lore.html>.

"U.S. Navy Marine Mammal Program." 2006. <http://en.wikipedia.org/wiki/U.S._Navy_Marine_Mammal_Program/>.

Weiss, Malcolm E. *Man Explores the Sea.* New York: Julian Messner, 1969.

Wood, Forrest G. *Marine Mammals and Man: The Navy's Porpoises and Sea Lions.* New York: Washington Publishers, 1973.

White Seabass

Buhr, Gabe. *Personal Interview*. Mar. 2006.

Dana, Richard Henry. *Two Years Before the Mast*. New York: Randon House. 1841.

Eschmeyer, William N. and Earl S. Herald. *Pacific Coast Fishes*. New York: Houghton Mifflin Company, 1999.

Hetzler, Robert. *Personal Interview*. June 2006.

Morris, Noelle. *Personal Interview*. Dec. 2005.

Rudolph, John Dennis. *Feeding and Predator Avoidance Strategies of Cultured White Seabass,* Atractoscion nobilis. San Diego: Montezuma Publishing, 1995.

Starr, Raymond. *The Impact of European Exploration and Settlement On Local Native Americans*. San Diego: Cabrillo Historical Association, 1986.

Stewart, Don M. *Frontier Port: A Chapter in San Diego History*. Los Angeles: The Ward Ritchie Press, 1965.

Thomas, James Calvin. *Management of the White Seabass* (Cynoscion nobilis*) in California Waters*. *Fish. Bull. 142*. Sacramento: California Dept. Fish Game, 1968.

"Timeline of San Diego History." *San Diego Historical Society*. 14 Oct 2006. <http://www.sandiegohistory.org/timeline/timeline.htm>.

"White Seabass." *Marine Sportfish Identification*. 14 Oct 2006. <http://www.dfg.ca.gov/mrd/mspcont3.html#seabass>.

"White Seabass." *California's Marine Living Resources: A Status Report*. 2001. *California Department of Fish and Game*. 20 Dec. 2006. <http://www.dfg.ca.gov/mrd/status/white_seabass.pdf>.

"White Seabass Information" *San Diego Oceans Foundation*. 14 Oct. 2006. <http://www.sdoceans.org/programs/wsb/info.php>.

Whitehead, S. S. *Analysis of Boat Catches of White Sea Bass* (Cynoscion nobilis*) at San Pedro, California*. *Fish. Bull. 21*. Sacramento: California Div. Fish Game, 1929.

Young, Parke H. *The Status of the White Seabass Resource and its Management*. *Tech. Rept. 15*. Sacramento: California Dept. Fish Game, 1973.

Abalone

Burton, Ronald S. "Conservation Genetics of California Abalone: Developing Tools for Management." July 2005. *California Sea Grant*. 8 Jan. 2007. <http://www.csgc.ucsd.edu/RESEARCH/PROJPROF_PDF/RF189.pdf>.

Culver, Carolynn S. *Identification and Management of the Exotic Sabellid Pest in California Cultured Abalone*. San Diego: California Sea Grant College System, 1997.

Gallegos, Dennis and Carolyn Kyle. *Archives of California Prehistory, Five Thousand Years of Maritime Subsistence at CA-SDI-48, on Ballast Point, San Diego County, California*. Salinas, CA: Coyote Press, 1998.

Hahn, K. O. *CRC Handbook of Culture of Abalone and Other Marine Gastropods.* Boca Raton, FL: CRC Press,1989.

Hobday, Alistair James. *Status Review of White Abalone (Haliotis sorenseni) Throughout its Range in California and Mexico.* Long Beach: National Marine Fisheries Service, 2000.

Howorth, David C. *The Abalone Book.* Happy Camp, CA: Naturegraph Publishers, 1978.

Lapota, David. *Biological and Regulatory Feasibility of Abalone Aquaculture in the California Coastal Zone.* San Diego: San Diego State University Press, 1982.

—. *Personal Interview.* June 2006.

Le Page, Steve. *Personal Interview.* Mar. 2006.

Leighton, David L. *The Biology and Culture of the California Abalone.* Pittsburgh: Dorrance Publishing Company, 2000.

—. *Personal Interview.* Mar. 2006.

Lundy, A.L.. *The California Abalone Industry.* Flagstaff: Best Publishing, 1997.

Morris, R. H., D.P. Abbot, and E. C. Haderlie. *Intertidal Invertebrates of California.* Stanford: Stanford University Press, 1980.

Morse, D.E., H. Duncan, N. Hooker, and A. Morse. "Hydrogen Peroxide Induces Spawning in Mollusks, with Activation of Prostaglandin Endoperoxide Synthetase." *Science.* Volume 196: pp.298–300. 1977.

Morse, D.E., H. Duncan, N. Hooker, and L. Jensen. "Gamma-Aminobutyric Acid, a Neurotransmitter, Induces Planktonic Abalone Larvae to Settle and Begin Metamorphosis." *Science.* Volume 204: pp.407–410. 1979.

Ryan, Connie, and Mary Patyten. "Annual Status of the Fisheries Report Through 2003." Dec. 2004. *California Department of Fish and Game.* 14 Oct. 2006. <http://www.dfg.ca.gov/mrd/status/status2003.html>.

Stacklin, Howard. *Personal Interview.* Jan. 2006.

Mussels

Becker, Bonnie J. *Personal Interview.* Dec. 2005.

"Common Mussel (*Mytilus Edulis*)." *ARKive.* 14 Oct. 2006. <http://www.arkive.org/species/ARK/invertebrates_marine/Mytilus_edulis/more_info.html>.

Cowles, David. "*Mytilus trossulus.*" 14 Oct. 2006. <http://www.rosario.wwc.edu/in-verts/Mollusca/Bivalvia/Mytiloida/Mytilidae/Mytilus_trossulus.html>.

Davis, John. *Personal Interview.* Mar. 2006.

Diamond, Jared. *Guns, Germs, and Steel.* New York: W.W. Norton & Company, 1999.

Dario, Don José. *The Journal of Padre Serra.* San Diego: Don Diego's Libreria, 1964.

James, George Wharton. *In and Out of the Old Missions of California.* Boston: Little, Brown and Company, 1905.

Kelly, Michael. *First Annual Report of the Board of Health of the City of San Diego.* 31 Dec. 1888. < http://www.sandiegohistory.org/journal/2002-4/1888.htm>.

Korringa, P. *Farming Marine Organisms Low in the Food Chain.* Amsterdam: Elsevier Scientific Publishing, 1976.

Moore, Thomas. *Personal Conversation.* Mar. 2006.

Morris, Robert H., Donald P. Abbott, and Eugene C. Haderlie. "*Mytilus Edulis.*" *Intertidal Invertebrates of California.* Stanford: Stanford University Press, 1980.

B "*Mytilus trossulus* — The Bay Mussel." 14 Oct. 2006. <http://www.nwmarinelife. com/htmlswimmers/m_trossulus.html>.

T B O'Connor, T.P. and B. Beliaeff. *Recent Trends in Coastal Environment Quality Results from the Mussel Watch Project.* Silver Spring, MD: NOAA, 1995.

B Stewart, Don M. *Frontier Port: A Chapter in San Diego History.* Los Angeles: The Ward Ritchie Press, 1965.

B Trevelyan, George A. "Aquacultural Ecology of Hatchery-Produced Juvenile Bay Mussels, *Mytilus edulis.*" Ph.D. diss., University of California, Davis, 1991.

Photo Credits

Laurel Rogers: map for geography sections of all chapters.

Native Americans

Gallegos 1998: page 25 (top and bottom).
High Tech High: pages 2–3, 4, 6, 6–11 (uppermost), 7, 8 (top and bottom), 9, 11, 12–13, 12 (top and bottom), 13 (top and bottom), 14 (top and bottom), 15, 16, 17, 18 (top and bottom), 19, 20, 21 (top and bottom), 22, 24, 26, 27, 28, 30 (top), and 31 (top, middle, and bottom).
San Diego Historical Society: page 29 and 30 (bottom).

Chinese Fishermen

Courtesy of Dr. Forest Rohwer: page 54 (middle).
Courtesy of Murray Lee: page 34.
High Tech High: 35 (bottom), pages 36–43 (uppermost), 38, 39, 40 (bottom), 42, 43 (bottom), 44 (third image down), 45 (top right), 46, 48, 50 (top and bottom), 51 (top and bottom), 52, 53 (top and bottom), 54 (top, middle, and bottom), 55 (top), 56, and 57.
Regulatory Fish Encyclopedia: page 55.
San Diego Historical Society: pages 32–33, 37, 40 (top), 43 (top), 44–45, 44 (top left), 47, and 49.

Waterfowl Hunting

Courtesy of David Hagerbaumer: pages 60, 64 (bottom), 67 (bottom), 70, 71, 72.
Courtesy of Jim Brown: page 73.
Courtesy of Jim Heather: pages 79 (top and bottom), and 80.
Courtesy of Ron Vavra: pages 65 (bottom), and 75.
High Tech High: pages 58–59, 61, 62–67 (uppermost), 62 (top and bottom), 63 (bottom), 64 (top), 65 (top), 66 (top and bottom), 67 (top), 68–69, 68, 69 (top, middle, and bottom), 74, 77, 78, 79 (top and bottom), 81–82 (top and bottom), 83 (top and bottom), and 84–85.
San Diego Historical Society: page 63 (top).

Tuna

Courtesy of Guy Bruni: pages 86–87 (photographed by Guy Bruni), 90, 93, 94, 107 (top and bottom), 108, 109, and 110 (top and bottom).
Courtesy of Jean Immenschuh: pages 92, 98, 100 (top and bottom), 101, 102, and 103 (top).
Courtesy of Russ Vetter: page 104 (top).
FAO/SIDP Species Identification Sheets: pages 112 (middle) and 113 (middle).
High Tech High: pages 88, 90–97 (uppermost), 95, 96, 97, 98–99, 99, 103 (bottom), 104 (bottom), 105, 106 (top and bottom), 111, 112 (top and bottom), and 113 (bottom).
NOAA Fisheries Collection: page 113 (top).

Salt

San Diego Historical Society: page 91.
Courtesy of Allen Jones: page 128 (top).

Courtesy of Jean Immenschuh: 127 (top).
Courtesy of Western Salt Company: pages 116, 119, 123, 126 (bottom), 128 (bottom), and 129.
High Tech High: pages 114–115, 118–124 (uppermost), 118, 120, 121, 122, 124, 125, 126–127, 126 (top), 127 (middle and bottom), 130, 131, 132 (top and bottom), 133, 134, 135, 136, 137, 138 (top and middle), 139 (top and bottom), 140 (top, middle, and bottom), 141 (top and bottom), 142 (top and bottom), and 143 (top and bottom).
Photographed by John Good: page 138 (bottom).

Kelp Additives

High Tech High: pages 144–145, 146, 147 (bottom), 148–151 (uppermost), 148, 149, 150, 151, 152–153, 152, 153 (top and bottom), 154 (top and bottom), 155, 156, 157 (top and bottom), 158 (top, middle, and bottom), and 159 (top and bottom).

Kelp to Gunpowder

Courtesy of Dr. Frank Sherwood: pages 168, 177, 179, and 180 (top).
High Tech High: pages 162, 163 (bottom), 164–171 (uppermost), 164, 167 (top), 169, 170 (top and bottom), 171, 172–173, 172 (top, middle, and bottom), 173 (top and bottom), 174, 175, 176 (top and bottom), 178, 180 (bottom), 181, 182 (top and bottom), and 183 (top and bottom).
San Diego Historical Society: pages 160–161, and 166–167.

Sea Lions

High Tech High: pages 184–185, 186, 187 (bottom), 188–193 (uppermost), 188 (top and bottom), 189, 190, 191, 192–193, 194–195, 194, 195, 196 (top and bottom), 197, 198, 199 (top, middle, and bottom), 200, 201 (top and bottom), 202, and 203.

Dolphins

Courtesy of Dave Koontz: page 220 (bottom).
High Tech High: pages 204–205, 206, 207 (bottom), 208–215 (uppermost), 209, 210 (HTH archives), 211, 212, 215, 216–217, 217, 218 (top and bottom), 219 (top and bottom), 220 (top), 221 (top and bottom), 222, 223 (top and bottom), 224 (top and bottom), 225, 226 (top and bottom), 227 (top and bottom), 228 (top and bottom), and 229.

White Seabass

Courtesy of Bob Hetzler: page 251.
High Tech High: pages 230–231, 232, 233 (bottom), 234–239, 234, 235, 236, 237, 238 (top and bottom), 239, 240–241, 241, 242 (top and bottom), 243, 244 (top and bottom), 245, 246 (top and bottom), 247 (top and bottom), 248, 249 (top and bottom), 250 (top and bottom), 252, 253, 254 (top, middle, and bottom), and 255.

Abalone

Courtesy of David Leighton: pages 273 (top and bottom), 275, and 280.
High Tech High: pages 256–257, 258, 260–265 (uppermost), 261, 262, 264, 265, 266–267, 266, 267, 268, 269, 270 (top and bottom), 271, 272, 274, 276, 277, 278 (top and bottom), 279 (top and bottom), and 281.
San Diego Historical Society: page 263.

Mussels

High Tech High: pages 282–283, 284, 286–291 (uppermost), 287, 288 (top and bottom), 289, 290, 291, 292–293, 292 (top and bottom), 293, 294, 295, 296, 297, 298, 299 (top and bottom), 300 (top and bottom), 301–303.